Evidentials and Relevance

Pragmatics & Beyond New Series

Editor

Andreas H. Jucker
Justus Liebig University Giessen, English Department
Otto-Behaghel-Strasse 10, D-35394 Giessen, Germany
e-mail: andreas.jucker@anglistik.uni-giessen.de

Associate Editors

Jacob L. Mey
University of Southern Denmark

Herman Parret
Belgian National Science Foundation, Universities of Louvain and Antwerp

Jef Verschueren
Belgian National Science Foundation, University of Antwerp

Editorial Board

Shoshana Blum-Kulka
Hebrew University of Jerusalem

Chris Butler
University College of Ripon and York

Jean Caron
Université de Poitiers

Robyn Carston
University College London

Bruce Fraser
Boston University

Thorstein Fretheim
University of Trondheim

John Heritage
University of California at Los Angeles

Susan Herring
University of Texas at Arlington

Masako K. Hiraga
St.Paul's (Rikkyo) University

David Holdcroft
University of Leeds

Sachiko Ide
Japan Women's University

Catherine Kerbrat-Orecchioni
University of Lyon 2

Claudia de Lemos
University of Campinas, Brazil

Marina Sbisà
University of Trieste

Emanuel Schegloff
University of California at Los Angeles

Deborah Schiffrin
Georgetown University

Paul O. Takahara
Kobe City University of Foreign Studies

Sandra Thompson
University of California at Santa Barbara

Teun A. Van Dijk
University of Amsterdam

Richard J. Watts
University of Berne

Volume 86

Evidentials and Relevance
by Elly Ifantidou

Evidentials and Relevance

Elly Ifantidou

University of Athens

John Benjamins Publishing Company
Amsterdam/Philadelphia

™ The paper used in this publication meets the minimum requirements of American National Standard for Information Sciences – Permanence of Paper for Printed Library Materials, ANSI z39.48-1984.

Library of Congress Cataloging-in-Publication Data

Ifantidou, Elly.
Evidentials and Relevance / Elly Ifantidou.
p. cm. (Pragmatics & Beyond, New Series, ISSN 0922-842X ; v. 86)
Includes bibliographical references and index.
1. Semantics. 2. Evidentials (Linguitics). 3. Pragmatics. 4. Speech acts (Linguistics). 5. Grammar, Comparative and general. 6. Relevance. I. Title. II. Pragmatics & beyond ; new ser. 86.

P325.5.E69 I35 2001
401.43--dc21   2001035507
ISBN 90 272 5105 3 (Eur.) / 1 58811 032 X (US) (Hb; alk. paper)

John Benjamins Publishing Co. · P.O.Box 36224 · 1020 ME Amsterdam · The Netherlands
John Benjamins North America · P.O.Box 27519 · Philadelphia PA 19118-0519 · USA

For my children,
Σοφία and Κίμων

Table of Contents

Acknowledgements

Many people have made this book possible. I would first like to express my deep gratitude to my supervisor, Deirdre Wilson, for commenting and discussing numerous versions of this work with unfailing interest and enthusiasm. I owe her an original perspective to semantic-pragmatic theory, philosophy of language and a challenging, inquiring approach to issues under research. I also owe her my first academic teaching, first conference papers, making them all exceptional events, as well as most of the inspiration underlying this book. Her wit, her kindness and generosity made studying Linguistics in UCL an enjoyable and exciting experience.

My research has been largely influenced by the work of Diane Blakemore, Regina Blass, Robyn Carston and Dan Sperber and I would like to take this chance of thanking them. I would like to especially thank Robyn Carston for valuable help and advice at various stages of this work as well as all the members of the Linguistics Department for making it a pleasure to study at UCL. The topic for this work was suggested by my supervisor in the Linguistics Department, University of Cambridge, Terence Moore, and I thank him for this. However, the incentive to pursue Linguistics was given by my tutors in the English Department, University of Athens, who first showed me how Linguistics can be fun. I would like to especially thank Sophia Marmaridou and Maria Sifianou for their guidance and support from undergraduate days until today.

In revising the manuscript for publication, I have benefited greatly from insightful comments and criticisms by two anonymous reviewers and useful suggestions by Andreas Jucker, who has been patiently waiting for the revised and final versions of the current one. I would also like to thank Isjtar Conen and Bertie Kaal for kindly offering their editorial assistance in all the technical and administrative aspects of this volume.

During the course of this work I received a great deal of help and support from my parents, Sophia Ifantidou and Vassilis Ifantides, to whom I would like to express my deepest gratitude. I should also like to thank my husband, Elias

Troukis, for making this work seem less burdensome through a great deal of practical help and encouragement.

Finally, I would like to express my gratitude to the British Council and the A.G. Leventis Foundation for providing the financial support for this research.

CHAPTER 1

Introduction

Evidentials: their nature and functions

1.1 Defining evidentials

In *A Dictionary of Linguistics & Phonetics* (1991), David Crystal defines *evidentiality* as

> A term used in SEMANTICS for a type of EPISTEMIC MODALITY where PROPOSITIONS are asserted that are open to challenge by the hearer, and require justification. Evidential constructions express a speaker's strength of commitment to a proposition in terms of the available evidence (rather than in terms of possibility or necessity). They add such nuances of meaning to a given sentence as "I saw it happen", "I heard that it happened", "I have seen evidence that it happened" (though I wasn't there), or "I have obtained information that it happened from someone else". ... (ibid.: 127)

There are two points worth noticing in Crystal's definition. First, he defines evidentiality as a semantic notion, although in the literature evidentials have been primarily examined in terms of their pragmatic function, e.g. modifying (weakening, or strengthening) the speaker's degree of commitment to the information communicated (Urmson 1963; Palmer 1986; Chafe 1986; Mayer 1990). This raises a fundamental question about the scope of the term 'evidential'. Crystal seems to be suggesting that the term 'evidential' should be exclusively used for constructions which *linguistically encode* information about the speaker's degree of commitment. This implies that the role of pragmatic inference in the interpretation of 'evidential' utterances can be safely ignored. Second, according to Crystal, the term 'evidential' does not apply to constructions that express possibility or necessity. Thus, modals such as *must, may, might, can, could, ought to, should*, are excluded. This raises the question of where the borderline between evidentiality and other types of epistemic modality is to be drawn. Presumably, adverbials such as *possibly* and *necessarily* are to be excluded: but what about expressions such as *perhaps* and *maybe*, or constructions such as '*I think/I suppose/I guess* John is in Berlin' and '*I know/*

I tell you that John is in Berlin'? Which 'nuances of meaning' are specifically evidential and which are not?

The answers to these questions can not be obtained from Crystal's brief and rather vague definition. A survey of the literature, however, shows two things. First, the notion of evidential is basically a functional one: that is, it is applied to linguistic expressions in virtue of their pragmatic function. Second, modals, adverbials and other epistemic modifiers of the type described above are standardly treated as evidentials (Urmson 1963; Givón 1982; Anderson 1986; Chafe 1986; Mithun 1986; Mayer 1990; Blakemore 1994). A sample of these approaches is given below.

Jacobsen (1986:3–28), in a concise historical review of evidentiality in linguistic description, points out that although the concept of evidentials as a category has existed in Americanist circles for some decades, the label EVIDENTIAL is relatively recent. The concept is traced back to the work of Franz Boas on Kwakiutl (1911a, 1911b, 1947, 1911 ed.), who examined certain "Suffixes denoting the source of information" (1911b:496). The term EVIDENTIAL occurs in Boas' posthumously published *Kwakiutl Grammar* (1947) as applied to just one of "a small group of suffixes [which] expresses source and certainty of knowledge ..." (ibid.:206). As Jacobsen shows, since then there has been a line of Americanist descendants of Boas who have referred to evidentiality (Sapir 1921; Swadesh 1939; Lee 1938, 1944, 1959; Jakobson 1944/1971, 1957/1971, 1959/1971, etc., and more recently Thompson 1979 and Chafe 1979). The concept of evidentials is absent, however, from linguistics textbooks and surveys of grammatical categories, mainly due to a lack of European and classical languages with distinctive evidential forms (Jacobsen 1986:7).

Chafe and Nichols (1986), in their Introduction to *Evidentiality: The linguistic coding of epistemology*,[1] introduce evidentiality as follows:

> There are ... things people are less sure of, and some things they think are only within the realm of possibility. Languages typically provide a repertoire of devices for conveying these various attitudes towards knowledge. Often enough, speakers present things as unquestionably true: for example, "It's raining". On other occasions English speakers, for example, may use an adverb to show something about the reliability of what they say, the probability of its truth: "It's probably raining" or "Maybe it's raining". Inference from some kind of evidence may be expressed with a modal auxiliary: "It must be raining". Or the specific kind of evidence on which an inference is based may be indicated with a separate verb: "It sounds like it's raining". The view that a

> piece of knowledge does not match the prototypical meaning of a verbal
> category may be shown formulaically: "It's sort of raining". Or an adverb may
> suggest that some knowledge is different from what might have been expected:
> "Actually, it's raining". (ibid.: vii)

The Evidentials Symposium at Berkeley in 1981 and the proceedings volume
(Chafe and Nichols eds 1986) was the first step towards broadening our
knowledge in this area. According to Chafe and Nichols, evidentials are devices
used by speakers to mark the source and the reliability of their knowledge. They
do not attempt to delimit the boundaries of evidentiality, and acknowledge that
the volume they are introducing represents a stage of exploration where
heterogeneous perspectives are presented. Again, they point out that the original
interest in evidentiality was aroused by American Indian languages, especially
those of Northern California, where the marking of evidentiality is systematized
mainly in verb suffixes. The book covers a wide range of such languages: for
example Kashaya (Northern California), Wintu (Northern California), Patwin
(Northern California), Maricopa (Arizona), Northern Iroquoian languages
(New York, Quebec, Ontario), Jaqi languages (Peru, Bolivia, Chile), Quechua
(Peru). Evidentiality is also examined in Turkish, Balkan languages, Tibetan
languages, Akha (Lolo-Burmese family), Japanese, and Chinese pidgin Russian.
The research was focused on these languages precisely because they exhibit
elaborated inflectional evidential systems, and hence lend themselves to relative-
ly straightforward investigation and neat results.

Let us examine the way some of the contributors to this volume define
evidentiality. Mithun (1986: 89–112) defines evidentials as

> ... markers [which] qualify the reliability of information communicated in
> four primary ways. They specify the source of evidence on which statements
> are based, their degree of precision, their probability, and expectations con-
> cerning their probability. (ibid.: 89)

Among what she calls "lexical evidential markers" in English, she includes *I
suppose, I guess, maybe, must have been, seems, looks, smells like, they say, I hear,
probably, it is highly improbable, he is sure to* (ibid.: 89–90).

Anderson (ibid.: 273–312) attempts a more precise definition, in four parts:

> (3a) Evidentials show the kind of justification for a factual claim which is
> available to the person making that claim, whether
>> direct evidence plus observation (no inference needed)
>> evidence plus inference
>> inference (evidence unspecified)

reasoned expectation from logic and other facts and
whether the evidence is auditory, or visual, etc.
(3b) Evidentials are not themselves the main predication of the clause, but are
rather a specification added to a factual claim ABOUT SOMETHING ELSE.
(3c) Evidentials have the indication of evidence as in (a) as their primary
meaning, not only as a pragmatic inference.
(3d) Morphologically, evidentials are inflections, clitics, or other free syntactic
elements (not compounds or derivational forms). (ibid.: 274–275)

On the basis of this "definition", Anderson claims that the bracketed constructions in (1a–e) are, indeed, evidentials:

(1) a. The toast [must have] burned.
     b. [I hear] Mary won the PRIZE.
     c. [I heard] (that) Mary won the PRIZE.
     d. [I understand that] Mary won the PRIZE.
     e. [I have it on good authority that] Mary won the PRIZE.
     f. [I smell] a pie baking.

(1f) qualifies as an evidential by definitions (3a,b,d) but not by (3c): perception
verbs are not primarily evidentials, i.e. they do not have the indication of
evidence as their primary meaning, but they often carry epistemically qualified
implicatures (ibid.: 276–277). Thus, Anderson considers (1f) a borderline case
and labels it as "evidential USAGE" (ibid.).

It is clear, then, that according to Anderson, (a) the term 'evidential',
although it is a special grammatical phenomenon which does not simply
include anything that might have an evidential function, *does* include constructions which are not primarily evidential but which have an evidential use, (b)
constructions that express possibility or necessity fall within the range of
evidentials, and (c) evidentials do not constitute the main point of the proposition expressed; they are specifications added to the proposition expressed.
According to Anderson, then, evidentials are used "… (a) to specify factual
claims and (b) indicate the justification available TO THE PERSON MAKING
THE CLAIM …" (ibid.: 277). Based on these claims, Anderson arrives at the
following generalizations:

(8) Evidentials are normally used in assertions (realis clauses), not in irrealis
clauses, nor in presuppositions.
(9a) When the claimed fact is directly observable by both speaker and hearer,
evidentials are rarely used (or have a special emphatic or surprisal sense).
(9b) When the speaker (first person) was a knowing participant in some event

(voluntary agent; conscious experiencer), the knowledge of that event is normally direct and evidentials are often then omitted.

(9c) Often, it is claimed, second person in questions is treated as first person in statements. (But such examples may contain ordinary perception verbs rather than archetypal evidentials, ...). (ibid.: 277–278)

Anderson's discussion still leaves a few questions unanswered. For example, are discourse connectives which mark the drawing of inference, such as *so* and *therefore*, to be considered as evidentials under his definition? Are intonation and prosodic features which indicate degree of speaker commitment to be included in the range of evidentials? Does the paralinguistic quotative device of two index fingers forming invisible quotation marks around part of the utterance, in combination with the right intonational features, constitute an evidentiality marker? And what about cases of pure pragmatic inference where nothing is linguistically encoded, prosodically signalled or bodily expressed? These are certainly cases where the context enables the hearer to infer that the information being communicated has a certain source, and hence a certain degree of strength. Crystal and Anderson apparently exclude such utterances from the range of evidentials; but is such a dividing line the most theoretically interesting one?

1.2   The functions of evidentials

We saw above that the notion of an evidential is basically a functional one. Let us look a little more closely at the functions that have been proposed. Most authors agree that evidentials have two main functions: they indicate the source of knowledge, and the speaker's degree of certainty about the proposition expressed:

a.   Evidentials indicate the source of knowledge (Bybee 1985; Chafe and Nichols eds. 1986; Mithun 1986; Chafe 1986; Mayer 1990; Givón 1982; Willett 1988). Information can be acquired in various ways, for example:

i.   By observation (sensory/perceptual evidence) (Chafe 1986; Anderson 1986; Woodbury 1986; Palmer 1986).

(2)   a.   *I see* him coming.
       b.   *I hear* her cooking.
       c.   *I feel* water in my shoes.
       d.   It *tastes* good.

and the less reliable

> e. He *looks like* he's drunk.
> f. She *sounds like* she's upset.
> g. It *feels like* a hot sauna.
> h. It *smells like* roasted chicken.

ii. By hearsay (from other people) (Chafe 1986; Anderson 1986; Mithun 1986; Palmer 1986; Blakemore 1994)

> (3) a. John *tells me* you got a job.
> b. *I hear* you got a job.
> c. *People say* he's trustworthy.
> d. *He is said* to have done it.
> e. *He is reputed* to be very learned.
> f. *Allegedly*, the computer has been stolen.
> g. *Reportedly*, he is the burglar.

and several less direct hearsay devices which primarily perform other functions (Chafe 1986; Mithun 1986; Blakemore 1994):

> h. *It seems* he is the burglar.
> i. It's *supposed to* be the best play of the year.
> j. *Apparently*, she is very efficient.

iii. By inference (Givón 1982; Chafe 1986; Mithun 1986; Mayer 1990; Blakemore 1994)

> (4) a. *Presumably*, he is capable of teaching 'A' levels.
> b. John *seems to/must be* here now.
> c. John *must have* arrived.
> d. *I gather* that Tom's in town.

Although not standardly included in evidential treatments, the inferential expressions in (4e–g) might be included in this class:

> e. *So* you've spent all your money.
> f. *I deduce* that he has worked hard.
> g. *Consequently*, I will give him a first.

iv. By memory. Although not standardly treated as evidentials, there is a class of expressions which indicate that information is simply recalled:

(5) a. *I remember* that John won the prize.
     b. *I recall* that it was raining on my wedding day.
     c. *As I recollect*, his childhood was not easy.

Since memory is variably reliable, such expressions have a claim to be considered as evidentials.

b. Evidentials indicate the speaker's degree of certainty (Derbyshire 1979; Givón 1982; Palmer 1986; Chafe 1986; Mayer 1990). People communicate information being aware, though not necessarily consciously aware, that not all knowledge is equally reliable. Thus, they qualify their statements by means of certain evidential constructions, for example:

i. By certain propositional attitude and parenthetical expressions (Urmson 1963; Givón 1982; Chafe 1986; Mithun 1986)

(6) a. *I think* that John is in Berlin.
     b. *I know* John is in Berlin.
     c. *I suspect* that he is the burglar.
     d. *I guess* that he will have to resign.
     e. *I suppose* that he will have to resign.

and

     f. John is in Berlin, *I think*.
     g. John is, *I know*, in Berlin.
     h. He is the burglar, *I suspect*.
     i. He will have, *I guess*, to resign.
     j. He will have to resign, *I suppose*.

ii. By certain adverbials (Urmson 1963; Givón 1982; Chafe 1986; Mayer 1990; Blakemore 1994)

(7) a. He is *probably* the best actor of the year.
     b. It is *certainly* very beautiful.
     c. John is *possibly* coming tonight.
     d. The answer is *undoubtedly* 'no'.
     e. *Surely*, you know what I mean.
     f. *Evidently*, the ball was over the line.
     g. The ball was, *obviously*, over the line.

iii. By epistemic modals (Givón 1982; Chafe 1986; Anderson 1986; Mayer 1990).

(8) a. I *may* not come tonight.
     b. He *might* tell us the truth.
     c. She *can* claim that you were there.
     d. He *could* be ill.
     e. Helen *must* be better today.
     f. That'*ll* be the postman.
     g. He *ought to/should* be there.

Generally, this functional criterion is combined with more or less restrictive linguistic criteria, which I shall consider below.

1.3 Linguistic properties of evidentials

1.3.1 Decoding versus inference

As we have seen, evidentials are generally treated as a *semantic* category, *linguistically encoding* information about the source and reliability of the information being offered. Before turning to the various linguistic criteria that have been proposed to distinguish evidentials, let me illustrate first how an utterance may function evidentially without this information being linguistically encoded at all. Consider (9):

(9) There are 2,712 beans in the bag.

If produced as a guess in a fairground competition, this would be understood as communicating a much lower degree of certainty than if produced in an official announcement of the results. Or consider (10):

(10) John is feeling miserable today.

The information in (10) would be understood as having different sources if produced by a speaker who had just seen John's miserable expression (observation), was reporting what John had said (hearsay), had just observed John's behaviour (inference), and so on; and such implicit assumptions about the source of the information might play a role in the interpretation of the utterance itself. Such pragmatic inferences about the source and reliability of information are interesting in their own right, and may well interact with the linguistic encoding of evidentiality.

Blakemore (1994) is one of the few linguists to draw attention to non-linguistic 'evidentials', such as intonation, prosodic features and the two-index-fingers quotation marks used to attribute the words quoted to someone else. Blakemore wonders whether the above should be considered as *grammatical* devices used to indicate the type of evidence the speaker has. Regardless of the answer to this question, Blakemore points out that there is a substantial element of pragmatic inference in the interpretation of evidentiality. On her view, those aspects of evidentiality which are derived pragmatically through the interaction of linguistic form with context, pragmatic principles and inference must be taken into account too.

Interestingly enough, in certain Balkan Slavic languages (e.g. Bulgarian) the expression of evidentiality relies to a considerable extent on the context. According to Friedman (1986: 168–187) evidentiality is "the chief contextual variant meaning (HAUPTBEDEUTUNG)" in Balkan Slavic languages. Here, certain forms can be used evidentially, and often are, but

> the fact that this is not always the case means that evidentiality is not inherent in these forms but results from a combination of whatever meaning is always present when the form is used (which meaning must then be sought) and the surrounding context. These forms are thus not special evidential forms but rather forms contextually capable of expressing evidentiality. (ibid.: 169)

In other words, he continues, in some Balkan Slavic languages

> … evidentiality does not constitute a generic grammatical category on a level with, for example, mood, tense and aspect. Rather, evidentiality is a meaning, whether contextual or invariant, expressed by the generic grammatical category which indicates the speaker's attitude toward the narrated event. (ibid.)

One point to notice is that the forms Friedman considers mark the speaker's *attitude* toward the information communicated. The other point is that identification of this attitude depends both on decoding *and* on inference, which must therefore be dealt with in any adequate account: "The question of whether the source of information was a report, deduction, direct experience, or something else is answered by the context in which the speaker's choice of form occurs." (ibid.: 185)

1.3.2   Syntax versus morphology

Among linguists who restrict their attention to linguistically encoded information, the most general definition is proposed by Chafe (1986: 261–272), Mayer (1990: 101–163), who treat as evidentials *all* linguistic expressions encoding evidential information — i.e. all the functionally evidential expressions listed in (a(i–iii)) and (b(i–iii)). Chafe (1986) considers a wide range of evidential linguistic expressions such as the ones in (a(i–iii)) and (b(i–iii)). Mayer (1990) defines evidentials as "items that have to do with the way information is graded in respect of certainty and source." (ibid.: 103)

He discusses the German equivalents of *must, obviously, surely/certainly, seem* and *supposedly* (ibid.). On this approach, the notion of an evidential is construed in the broadest possible terms.

1.3.2.1   *Morphological criteria*

At the opposite extreme are linguists like Levinsohn (1975), Derbyshire (1979), Givón (1982), Barnes (1984), Willett (1988), Palmer (1986), Chafe and Nichols (eds) (1986) who treat as evidentials only those expressions which encode evidential information as part of the inflectional morphology. Tuyuca (Colombia and Brazil), for example, is famous for its complex system of five evidentials which enables the speaker to communicate how and when he obtained his information (Barnes 1984). It is obligatory that speakers of Tuyuca indicate whether they obtained their information in one of the following ways: (i) visually (ii) nonvisually (iii) through evidence of the state or event ('apparent') (iv) by being told about the state or event ('secondhand') and (v) by assuming what happened ('assumed'). A typical example is given in (11):

(11)   a.   *díiga apé-wi*
            'He played soccer' (I saw him play).
       b.   *díiga apé-ti*
            'He played soccer' (I heard the game and him, but I didn't see it or him).
       c.   *díiga apé-yi*
            'He played soccer' (I have seen evidence that he played: his distinctive shoe print on the playing field. But I did not see him play).
       d.   *díiga apé-yigi*
            'He played soccer' (I obtained the information from someone else).
       e.   *díiga apé-higi*
            'He played soccer' (It is reasonable to assume that he did)
            (Barnes 1984:257).

Within this overall morphological approach, further subdivisions are possible. Palmer (1986) draws a distinction between two systems of epistemic modality: judgements and evidentials (ibid.: 51–76). The system of judgements includes the notions of possibility/necessity which are expressed by modals, e.g. *may, must, will, can, might, would, ought to, should,* or by mood, e.g. subjunctive (ibid.: 57–66). The system of evidentials typically includes the 'hearsay' and 'sensory' types of evidence which, in English at least, are conveyed by expressions such as *It is said that, X said that, It appears that, I saw, I heard* (ibid.: 52 and 66–76). The two systems are quite closely connected and often overlap. Both are concerned with the indication by the speaker of his degree of commitment to the truth of the proposition expressed (ibid.: 51). Thus, in English for example, it is possible to have combinations of the two systems as in *I can see, I can hear, I could tell, I wouldn't know, it might be thought that, it might seem, it can possibly be said.* Still, Palmer thinks it is worth drawing the distinction and pointing out that certain languages, e.g. English, only grammaticalize judgements, whereas others, e.g. Tuyuca, only grammaticalize evidentials, and others, e.g. German, combine the two in their system of grammatical marking.

Palmer's (1986: 51–54, 66–76) survey of evidentials is restricted to languages which grammaticalize evidentiality in terms of formal markers (inflections, particles, clitics) indicating whether information is 'visual', 'reported', 'deduced', 'speculative', and other finer evidential distinctions such as 'witnessed positive', 'witnessed negative', 'firsthand information' and 'emphatic firsthand information'. One of the languages he considers is Hixkaryana (Carib, N. Brazil — Derbyshire 1979: 143–145), which has specific particles for expressing:

(12) a. hearsay: *-ti*
          nomokyan ha-ti
          'He's coming' (they say)
      b. uncertainty: *-na*
          nomokyan ha-na
          'Maybe he'll come'
      c. deduction: *-mi*
          nomokyan ha-mi
          'He's evidently coming' (on hearing the sound of an outboard motor)
      d. positive doubt, scepticism: *-mpe*
          nomokyatxow ha-mpe
          'They're coming! I don't believe it'
          (Palmer 1986: 54)

Palmer also refers to Inga (a Quechuan language of Colombia) (Levinsohn 1975: 14–15), which has five particles for encoding evidentiality. Examples of three of them are given in (13):

(13) a. action witnessed: *-mi*
          nis puñuncuna-mi
          'There they slept'
      b. action deduced by the speaker: *-cha*
          chipica diablo-char ca
          'A devil was presumably there'
      c. action reported to the speaker: *-si*
          chacapi-si yallinacú
          'They were crossing the bridge'
          (Palmer 1986:52)

Between the two extremes set out so far, one can imagine a whole range of linguistic criteria for evidentiality, most of which are more relevant than Palmer's morphological restrictions to the issues I want to discuss in this book.

1.3.2.2 *Syntactic criteria*

One distinction worth noting is between evidential expressions which are syntactically parenthetical, i.e. in some sense syntactically independent of the main clause, and those that are not. Consider, for example, true parentheticals versus their main-clause counterparts as in (14):

(14) John is, *I think*, in Berlin.   vs.   I think John is in Berlin.

This is a distinction which has hardly ever been drawn by linguists dealing with evidential expressions, yet it might have significant effects on interpretation.

Similarly, consider parenthetical sentence adverbials versus integrated VP-adverbials (Hartvigson 1969; Schreiber 1972; Jackendoff 1972; Goral 1974), as in (15):

(15) *Obviously*, John was stealing   vs.   John was obviously (=openly) stealing.

What is the relation between the two occurrences of *obviously*? Generally, the sentence adverbial is seen as an evidential, whereas the VP manner adverbial is not. Yet the meanings of the two adverbials are clearly related, and in fact either occurrence can be interpreted in either way. Can some systematic statement be made?

From a syntactic point of view, evidentials of the type illustrated above, i.e. true parenthetical verbs, as in (14), and sentence adverbials, as in (15), belong to a more general class of parenthetical constructions. Examples of such constructions are given in (16):

(16) a. John, *who is an economist,* registered for an MA in Linguistics.
      b. Peter was there, *if that makes any difference.*
      c. Bill has, *by the way,* accepted the invitation.
      d. Mary seems, *to put it mildly,* to be quite inefficient.
      e. Frankly, *my dear,* I don't know how to handle that.
      f. Mary's book, *a best seller,* hasn't impressed me in the least.
      g. Bill, *and prepare yourself for a shock,* is getting married.
      h. Three people, *or maybe more,* came to the party.
      i. It has been raining, *because the grass is wet.*
      j. It was raining, *but the grass is not wet!*

Similarly, evidential sentence adverbials belong together syntactically with a much broader range of sentence adverbials. Examples are given in (17):

(17) a. *Frankly,* he is a bore.
      b. John has, *unfortunately,* failed the exam.
      c. I don't care, *honestly!*
      d. *Confidentially,* Peter broke up with Jane.
      e. *Very sadly and regrettably,* he lost his job.

Recently, it has been suggested that none of these constructions are syntactically integrated with the sentences they modify (Mittwoch 1977, 1979, 1985; Haegeman 1984, 1991; Fabb 1990; Espinal 1991; Burton-Roberts 1999). The suggestion is that the two syntactically separate parts form a unit only in discourse structure; their relation is, in other words, established at the level of utterance interpretation rather than in the syntax.

This raises the following questions: (a) what is the relation between the truly parenthetical evidentials and their non-parenthetical counterparts? and (b) what is the relation between the truly parenthetical evidentials and the broader class of parenthetical constructions illustrated in (16) and (17)? They are certainly syntactically similar. Are they semantically similar too?

1.3.3 Semantic criteria

The syntactic distinction between parenthetical and non-parenthetical constructions seems to correlate to some degree at least with a semantic distinction between truth-conditional and non-truth-conditional expressions. Roughly, expressions which are syntactically external to the main clause seem to be semantically external to the proposition expressed and hence to make no contribution to the truth conditions of the utterances in which they occur. On this view, (18), for example, would be true or false depending on whether John did or did not leave, and the evidential *obviously* would merely indicate the speaker's degree of certainty or source of evidence, but make no contribution to the truth conditions of the utterance itself:

(18)   *Obviously*, John left.

By contrast, the manner adverbial *obviously* in (15) above is truth-conditional in the regular way. A hypothesis I would like to examine is the one outlined above: that only the truly parenthetical evidentials are non-truth-conditional, whereas their main-clause counterparts such as those in (19) are not:

(19)   a.   I think she is ill.
            b.   Bill tells me she is ill.

This is not a hypothesis that has generally been made in the semantic literature on evidentials. Many semanticists seem to assume that *all* evidentials, both main-clause and parenthetical, are non-truth-conditional (Benveniste 1971 [19-58]; Austin 1962; Urmson 1963; Holdcroft 1978; Anderson 1986). These two hypotheses need further investigation, and one of my main aims is to explore them further. Because my central interest is in the truth-conditional or non-truth-conditional status of evidentials, I will feel free to compare my chosen evidentials with a variety of non-evidential phenomena which are standardly treated as non-truth-conditional and which seem to fall into the same syntactic class as the evidentials I will be considering. Parentheticals in general, as in (16), and sentence adverbials in general, as in (17), are cases in point.

One of the reasons for looking at evidentials, then, is to see whether their similarities in function reflect deeper similarities in their semantic status, and whether these similarities are shared by other items with similar syntactic properties, or not. Moreover, can some pragmatic statement be made regarding truly parenthetical evidentials and parenthetical constructions in general?

As regards the definition of evidentiality, I shall take the broadest possible approach, allowing myself to consider both semantically encoded and pragmatically inferred aspects of meaning. Within this framework, there are three main questions which I would like to investigate.

1.4   The issues[2]

1.4.1   Pragmatic inference and evidentials

As we have seen, linguists dealing with evidentiality have been primarily, if not solely, concerned with *linguistically encoded* information about the source and reliability of the information being offered. One of the issues I will be investigating is the extent to which evidential information can be communicated in ways other than encoding/decoding. It has hardly ever been pointed out that the source of knowledge or the speaker's degree of certainty about the proposition expressed, can be *pragmatically inferred*. Granting that this is so, it would be interesting to know whether there is a pragmatic framework which can account for such pragmatically inferred evidential information, and its interaction with what is linguistically encoded.

1.4.2   Truth-conditional versus non-truth-conditional semantics

Standardly, semanticists distinguish between *truth-conditional* and *non-truth-conditional* meaning. Evidentials in general have been treated in non-truth-conditional terms, i.e. as contributing not to the proposition expressed by the utterance, its truth-conditional content, but to indicating the source and reliability of the information being offered. Is this, indeed, true for all evidential sentence adverbials and verbs, both truly parenthetical and main-clause ones, as semanticists have claimed? As already suggested, it may turn out that only the truly parenthetical evidentials are non-truth-conditional, whereas the main-clause ones are not.

1.4.3   Explicit versus implicit communication

Standardly, pragmatists distinguish between *explicit* and *implicit* communication. Is the information which speakers successfully communicate about the evidential status of their utterances typically explicit or implicit? Does the distinction between explicit and implicit communication coincide with those between decoding and inference, or between truth-conditional and non-truth-conditional status? These questions will be another main focus of my research.

In the next chapters, three approaches to pragmatic inference, to non-truth-conditional semantics, and to the distinction between explicit and implicit communication will be outlined: the speech-act approach, Grice's approach and the relevance-theoretic approach developed by Sperber and Wilson. In subsequent chapters, the application of these approaches to various evidential constructions will be investigated in more detail.

CHAPTER 2

Speech-act theory

2.1 Speech acts, language and communication

My aim in this chapter is not to provide yet another introduction to speech-act theory, since several good ones exist (Lyons 1977; Bach and Harnish 1979; Recanati 1987; Vanderveken 1990; Tsohatsidis 1994). My aim is, instead, to see what light speech-act theory can shed on the specific questions raised in the previous chapter, about (a) the nature of pragmatic inference, (b) the distinction between truth-conditional and non-truth-conditional semantics, and (c) the distinction between explicit and implicit communication. More detailed discussion of the speech-act approach to evidentials will be given in chapters 4 and 5.

Following Wilson (1998–9), I shall draw a distinction between speech-act theory (the study of speech acts), speech-act pragmatics (the view that utterance interpretation is largely a matter of recognizing what speech acts the speaker intended to perform) and speech-act semantics (the view that speech-act information is often linguistically encoded). Since this distinction is central to the three questions that concern me, I will say a word about each.

2.1.1 Speech-act theory

As is well known, speech-act theory developed as a reaction to what was seen as an over-emphasis on the descriptive use of language in truth-conditional approaches to sentence meaning. Austin, in *How to do things with words* (1962), claimed that language is used not only to describe the world, but to act upon, or in, it: language is used to perform actions — speech acts: making statements, giving commands, asking questions, making promises, predicting, warning, apologizing, guessing, congratulating, begging, baptizing. In other words, language is not only a tool for representing reality or expressing thoughts; it is also used to change the world: to influence others, to create new states of affairs, to express social roles, to arouse emotions. It is primarily a social phenomenon, reflected in social institutions which enable a wide variety of actions to be performed (Lyons 1977: 725; Bach and Harnish 1979; Sperber and Wilson 1986/95; Recanati 1987; Tsohatsidis 1994).

Speech-act theorists have been much concerned with describing and classifying speech acts. Their focus has been on illocutionary acts (e.g. asserting, promising, warning, ordering, requesting, threatening, etc.) In *Expression and meaning* (Searle 1979: 1–29), Searle distinguishes five major categories of illocutionary acts:

i.   *Assertives* (e.g. statements), which are defined as committing the speaker (in varying degrees) to the truth of the proposition expressed by the utterance. Assertive speech acts include *asserting* that *p*, *swearing* that *p*, *insisting* that *p*, *boasting* that *p*, *complaining* that *p*.[1]

ii.   *Directives* (e.g. orders), which are defined as attempts (of varying degrees of strength) to get the hearer to do something. Directive speech acts include *advising* someone to do something, *requesting* someone to do something, *entreating* someone to do something. Questions come under this category of speech acts, according to Searle, since they are attempts by the speaker to get the hearer to do something, namely answer the question.

iii. *Commissives* (e.g. promises), which commit the speaker to some future course of action, e.g. *undertaking* to do something.

iv.   *Expressives* (e.g. apologies) which are defined as communicating the speaker's emotional attitude to the state of affairs described by the utterance, e.g. *congratulating, thanking, welcoming* someone.

v.   *Declarations* (e.g. declaring the court open) which are defined as bringing about the state of affairs described in the proposition expressed by the utterance, e.g. *firing* someone, *declaring* war, *baptizing* someone.

Searle's definition of assertive speech acts, and in particular his claim that these commit the speaker *with varying degrees of strength* to the truth of the proposition expressed, should shed some light on the analysis of evidentials. According to Searle, assertives are "assessable" or "determinable" on a true-false dimension, and the speaker should specify the extent to which he commits himself to the truth of the proposition expressed. This degree of commitment may vary between *suggesting* or *putting forward as a hypothesis*, on the one hand, and *insisting*, or *swearing*, on the other (Searle 1979: 12–13). On this approach, evidentials might be seen as providing a linguistic means of specifying degree of commitment.

In the same descriptive vein, speech-act theorists have defined various *felicity conditions* which illocutionary acts must fulfil if they are to be successful and non-defective. Searle (1969: 57–61) classified felicity conditions under three main heads, as *preparatory* conditions, *sincerity* conditions and *essential* conditions. To satisfy preparatory conditions, the person and the situation must be appropriate for the performance of the act. If not, the act will be, in Austin's terms, a misfire. For example, the person who pronounces two people man and wife must be authorized to do so, and the utterance should be produced in the course of a more or less established procedure. To satisfy sincerity conditions, the person performing the act must do so sincerely, i.e. with the appropriate beliefs or feelings. If not, the act will be, in Austin's terms, an abuse. For example, the person who thanks someone for a service must feel gratitude or appreciation towards him. Essential conditions are those that must be satisfied for the act to be performed at all. For example, the person who promises essentially undertakes the obligation or expresses the intention to perform a certain act. If the speaker can show that he did not have this intention, he can prove that the utterance was not a promise.

It is not clear where evidentials would fit into this framework of felicity conditions. According to Austin, our assertions are not valid unless we have evidence for them (Lyons 1977:733–734). According to Searle (as noted above), the speaker of an assertive speech act makes a stronger or weaker commitment to the proposition expressed. Both these conditions can be explicitly signalled by use of evidentials. But it is hard to tell whether the conditions imposed by evidentials are preparatory conditions, sincerity conditions or essential conditions on speech acts such as *asserting, suggesting, guaranteeing.* One might say, perhaps, that having an appropriate degree of evidence is an essential condition on suggesting, that *believing* one has an appropriate degree of evidence is a sincerity condition on suggesting, and that being *regarded* as having access to an appropriate degree of evidence is a preparatory condition on suggesting. Discussions of felicity conditions generally do not look in detail at speech acts of this type. However, the standard speech-act position is that *believing* the proposition expressed by an utterance is the sincerity condition on *asserting, having a basis for* presenting the asserted proposition as true is the preparatory condition on asserting and the proposition's *representing an actual state of affairs* is the essential condition on asserting (Searle 1969:64; Vanderveken 1990:117–118). Sincerity conditions come with varying degrees of strength (Vanderveken 1990:119–121). Thus, it has been claimed that *putting forward as a positive assertion* that the state of affairs represented by the proposition expressed is (or will be) true is a special sincerity condition expressed by *guaranteeing,* and *putting forward as a tentative assertion* is a special sincerity condition expressed by *suggesting.* Adverbs such as *frankly* or *sincerely* are seen as expressing these sincerity conditions with a higher degree of strength (Vanderveken 1990:119). It seems, then, that on the speech-act approach, evidentials would be analysed as providing a linguistic means of expressing the degree of strength of the sincerity conditions of assertions, i.e. the degree with which the speaker asserts: weaker for *suggest*, stronger for *guarantee* (Vanderveken 1990:172, 183).

2.1.2 Speech-act pragmatics

Speech-act theory has been seen as providing a useful framework for studying pragmatics. Within this framework, utterance interpretation is seen as largely a matter of identifying the set of speech-acts, and in particular illocutionary acts, the speaker intended to perform (Wilson 1998–9, Lecture 2). Consider (1):

(1) I'll stay until 5.00.

For speech-act pragmatics, having identified the intended locutionary act (or proposition expressed), the hearer's main task in interpreting (1) is to decide which illocutionary act the speaker primarily intended to perform: a straightforward assertion, a promise, a warning, a threat, and so on. This approach is well illustrated in Bach and Harnish's book *Linguistic communication and speech acts* (1979), which discusses in some detail how such a pragmatic theory might work. According to Bach and Harnish, the hearer should reason along the following lines in inferring the illocutionary act primarily intended by the speaker of (1):

L1 *S* is uttering *e*.
L2 *S* means 'S will stay until 5.00' by *e*.
L3 *Mary* is saying that she will stay until 5.00 at ... *place* on ... *day*.
L4 *Mary*, if speaking literally, is constating that she will stay until 5.00.
L5 *Mary* could be speaking literally.

and ending with

L6 *Mary* is promising that she will stay until 5.00.
       (Bach and Harnish 1979:61)

On this approach, appeals to pragmatic inference are made at various points. For example, some account of pragmatic inference is needed to deal with disambiguation and reference assignment, and more generally the identification of the intended locutionary act, which in Bach and Harnish's schema occurs at

L3. There are also cases where utterances do not encode a full proposition: e.g. "Red light", "Hurrah for Manchester United" or "Down with Caesar" (Searle 1969:31; Vanderveken 1990:23–24). Such cases presumably call for further pragmatic inference in order to be interpreted. Similarly, some account of pragmatic inference is needed to account for indirect speech acts, which are a major feature of speech-act pragmatics. Bach and Harnish further develop the above schema in order to show how hearers reason in inferring indirect speech acts. How, for example, might the hearer H infer that (1) was intended as an offer to help him prepare a dinner party? On Bach and Harnish's account, the hearer might reason along the following lines:

L7 Mary could not be merely stating that she will be staying until 5.00. (It is mutually believed that H is having a dinner party and needs some help.)
L8 There is some F-ing that P connected in a way identifiable under the circumstances to stating that Mary will stay until 5.00, such that in stating that Mary will stay until 5.00 Mary could also be F-ing that P.
L9 Mary is stating that she will stay until 5.00 and thereby offering to help H with preparations for the dinner party.
(Bach and Harnish 1979:73)

Moreover, in cases such as (1) where the direct illocutionary acts are not linguistically encoded, speech-act pragmatics must provide an account of how hearers infer them: how they choose, in context, an actual illocutionary force from a range of semantically possible illocutionary forces assigned to the sentence uttered. This is directly relevant to my work on evidentials, since, as I have shown in chapter 1, the degree of strength of an assertive speech-act often appears to be contextually inferred. The question I will be asking in a later section is what light speech-act pragmatics sheds on this process of pragmatic inference.

2.1.3 Speech-act semantics

Speech-act semantics is the study of how speech-act information is linguistically encoded (Wilson 1998–9, Lecture 2). The obvious way to encode such information is by means of performative verbs. These can be used precisely to *name* the illocutionary act that is being performed. Examples are given in (2):

(2) a. I promise you that I'll stay until 5.00.
     b. I warn you that I'll stay until 5.00.

Speech-act theorists generally treat such verbs in their first-person present-tense uses as making no contribution to the truth conditions of the utterances in which they occur. (2a) and (2b) are true if and only if the speaker will stay until 5.00, and they are truth-conditionally equivalent to (2c):

    c.   I'll stay until 5.00.

All three utterances express the same proposition, and hence perform the same locutionary act. Performative verbs are devoid of descriptive meaning; their only function is to disambiguate the illocutionary force of the utterance by *indicating* what speech act is being performed.

On this approach, a fundamental distinction is made between two types of information that can be linguistically encoded: some words contribute to the *proposition expressed* by an utterance, whereas others encode information about *illocutionary force*. Hence Searle's famous representation of sentence/utterance meaning as F(P) — i.e. as illocutionary force applied to a propositional content. On this approach, (2a–c) above would have the same propositional content, but might differ as to their illocutionary force, encoded in (2a) and (2b) by the performative verbs. However, most speech-act theorists claim to be doing more than mere lexicology of performative verbs. Speech-act semanticists claim that the class of linguistic constructions which encode speech-act information — i.e. the class of illocutionary force indicators — is much wider than the class of performative verbs. Mood indicators, i.e linguistic features that distinguish declarative, interrogative, imperative, exclamative, optative, subjunctive, conditional sentence types, are seen as a further device for encoding speech-act information. For example, interrogatives are seen as asking questions, or requesting information, and imperatives are seen as issuing commands, or requesting action. 'Asking whether' and 'telling to' are speech acts belonging to the *directive* class: to 'ask whether' is to attempt to get the hearer to answer the question, and to 'tell to' is to attempt to get the hearer to perform some action (Searle 1979: 13–14; Bach and Harnish 1979: 48; Sperber and Wilson 1986/ 95: 246; Wilson and Sperber 1988: 80, 91; Vanderveken 1990: 15; Bach 1994a).

According to Vanderveken (1990: 16), the speech acts performed by different imperative sentences can be narrowed down by means of further illocutionary-force indicators. Examples are given in (3a–b):

  (3) a.   Frankly, do it!
       b.   Please, do it!
       c.   Whether you like it or not, do it!

(3a–c) have different directive illocutionary forces encoded by specific linguistic indicators such as *frankly*, *please* and conditionals. *Frankly* in (3a) indicates that the speaker is granting honest permission to the hearer to do something. This imperative sentence has the illocutionary force of permitting and indicates a special (sincere) type of directive speech act. *Please* in (3b) indicates that the speaker gives an option of refusal to the hearer. This imperative sentence has the illocutionary force of a request, and indicates a special (polite) type of directive speech act. The conditional *Whether ... or not* in (3c) indicates that the speaker does not give an option of refusal to the hearer. This imperative sentence has the illocutionary force of an order and indicates a special (enforcing) type of directive speech act.

Thus, speech-act semantics is the study, on the one hand, of the linguistically encoded aspects of the locutionary act, and on the other, of the various illocutionary-force indicators available for encoding information about intended illocutionary acts. Evidentials, as we will see, are generally regarded as contributing to the illocutionary force of an utterance rather than to the proposition expressed (the locutionary act). This is one of the claims I propose to investigate in later chapters. In the rest of this chapter, I will consider how much light this general framework sheds on the three specific questions that interest me: about the nature of pragmatic inference, the distinction between truth-conditional and non-truth-conditional semantics, and the distinction between explicit and implicit communication.

2.2   Speech acts and pragmatic inference

The main questions to be addressed in this section are (a) whether speech-act theorists subscribe to a distinction between semantic decoding and pragmatic inference; (b) whether they acknowledge the extent to which pragmatic inference is necessary for utterance interpretation; (c) whether they shed any light on the nature of the pragmatic inference processes involved; and (d) whether they offer any criterion for choosing the intended interpretation from a range of possible ones.

Early (pre-Gricean) speech-act theorists such as Austin, Strawson, Urmson and early Searle do not seem to subscribe to a semantics-pragmatics distinction. Sentence meaning is identified with illocutionary-force potential: to give the meaning of a sentence is to specify the range of speech acts that an utterance of that sentence could be used to perform (Wilson and Sperber 1988:77). Thus,

Searle (1969) concludes that utterance interpretation can be reduced to sentence interpretation: to interpret an utterance, i.e. to determine the illocutionary act performed by the speaker, it is sufficient in principle to understand the sentence uttered — or at least some sentence that *could* have been uttered (Recanati 1987:26). According to Searle:

> Wherever the illocutionary force of an utterance is not explicit it can always be made explicit. This is an instance of the principle of expressibility, stating that whatever can be meant can be said. Of course, a given language may not be rich enough to enable speakers to say everything they mean, but there are no barriers in principle to enriching it. ... whatever can be implied can be said, ... (Searle 1969:68)

Essentially, the interpretation of utterances was seen as a matter of linguistic decoding. Hence the emphasis on illocutionary-force indicators such as performative verbs, verb mood, and other devices mentioned above.

However, some features of speech acts are clearly pragmatically inferred: indirect speech acts are the paradigm examples of pragmatically-inferred speech acts. The question is, how do speech-act theorists account for them?

Searle, in his early work (1969), analysed indirect speech acts in terms of felicity conditions: performing an indirect speech act is, essentially, indicating the satisfaction of an essential condition by asserting or questioning one of the other conditions: preparatory conditions, propositional content conditions and sincerity conditions (Searle 1969, chapter 3:68). Thus, (4) indicates the satisfaction of the essential condition for a request by questioning whether the preparatory condition that the hearer has the ability to perform the act holds (see also Searle 1975:60, 1979:31; Lyons 1977:784–785). It is still not clear how hearers infer the indirect speech act, although it might be clear how speakers reason in producing them, how "it is possible for the speaker to say one thing and mean that but also to mean something else" (Searle 1979:31). In later work, Searle (1975, 1979) specifically uses Gricean machinery to deal with indirect speech acts. He admits that the above account is "incomplete" and modifies it by taking into consideration Grice's principles of cooperative conversation, mutually shared background information and the hearer's ability to infer (Searle 1975:59–82, 1979:30–57).

Pragmatic inference as it has been dealt with by contemporary pragmatists (e.g. Bach and Harnish, Recanati, Sperber and Wilson) is not part of the pre-Gricean theorists' machinery at all. After all, even when it is not explicitly indicated which illocutionary act was intended, the speaker *could have chosen* to use an explicit performative, which reinforces the same idea, namely that utterance interpretation is, in principle at least, a matter of sentence interpretation (Recanati 1987:26). This emphasis on linguistic decoding, or linguistically encoded illocutionary forces, gave pragmatics a minimal or non-existent role in early speech-act theory.

How, then, do speech-act theorists deal with disambiguation and reference assignment, which are needed in order to recover the locutionary act performed; and how do they say hearers choose among a variety of speech acts all compatible with the linguistic properties of the sentence uttered? Pre-Gricean theorists usually appeal to 'context' when it comes to dealing with these issues, but they never really explain what they mean by it. According to Austin "... the occasion of an utterance matters seriously, and ... the words used are to some extent to be 'explained' by the 'context' in which they are designed to be or have actually been spoken in a linguistic interchange." (Austin 1962:100)

Similarly, Searle, in discussing reference, claims:

> In the above example ["That criminal is your friend"] ... it is clear that the context is sufficient to provide an identifying description, for the word "that" in "that criminal" indicates that the object either is present or has already been referred to by some other referring expression ... (Searle 1969:90)

In later work, Searle goes into the issue at greater length:

> ... the sentence only determines a definite set of truth conditions relative to a particular context. That is because of ... some indexical element, such as the present tense, or the demonstrative "here", or the occurrence of contextually dependent definite descriptions, such as "the cat" and "the mat". (Searle 1979:79)

In fact, Searle's chapter on Literal meaning (1979:117–136) is dedicated to defending the thesis that the meaning of a large number of sentences depends on "certain factual background assumptions which are not part of the literal meaning" or part of "the semantic content of the sentence" (ibid.:80). He refers to vagueness, indexicality and ambiguity as some of the indeterminacies that have to be resolved. It is not clear, though, how exactly hearers identify the required background assumptions and use them to disambiguate, assign reference, resolve vagueness etc. We are still a long way from having a pragmatic inference process described, let alone explained.

Regarding the disambiguation of illocutionary force, Searle claims, as vaguely as Austin, that: "Often, in actual speech situations, the context will make it clear what the illocutionary force of the utterance is, without its being

necessary to invoke the appropriate explicit illocutionary force indicator."
(Searle 1969:30) Again, it is not enough to know that in cases where an explicit
illocutionary force marker is absent, the 'context' will do the work. We need to
know how this is so.

In more recent work, speech-act theorists have been slightly more specific
about the nature of 'context':

> Context is, … one of the determinants of the illocutionary act performed by an
> utterance. For the purposes of formalization a context of utterance consists of
> five distinguishable elements and sets of elements: a speaker, a hearer, a time,
> a place, and those various other features of the speaker, hearer, time and place
> that are relevant to the performance of the speech acts. Especially important
> features are the psychological states — intentions, desires, beliefs, etc. — of the
> speaker and the hearer. (Searle and Vanderveken 1985:27)

This is essentially the definition of context used in most formal approaches to
semantics, but it still leaves many questions unanswered. In particular, if the
intentions, desires and beliefs of the speaker and hearer affect utterance
interpretation, as they obviously do, how exactly do they do this? How, for
example, do hearers recognize the intentions, desires or beliefs of the speaker
that are intended to play a role in the interpretation process and how, once
identified, do they help with disambiguation, reference assignment and
identification of illocutionary force? No answer to these questions is provided
by early speech-act accounts.

It seems, then, that (a) early speech-act theorists acknowledge the importance of general pragmatic factors such as 'context' in utterance interpretation,
but do not specify their nature or how they operate. Pragmatic inference
processes as such are not part of their machinery, hence (b) they do not shed
any light on the nature of the pragmatic processes involved, and (c) they do not
offer any criterion for choosing the intended interpretation from a range of
possible ones.

Post-Gricean speech-act theorists, such as Searle (1975) and Bach and
Harnish (1979) do distinguish between semantic decoding and pragmatic
inference, and rely on Gricean pragmatics to deal with the pragmatic side. Bach
and Harnish acknowledge the extent to which pragmatic inference is necessary
for utterance interpretation, and propose an inference pattern, the *speech act
schema* (SAS), for use in resolving linguistic underdeterminacies which arise at
the level of the locutionary act, or 'what is said'. This inference pattern is also
designed to describe how hearers identify the illocutionary act, the force or
attitude expressed. Here, *mutual contextual beliefs* (MCBs), and in particular the

assumption that the speaker has spoken *contextually* or *conversationally appropriately,* play an important role. A speaker's contribution is conversationally appropriate if and only if it accords with certain maxims — *conversational presumptions* in Bach and Harnish's terms — which are in effect at that time (ibid.: 62–65). Central to these are the *Communicative Presumption* (CP):

> *Communicative Presumption* (CP): The mutual belief in C_L [linguistic community] that whenever a member S says something in L to another member H, he is doing so with some recognizable illocutionary intent. (ibid.: 7)

and the *conversational presumptions*:

> *Relevance* (RE): The speaker's contribution is relevant to the talk-exchange at that point.
>
> *Sequencing* (SE): The speaker's contribution is of an illocutionary type appropriate to that stage of the talk-exchange.
>
> *Sincerity* (SI): The speaker's contribution to the talk-exchange is sincere — the speaker has the attitudes he expresses. (ibid.: 63)

When these presumptions are in effect, speakers will be presumed to be speaking with recognizable illocutionary intent and hearers should be able to recognize the intended illocutionary force (ibid.: 65). In Bach and Harnish's schema, then, mutual contextual beliefs and the communicative and conversational presumptions interact with what is said to enable the hearer to infer a specific illocutionary force.

However, a number of issues remain unresolved: Bach and Harnish admit, for example, that the presumption of Relevance is a very "powerful" one, but also very "vague": they do not specify what "being relevant" really means. Moreover, although the SAS represents the pattern of inference followed by the hearer, they acknowledge that it does not represent *how* the inference is actually made (Bach and Harnish 1979: 18, 76–81), or explain why hearers follow it. A related question is whether hearers *do* always follow the inference process described by the SAS, which looks like a deliberate, conscious process rather than something that hearers might spontaneously and unconsciously perform. These are questions also raised by Grice's approach to pragmatic inference. Since later *speech-act pragmatics* is really a combination of speech-act semantics with Gricean pragmatics, I will defer further discussion of the pragmatic inference processes involved until the chapter on Grice.

2.3 Speech acts and non-truth-conditional semantics

As noted above, for speech-act theorists, the *propositional content*, or *truth-conditional content*, of an utterance is distinguished from its *illocutionary force*. The point is clearly made by Searle:

> ... I am distinguishing between the illocutionary act and the propositional content of the illocutionary act. ... From this semantical point of view we can distinguish two (not necessarily separate) elements in the syntactical structure of the sentence, which we might call the propositional indicator and the illocutionary force indicator. The illocutionary force indicator shows how the proposition is to be taken, or to put it another way, what illocutionary force the utterance is to have: that is, what illocutionary act the speaker is performing in the utterance of the sentence. Illocutionary force indicating devices in English include at least: word order, stress, intonation contour, punctuation, the mood of the verb, and the so-called performative verbs. I may indicate the kind of illocutionary act I am performing by beginning the sentence with "I apologize", "I warn", "I state", etc. (Searle 1969: 30)

The standard way to represent this distinction is:

$$F(p)$$

where F is a variable for illocutionary force-indicating devices and p is a variable for propositions expressed (Searle 1969: 31; Searle and Vanderveken 1985: 1–2, 8–9; Vanderveken 1990: 13). Thus, utterances such as (4a–e):

(4) a. Paul will do it.
    b. Please, Paul, do it.
    c. Will Paul do it?
    d. If only Paul would do it!
    e. Whether you like it or not, Paul, do it!

are seen as having the same propositional content, namely that Paul does something, but different potential illocutionary forces: (4a) can have the illocutionary force of a prediction, (4b) the force of a polite request, (4c) the force of a request for information, (4d) the force of a wish and (4e) the force of an order (Vanderveken 1990: 11, 14, 16).

Consider now the truth-conditional status of the illocutionary-force indicators listed above. According to Austin (1962), utterances (5a) and (5b):

(5) a. George didn't come.
    b. I state that George didn't come.

have the same truth conditions and represent the same state of affairs, namely one in which George didn't come. It follows that the performative prefix 'I state' does not contribute to the truth-conditional content of the utterance it introduces. It is devoid of any descriptive meaning; its only function is to render the illocutionary force of the utterance unambiguously explicit (Recanati 1987:21).

On this approach, propositional contents have truth conditions, whereas illocutionary acts have *conditions of success and satisfaction*. What is important to notice here is that speech-act theorists were genuinely interested in the distinction between truth-conditional and non-truth-conditional meaning. However, later work seems to have shown that they often got it wrong. It has been repeatedly argued (Lemmon 1962; Hedenius 1963; Lewis 1970; Wiggins 1971; Warnock 1971; Bach 1975; Ginet 1979; Cresswell 1979; Bach and Harnish 1979; Recanati 1987) that Austin was wrong to say that performative verbs make no contribution to truth-conditional content. Performative verbs do have a descriptive content and, moreover, they are truth-conditional. Surely, the utterances in (6) and (7) below do not have the same truth conditions, as they would on the performative analysis:

(6)   A: I tell you that the rain has stopped.
      B: And I tell you it hasn't.

(7)   A: The rain has stopped.
     *B: And it hasn't.

Recanati (1987) makes this point by noting that (i) performative verbs differ from mood (another illocutionary force indicator) precisely because they have a descriptive meaning, which mood clearly does not; in this respect they are similar to any ordinary lexical item, in a way moods are not; (ii) the utterance 'Mary states that the rain has stopped' differs from 'I state that the rain has stopped' only in replacing the name of the speaker, i.e. 'Mary', for 'I'. Surely the truth conditions of the utterances should not change under this substitution: both represent a state of affairs in which Mary claims that the rain has stopped (Recanati 1987:23–24); (iii) omitting certain performative verbs clearly shows that the truth conditions of an explicit performative do differ from those of the associated primary performative, e.g. 'I deny that this is so' does not include the corresponding primary performative 'This is not so'. Similarly, 'I promise to come' does not include the corresponding primary performative 'I will come' (Recanati 1987:48–49); and (iv) in the case of 'I believe', if I am asked in a poll to give my belief(s), I might say 'I believe that the new tax system is unfair', in which case I am clearly describing one of my beliefs (Recanati 1987:49).

These and other arguments suggest that performative verbs contribute to the truth conditions of utterances in the same way as any truth-conditional item does. They are used to perform a *direct act* of declaration and *indirect acts* of commanding, promising, threatening, predicting, etc. Recanati (1987) defends this conclusion in great detail. If he is right, then the truth-conditional status of other "illocutionary force indicators" — including evidentials — may need reconsideration.

Performative verbs are the best-known illocutionary-force indicators. Other types of expression which have been standardly seen as falling into the same category are mood indicators, word order, intonation and punctuation signs. These are not always seen as precise enough to determine the exact illocutionary force intended by the speaker (Searle and Vanderveken 1985: 1–7; Vanderveken 1990: 16–17, 23–25). More complex illocutionary forces may be conveyed by means of additional linguistic indicators: illocutionary adverbials e.g. *frankly, moreover, if I may say so, by the way, speaking of ...*, (Bach and Harnish 1979: 219–225), other types of adverbial e.g. *please, alas, yes, to be sure* (Vanderveken 1990: 16–17; Recanati 1987: 21) connectives e.g. *and, but, after all, if, even* (Searle and Vanderveken 1985: 3, 5; Vanderveken 1990: 259; Recanati 1987: 15–16, 21), and performative verbs in a parenthetical use, e.g. *I'll be there, I promise* (Urmson 1963: 220–246; Lyons 1977: 738). The meaning of these indicators is seen as determining the specific illocutionary forces of the utterances that include them by expressing additional components of illocutionary force, e.g. *"an increase or decrease in the degree of strength of illocutionary point"* (emphasis added) (Vanderveken 1990: 17). As noted above, evidentials would presumably be treated along these lines, as specifying the degree of strength of the speaker's commitment (Urmson 1963; Palmer 1986).

One class of items I will be looking at more closely contains the attitudinal adverbials, e.g. *happily, unfortunately, luckily*. These have also been dealt with by speech-act theorists (Urmson 1963: 220–246) as illocutionary-force indicators. On Urmson's approach, the attitudinal adverbial *happily* is treated as indicating that a speech act of rejoicing or felicitating is being performed, the attitudinal adverbial *unfortunately* as indicating that a speech act of complaining or lamenting is being performed, and so on. These are *expressive* speech acts which "express the psychological state specified in the sincerity condition about a state of affairs specified in the propositional content" (Searle 1979: 15). Examples of expressive verbs are *thank, congratulate, apologize, condole, deplore* and *welcome*. It might be questioned whether the expression of attitudes — thoughts and emotions — is really best analysed in speech-act terms. Typically, speech acts are acts that can not be performed without speaking — or at least without acting publicly. Warning, threatening, promising, asserting are examples. Thoughts and emotions, though, are primarily private. You may be sitting quietly, and I may nonetheless infer that you believe something, or suspect something, or regard something as fortunate or unfortunate. I cannot infer in the same way that you are warning me, or promising me, or asserting something. Attitudinal adverbials, then, fit much less naturally into the speech-act framework than the other "illocutionary-force indicators" discussed above. I will return to these points in chapters 4 and 5.

To conclude, speech-act theorists systematically distinguish between (truth-conditional) propositional content and (non-truth-conditional) illocutionary force indicators. Such indicators have been claimed to include performative verbs, illocutionary, evidential and attitudinal adverbials, and various types of parenthetical construction. The claim that performatives are non-truth-conditional has been seriously challenged. My aim in later chapters is to establish whether speech-act theorists might have been as mistaken about evidentials as they appear to have been about performative verbs themselves.

2.4 Speech acts and explicit vs. implicit communication

The main questions to be raised in this section are whether speech-act theorists have a conception of *explicit* versus *implicit*, and if so, whether illocutionary-force indicators are seen as falling on the explicit or the implicit side. To answer these questions, we need to know how the distinction between explicit and implicit communication should be drawn. In general, it has been drawn in two different ways: (a) by claiming that anything that is linguistically encoded is explicitly communicated and anything that is pragmatically inferred is implicitly communicated; and (b) by basing the distinction on Grice's distinction between saying and implicating.[2]

Both approaches capture a central, pre-theoretical intuition about the distinction between explicit and implicit communication. Most of us would agree that in the exchange in (8):

(8) *Peter*: Would you like to go to the movies?
     Mary: I'm handing in an essay tomorrow.

Mary has explicitly communicated (for example) the information in (9):

(9)   Mary is handing in an essay on 11th May 1999.

and implicitly communicated the information in (10):

(10)   Mary doesn't want to go to the movies.

However, as Wilson 1998–9 points out, these pre-theoretical intuitions may not be so clear in other cases. Consider (11):

(11)   a.   *Peter*:   Is Bill awake?
       b.   *Mary*:   He is.

What Mary communicates by uttering (11b) is that Bill is awake. But does she communicate it explicitly or not? Here, our pre-theoretical intuitions may pull us in different directions. One reaction to (11b) is to say that the communication is implicit because Mary has not linguistically *encoded* the information that Bill is awake: she has used the pronoun *he* rather than the name *Bill*, and the predicate is not overtly realized. As a result, the hearer will have to go through some pragmatic inferencing in order to derive the information that Bill is awake; hence the tendency to say that this information has *not* been explicitly communicated. This idea is reinforced by the intuition that Mary could have made her utterance *more* explicit by saying *Bill* rather than *he*, and by saying *awake* rather than leaving an empty predicate. It would be possible, then, to argue that only what is linguistically encoded is explicitly communicated, and any element of pragmatic inference falls on the implicit side. Similar intuitions arise with disambiguation in (12a) and (12b):

(12)   a.   Bill bought a bat.
      b.   Bill said he was leaving on Tuesday.

(12a) is a case of lexical ambiguity and (12b) a case of syntactic ambiguity. Suppose that in saying (12a), Mary communicates that Bill has bought a cricket bat rather than a flying rodent, and in saying (12b), Mary communicates that Bill is leaving on Tuesday rather than that he spoke on Tuesday, the question is, has she communicated this information explicitly or implicitly? As in (11b) above, an element of pragmatic inference is involved; hence the tendency to say that this interpretation has been implicitly rather than explicitly communicated. This tendency is reinforced by the fact that Mary could have made her utterances more explicit by encoding the intended interpretation in an unambiguous way. This could be seen as further evidence for the claim that the distinction between explicit and implicit communication is coextensive with the distinction between linguistic decoding and inference. Notice that on this approach, the overt illocutionary-force indicators would fall on the explicit side, since what they communicate is linguistically encoded. By contrast, disambiguating the illocutionary force of utterances when no illocutionary-force indicator appears in the utterance would fall on the implicit side.

The second way of drawing the distinction between explicit and implicit communication is to base it on Grice's distinction between saying and implicating. Here, I shall simply sketch the lines along which this distinction is drawn, since a detailed account of Grice's theory of meaning will be given in chapter 3. Grice distinguishes between what is said, i.e. the proposition expressed by an utterance, and what is implicated, i.e. everything communicated by an utterance that is not part of what is said. For Grice, reference assignment and disambiguation are resolved at the level of 'what is said'. Thus, he would claim that in uttering (11b), Mary may say that Bill is awake, in (12a) she may say that Bill bought a cricket bat and in (12b) she may say that Bill is leaving on Tuesday. If the saying/implicating distinction roughly coincides with the explicit/ implicit distinction, then explicit communication will clearly involve an element of pragmatic inference. Moreover, Grice treats standard non-truth-conditional words, such as the discourse connectives *but, moreover* and *so*, as carrying conventional implicatures, i.e. as falling on the implicit side, although the information they communicate is linguistically encoded. Thus, Grice's distinction allocates truth-conditional information (whether decoded or inferred) to the level of what is said, and non-truth-conditional information (whether decoded or inferred) to the level of what is implicated. On this approach, non-truth-conditional illocutionary force indicators would fall on the implicit side. The issue of how Grice would analyse a variety of illocutionary-force indicators will be discussed in more detail in later chapters.

As Wilson points out (1998–9, Lecture 5), for someone interested in a theoretically adequate distinction between explicit and implicit communication, approach (a) above has little to recommend it. In the first place, there is no point in proliferating distinctions by developing an explicit/implicit distinction that simply coincides with the already existing one between decoding and inference. In the second place, what is linguistically encoded is very often only a fragmentary logical form which does not amount to a full proposition. Surely, when considering what is communicated, we think of the communication of full propositions rather than fragmentary linguistically encoded information. Thus, approach (b), which involves developing Grice's distinction between saying and implicating, looks more adequate as the basis for a full-fledged explicit/implicit distinction.

Early (pre-Gricean) speech-act theorists apparently do not draw a theoretical distinction between explicit and implicit communication. Instead, they use the terms in various pre-theoretical, intuitive ways that allow at least some illocutionary force indicators to fall on the explicit rather than the implicit side. Thus, according to Austin (1962) "... performative verbs serve the special purpose of *making explicit* (which is not the same as stating or describing) what precise action it is that is being performed by the issuing of the utterance: ..." (Austin 1962:61)

Austin contrasts *explicit* performatives, e.g. "I order you to go", with *implicit* ('inexplicit') performatives, e.g. "Go", where it is unclear whether the speaker is ordering or advising or pleading with the hearer to go and where the "circumstances", the "given situation" will do the work of the absent explicit performative (Austin 1962:32). This way of drawing the *explicit/implicit* distinction seems to run more along the lines of (a) than (b) above, i.e. anything that is linguistically encoded is explicitly communicated, whereas anything that is pragmatically inferred is implicitly communicated.

However, it is not clear exactly how Austin would have drawn the distinction. In his view, doing something non-verbal, e.g. bowing and raising one's hat, could count towards making explicit the intended illocutionary force, i.e. paying respects, as much as saying something would (Austin 1962:69–70). His claim that: "To do or to say these things is to make plain how the action is to be taken or understood, what action it is. And so it is with putting in the expression 'I promise that'" (Austin 1962:70) might suggest that 'explicit', in the way Austin used it, is a quite broad term covering not only linguistic devices that make clear the illocutionary force of the utterance, but any type of paralinguistic device that serves the same purpose, hence pragmatically inferred information too. If so, the mapping between explicit/implicit and decoding/inference breaks down. In any case, our speculations about how Austin would draw the explicit/implicit distinction merely suggest that he was far from having a technical working distinction. Moreover, as Lyons observes:

> ... Austin certainly argues throughout [Austin 1962] as if the only way in which the illocutionary force of the utterance can be made explicit is by means of a performative verb (in the first-person singular); and his examples all suggest that this is so. It very much looks, in fact, as if Austin is covertly and perhaps illegitimately restricting the interpretation of "making explicit". ... Presumably, it is a precondition of something being an explicitly performative element for Austin that it should be part of what we say (in the sense "say₂" [uttering, pronouncing]) rather than part of our manner of saying it; and he

does operate with this distinction between what is said and the manner of its being said. But the distinction itself is never made precise. (Lyons 1977:743–744)

Lyons concludes that Austin was using a notion of 'explicit' which does indeed map onto linguistic decoding. If so, illocutionary force indicators, being linguistically encoded, would fall on the explicit side.

Another way in which the terms have been extensively used in speech-act theory is in describing indirect illocutionary acts. Here, 'implicit' is generally equivalent to 'indirect' and 'explicit' to 'direct'. Thus, for example, in saying (13a)–(13c):

(13) a. Can you open the window?
       b. Do you know the way to Oxford Circus?
       c. You are sitting on my linen dress!

the speaker is probably not primarily intending to perform the direct speech act of asking a straightforward question, i.e. requesting information about the hearer's physical ability to open a window in (13a), or requesting information about whether the hearer does or does not know the way to Oxford Circus in (13b). Similarly, in (13c) the speaker is probably not primarily intending to perform the direct speech act of making a simple assertion. Instead, utterances such as (13a–c) are typically used as indirect requests for action (i.e. as equivalent to *Open the window, Show me (or tell me) how to get to Oxford Circus* and *Get off my linen dress*). For speech-act theorists the terms 'implicit' and 'indirect' are interchangeable: "Such implicit acts are called *indirect speech acts.*" (Searle and Vanderveken 1985:10). On this view, the speech-act that is 'directly' performed, i.e. 'explicitly' expressed, is linguistically encoded, and the speech act that is 'indirectly' performed, i.e. implicitly conveyed, is pragmatically inferred.

Notice, moreover, that for speech-act theorists the use of 'indirect' in the phrase 'indirect speech acts' is parallel to the use of 'indirect'/'implicit' in describing exchanges such as (8) above. Here is how Searle begins the main part of his chapter on Indirect speech acts:

Let us begin by considering a typical case of the general phenomenon of indirection:

1. Student X: Let's go to the movies tonight.
2. Student Y: I have to study for an exam.

The utterance of (1) constitutes a proposal in virtue of its meaning, in particular because of the meaning of "Let's". ... The utterance of 2 in the context just given would normally constitute a rejection of the proposal, but not in virtue of its meaning. In virtue of its meaning it is simply a statement about *Y*. (Searle 1979:33)

But this is exactly how 'implicit' is understood in approach (a): as co-extensive with 'pragmatically inferred'. Speech-act theorists tended to concentrate on illocutionary force indicators that make the illocutionary force of an utterance explicit, i.e. linguistically encode it. Hence the emphasis on performative verbs, word order, verb mood, exclamatory adverbs, illocutionary connectives, punctuation signs. This is a further indication that some speech-act theorists at least operated with something like criterion (a).

This view is reinforced by later work in speech-act pragmatics. The performance of *indirect speech acts* is explained by post-Gricean speech-act theorists (e.g. Vanderveken) in terms of *conversational maxims* such as "Speak truly!", "Be sincere", "Let your utterance be a successful and non-defective illocutionary act!", "Let your utterance be an appropriate linguistic means to attain your ends!" (Vanderveken 1990:72–73). When the speaker intends to perform an indirect speech act, he *exploits* some such conversational maxim and the hearer recognizes the intended speech act by reasoning (calculating the indirect speech act) along familiar Gricean lines. Clearly, 'indirect/implicit' meaning must here be understood as 'pragmatically inferred' meaning. Illocutionarily ambivalent utterances, i.e. utterances with no explicit illocutionary force indicator, fall on the implicit side, while illocutionary force indicators fall on the explicit side.

However, the fact that later speech-act theorists appeal to Gricean Maxims does not show that they have adopted Grice's approach to the explicit/implicit distinction. Indeed, Bach (1994a, 1994b) argues that pragmatically inferred truth-conditional meaning is not explicit but implicit (an 'implicature', in his terms). Clearly, some theoretical work remains to be done in this area. In the next chapter, I will look at Grice's approach to the central questions raised in this study, which should shed further light on post-Gricean speech-act accounts.

CHAPTER 3

Grice and communication

3.1 Introduction

There are several good introductions to Grice's work on meaning and com-munication (Bennett 1976; Harnish 1977; Bach and Harnish 1979; Levinson 1983; Blackburn 1984; Sperber and Wilson 1986/95; Recanati 1987; Avramides 1989; Neale 1992). My aim in this chapter is not to add to them but to pick out the features of Grice's approach that seem to me most relevant for the study of evidentials.

As pointed out in the introduction, the interpretation of utterances containing evidentials involves considerable interaction between linguistic encoding and pragmatic inference. While speech-act theorists have been mainly interested in the linguistic encoding side, Grice was particularly interested in the borderline between encoding and inference, and the nature of the pragmatic inference processes themselves. He was the first to develop a theory of com-munication that showed how communication could take place in the absence of a code, and I will be considering what light this might shed on the role of pragmatic inference in evidential constructions. In addition, he proposed a new analysis of a class of non-truth-conditional expressions such as *but, so, more-over,* which seems to bear some relation to evidential expressions, and I will be considering to what extent his approach might shed light on the semantics of evidentials.

3.1.1 Grice on communication

Grice, in his *William James Lectures* (1967), offered the first known alternative to the code model of communication. Pre-Gricean theories viewed communi-cation as a process of coding and decoding. A *code* is a set of shared rules, or conventions, pairing *messages* with *signals*. In verbal communication, the *messages* would be the thoughts the speaker intends to communicate, and the *signals* would be the utterances she produces. On this approach, verbal com-munication involves the speaker encoding her private thoughts into public utterances, which the hearer observes and decodes.

Grice paved the way for an *inferential* model of communication, where communication is viewed as *intentional* behaviour, and understanding an utterance as recognizing the intentions behind it. For Grice, utterance interpretation need not involve the use of any code. He uses the term 'utterance' to refer to any type of communicative behaviour, verbal or non-verbal. As Avramides points out: "Under Grice's broad reading of 'utterance' can be included such things as flag waving, air raid whistles, nods of the head, hand waving, etc., as well as sentences of a language." (Avramides 1989:42).

And it is clear that many cases of non-verbal communication do not involve the use of a code. To illustrate, suppose Mary asks Peter whether he enjoyed his skiing holidays in France and Peter, instead of giving a straightforward answer, shows Mary his leg in plaster. Mary will clearly infer the answer, which will be along the lines of 'Breaking my leg ruined my skiing holidays in France'. Similarly, if Mary asks Peter how he feels, he might simply cough, thus allowing her to infer that he has a chest cold. Clearly, no code is involved here and such types of communication fall outside the scope of a code model.

Even in verbal communication, which involves the use of a grammar or code, the thoughts the speaker intends to communicate are far from fully decodable. They are partly decoded, but partly inferred on the basis of contextual information: the form of the utterance falls far short of encoding a full-fledged speaker's meaning.

The code model of communication offers little insight into these two types of case: in the first, there is nothing for hearers to decode, and in the second, the speaker's meaning is only partially encoded. What is crucial to both cases, according to Grice, is recognition of the communicator's *intention* to convey one piece of information rather than another. Grice's most basic claim is that recognition of the communicator's intention — by whatever means — is enough for communication to succeed (Bach and Harnish 1979: Introduction xiv–xv; Sperber and Wilson 1986/95:21–28; Recanati 1987:177–178; Avramides 1989:15–16).

How do we recognize the intentions of others? Suppose, for example, that Mary sees me approach the counter of a shop and open my bag. She will assume that I intend to pay for the items I have chosen, rather than simply put the items in my bag and leave. Mary does not *decode* my intentions: there is no code according to which opening a bag means that I intend to pay. In general, intentions are not decoded but inferred on the basis of observable evidence, by a process of *non-demonstrative inference* involving hypothesis formation and evaluation. Grice's main contribution to pragmatics was to show how the pragmatic inference process might go.

The cases of communication that Grice was primarily interested in go beyond the mere recognition of an intention. Grice was interested in distinguishing a certain 'overt' type of communication from a variety of more covert forms of information transmission involving an element of manipulation or concealment (for examples and discussion, see Sperber and Wilson 1986/95: 28–31). There has been considerable debate on how the relevant notion of overtness can be characterized. What is most important about this debate is the assumption that lay behind it: that in 'overt' communication, humans have special help in recognizing the communicator's intentions. In other words, 'overt' communication is a separate domain, with its own theoretical principles and generalizations.

Granted the existence of a special domain of overt communication, the question arises: how are communicators' intentions recognized at all? As we have seen, Grice sketched a general answer: these intentions are *inferred*, by a non-demonstrative inference process in which the fact that overt communication is being attempted provides some special help. In overt communication, according to Grice, the audience is entitled to assume that the communicator is aiming at certain standards. These are described in his famous Co-operative Principle and Maxims, to which I will now turn.

3.1.2   The CP and maxims

Before looking at the co-operative principle and maxims, let me first set out a general picture of the various categories of overtly communicated (non-natural) meaning that, in Grice's framework, an utterance can convey:

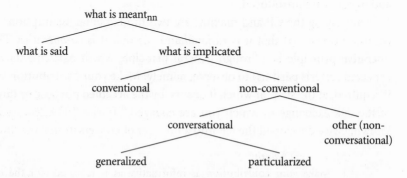

I will comment briefly on each of the categories before considering where the CP and maxims fit in.

As noted in chapter 2, a fundamental distinction in Grice's framework is between *saying* and *implicating*. Grice uses the expression 'what is said' to refer to the truth-conditional content of utterances, i.e. to what is explicitly or literally said (Levinson 1983:97). What is implicated is everything that is overtly communicated by an utterance but is not part of what is said.

Grice also distinguished between various types of implicatures. *Conventional* implicatures are linguistically encoded, and hence semantic, but do not affect the truth conditions of the utterance (Blakemore 1992:148). To illustrate the distinction between saying and conventionally implicating, consider (1):

(1) *Mary*: She was poor but she was honest.

What Mary has 'said', according to Grice, is given in (2):

(2) a. She was poor.
     b. She was honest.

What Mary has conventionally implicated is given in (3):

(3) There is a contrast between (2a) and (2b).

The information in (3) does not affect the truth conditions of the utterance in (1), and hence *but* is non-truth-conditional. It is precisely the fact that conventional implicatures are non-truth-conditional that distinguishes them from other types of linguistically-encoded meaning.[1]

Non-conventional implicatures fall into further sub-types, of which the best known are the *conversational* ones. These are crucially not decoded but inferred. It is partly to explain the recovery of conversational implicatures that Grice's CP and maxims are introduced.

Underlying the CP and maxims are two fundamental assumptions about communication: (i) that it is *rational* and (ii) that it is *co-operative*. The co-operative principle is a "rough general principle which participants will be expected (ceteris paribus) to observe, namely: Make your contribution such as is required, at the stage at which it occurs, by the accepted purpose or direction of the talk exchange in which you are engaged." (Grice 1989:26). As is well known, Grice developed the CP into a number of conversational maxims:

Maxims of Quantity
1. Make your contribution as informative as is required (for the current purposes of the exchange).
2. Do not make your contribution more informative than is required.

Maxims of Quality: Try to make your contribution one that is true.
1. Do not say what you believe to be false.
2. Do not say that for which you lack adequate evidence.

Maxim of Relation
Be relevant.

Maxims of Manner: Be perspicuous.
1. Avoid obscurity of expression.
2. Avoid ambiguity.
3. Be brief (avoid unnecessary prolixity).
4. Be orderly.

(Grice 1989: 26–27)

The central role of the CP and maxims is to explain how it is possible for speakers to communicate more than they actually say. According to Grice, conversational implicatures are beliefs that have to be attributed to the speaker to preserve the assumption that she was obeying the CP and conversational maxims in saying what she said. Notice that the maxims of Quality have a clear connection to evidentiality; thus, a Gricean approach to evidentials might start from the Quality maxims. I will be discussing possible Gricean analyses of evidentials in the next section.

Grice seems to have seen the CP and maxims as functioning solely in the recovery of implicatures, and as making no contribution at the level of what is said. However, we need to know how hearers identify the proposition expressed by an utterance: how reference is assigned, ambiguities resolved, and elliptical material restored. It is worth considering whether pragmatic principles or maxims might play a role in determining what is said. This issue is discussed in the next section.

According to Grice, speakers are expected to observe the maxims and hearers to assume, in turn, that speakers are doing so. His idea was that even if speakers appear to be violating a particular maxim at the level of what is said, hearers will provide any assumptions needed to make the utterance satisfy the maxims, or at least the CP. They will, in other words, fill in the thought behind the utterance so that the assumption that the speaker is both rational and co-operative is maintained.

Grice's account of utterance interpretation, important and exciting as it might be, raises a number of problems and leaves many questions unanswered. Regarding the co-operative principle itself, it is not clear that every conversation has an "accepted purpose or direction". Moreover, as Wilson (1994) observes, it is not clear in Grice's framework how the purpose or direction of a conversation would be identified, or how, once identified, it would help with comprehension:

> ... how is the accepted purpose of an utterance identified? Grice gives no answer to this. Like many theorists of communication, he seems to have assumed that the purpose of an utterance, like the set of intended contextual assumptions, is somehow given in advance of the comprehension process, or identifiable independently of it. In fact, it could not be identified by the use of the Co-operative Principle itself, on pain of circularity: to identify the purpose of an utterance by use of the Co-Operative Principle, one would already have to know it ... (Wilson 1994: 56)

Another problem is the source of the CP and maxims: what is their origin and nature? Why should speakers obey them? Are they universal? Are they innate? Or are they socially variable and hence, culture specific? If so, we need an account of the social parameters that cause this variation. Is the CP really the overarching principle governing conversation? Is the number of the maxims adequate? Do we need more? Or could we do with less? (Sperber and Wilson 1986/95: 35–38; Blakemore 1992: 26; Smith and Wilson 1992; Wilson 1994).

Grice acknowledged many of these problems, and proposed answers to some. As we have seen, he considers the CP and maxims as universal and rational: "... I would like to be able to think of the standard type of conversational practice not merely as something that all or most do *in fact* follow but as something that it is *reasonable* for us to follow, that we *should not* abandon." (Grice 1989: 29)

He adds:

> So I would like to be able to show that observance of the Cooperative Principle and maxims is reasonable (rational) along the following lines: that anyone who cares about the goals that are central to conversation/communication ... must be expected to have an interest, given suitable circumstances, in participation in talk exchanges that will be profitable only on the assumption that they are conducted in general accordance with the Cooperative Principle and the maxims. Whether any such conclusion can be reached, I am uncertain; in any case, I am fairly sure that I cannot reach it until I am a good deal clearer about the nature of relevance and of the circumstances in which it is required. (Grice 1989: 29–30)

Which brings us to another widely recognized problem with Grice's maxims: their vagueness. According to Lyons:

The usefulness of Grice's maxims is further reduced by the generality, not to say vagueness, with which they are formulated. ... As for relevance and perspicuity, it is, if anything, far more difficult to evaluate utterances in terms of these two properties than it is to quantify the amount of semantic information in the utterance. The fact that Grice's maxims have not been, and perhaps cannot be, fully formalizable makes his notion of implicature rather less precise ... (Lyons 1977:594)

The most famous indeterminacy is one that Grice himself recognized: the lack of a definition of relevance (Grice 1989:30). The problem has been acknowledged by some of his successors, e.g. Bach and Harnish, but in general they have chosen to concentrate on questions of informativeness (see e.g. Levinson, Horn). Or consider the Manner maxims. Here, Grice does not specify what "Be brief" and "Avoid obscurity of expression" really amount to. How is brevity to be measured: in terms of words, syllables, phonemes, letters? When is an expression obscure or "perspicuous"? As regards the Quantity maxims, what makes our contribution "as informative as is required (for the current purposes of the exchange)", and how should we formulate it so that it is not "more informative than is required"? As they stand, then, the CP and maxims raise as many questions as they answer.

But while Grice's account is vague in many respects, he clearly establishes an alternative to the code model of communication. There is no denying his central achievement: to show how inferential communication is possible at all. In later chapters, I will adopt the framework of relevance theory, which was directly inspired by Grice's work. In the rest of this chapter, I will consider what light Grice's framework can shed on the analysis of evidentials.

3.2 Pragmatic inference and evidentials

In this section I will consider how a Gricean would answer one of the questions I have set myself: how are degrees of speaker commitment pragmatically inferred? The first problem is that they are — at least primarily — degrees of commitment to *what is said*, i.e. the proposition expressed. As we have seen, although the Quality maxims refer specifically to what is said, Grice did not explicitly consider what role his CP and maxims might play at this level. As noted in the previous section, in discussing the CP and maxims, he concentrated on the implicit aspect of communication rather than the recovery of what is said.

However, it has been claimed that the CP and maxims can be seen as playing a role at the level of what is said, and in particular in disambiguation and reference assignment (Katz 1972: 449–450; Walker 1975: 156–7; Wilson and Sperber 1981: 156–159). According to Walker (1975) "…, in ordinary cases of ambiguity we rely on that principle [the co-operative principle] to determine which sense is intended; …" (Walker 1975: 156) and "The Co-operative Principle often helps to determine to what item a speaker is referring when he uses a proper name or a definite description, because there is more than one object in the world that satisfies the predicate from which the description is formed." (ibid.: 157)

On this approach, we cannot disambiguate the meaning of 'bank' in 'I am going to the bank' or recover the referent for 'Bill' in 'Bill left' unless we assume that the speaker was obeying the co-operative principle and maxims. The assumptions that the speaker is being truthful, informative, relevant and clear enable us to recover the 'financial institution' sense for 'bank', and identify the Bill we both know, rather than the president of the USA.

An example similar to (4) below was used by Katz (1972) to make essentially the same point. Suppose someone says on public television:

(4)   Bill Clinton is a crook.

When he is prosecuted for libelling the president of the USA, his defence lawyer argues that he was not referring to the President of the USA but to a local shopkeeper who had cheated him. Katz argues that such a defence is bound to fail: in the circumstances, the audience were entitled to assume that the speaker was referring to their President. If this was not what he intended to say, he ought to have used some qualifying expression such as: 'who runs a shop in my neighbourhood'. This line of argument depends on the assumption that the speaker is expected to obey the CP and maxims in saying what he said. Katz concludes "… the machinery of Grice's theory enters into not only what is conversationally implied but also into what is said, …" (Katz 1972: 450)

Wilson and Sperber (1981) took the same point further by pointing out that it is not only in disambiguation and reference assignment that the CP and maxims have a role to play. There are other aspects of what is said that are determined by pragmatic principles too. Suppose that while John Smith is playing the violin, I say:

(5)   John plays well.

You will recover 'what I said' as in (6):

(6) John Smith plays the violin well.

Yet all that is warranted by reference assignment and disambiguation alone appears to be the much weaker proposition in (7):

(7) John Smith plays some musical instrument well.

The idea that pragmatic principles play a major role in determining not only what is implicated, but also what is said, has been an important feature of the relevance-theoretic approach (see Sperber and Wilson 1986/95; Carston 1988, 1998; Blakemore 1992).

Having established that the CP and maxims can play a role in determining what is said, I turn now to the question that is central to the analysis of evidentials: can the CP and maxims help to determine the speaker's degree of commitment to its truth? This is a question not about what the speaker has said, but about the speaker's *attitude* to what was said. It therefore raises a further question: where, in Grice's framework, does the communication of propositional attitudes fit in?

Consider first the fact that in saying (8a), Mary would typically communicate the information in (8b):

(8) a. The sun is shining.
    b. Mary believes that the sun is shining.

In Grice's terms, (8b) is not part of what Mary has said. Hence, according to our diagram above (p. 39), it must be part of what she has implicated. Yet Grice specifically denies that (8b) is a conversational implicature of (8a). The passage is an interesting one, because it makes clear the link between the maxims of Quality and expressions of propositional attitude such as belief:

> On my account, it will not be true that when I say that p, I conversationally implicate that I believe that p; for to suppose that I believe that p (or rather think of myself as believing that p) is just to suppose that I am observing the first maxim of Quality on this occasion. (Grice 1989:42)

What Grice is saying is that (8b) above follows from the CP and maxims, but is nonetheless not a conversational implicature. Since it is clearly not part of what is said, nor is it a conventional implicature (since its recovery depends on the CP and maxims), it appears that there is no place at all for it in Grice's framework. Thus, the framework must be extended in some way to accommodate this very basic information about propositional attitude. I will return to this point below.

By invoking the maxims of Quality, from the fact that the speaker says 'P', the hearer can infer not only (a) that she believes that P, but also (b) that she has adequate evidence for 'P'. Bach and Harnish (1979, chapter 4) use this assumption to explain how various types of assertive speech acts are recognized. Different types of assertive speech act (e.g. assertives, predictives, confirmatives, suggestives) are linked to differences in the strength of belief or amount of evidence involved (ibid.: 41–2). Thus, if the speaker is *asserting*/claiming/ declaring that P, she must believe that P; if she is *confirming*/concluding/ assessing that P, she must believe that P on the basis of some truth-seeking procedure, which arguably results in a stronger degree of commitment; if she is *suggesting*/guessing/speculating that P, she must believe that there is not suffi- cient reason to believe that P, which is the weakest degree of commitment (Bach and Harnish 1979: 42–46). Thus, the CP and maxims play a role in the recovery of speech-act descriptions in just the same way as they contribute to the recovery of propositional-attitude descriptions. Hence, from the fact that Mary has said (8a) above, and the assumption that she is obeying the maxims of Quality, together with further contextual assumptions, the hearer is entitled to infer (9):

(9)   Mary asserts that the sun is shining.

Again, this falls outside Grice's framework, being neither part of what is said nor (arguably) a conversational implicature. This point will be taken up in a later section.

Recanati (1987) discusses how a particular type of assertive speech act might be identified on the basis of the linguistic content of the utterance, the CP and maxims, and contextual information: "... having to select the direct speech act among several possible candidates, the hearer uses the conversational maxims as a guide; he eliminates the speech acts that, if performed by the speaker, would (even apparently) violate them." (ibid.: 225)

Thus, if it is clear in the circumstances that the speaker has minimal evidence for the truth of her utterance, and if a guess would, in the circum- stances, be appropriate, he might interpret her utterance as a guess. Against such a background, the evidential markers might be appropriately analysed as overt indicators of the type of speech act the speaker has in mind, to be used where purely inferential mechanisms might lead the hearer astray. Thus Grice's inferential account of degrees of speaker commitment fits well with the speech- act account of evidentials discussed in chapter 2.

Grice dealt with the speaker's propositional attitudes to implicatures in much greater detail, and he saw the CP and maxims as playing a crucial role in this aspect of comprehension. For example, he analyses the use of the disjunctive 'or' in 'P or Q' as *conversationally implicating* that the speaker does not know that P, and does not know that Q. He comments:

> The fact that it would be inappropriate to say "My wife is either in Oxford or in London" when I know perfectly well that she is in Oxford has led to the idea that it is part of the meaning of "or" (or of "either ... or") to convey that the speaker is ignorant of the truth-values of the particular disjuncts. (Grice 1989: 8–9)

He goes on to argue against a decoding account of this phenomenon and for an inferential account:

> One who says that A or B, ... could be shown in normal circumstances to implicate (conversationally) that there are non-truth-functional grounds for supposing that AvB. For to say that A or B ... would be to make a weaker and so less informative statement than to say that A or to say that B, and ... would therefore be to make a less informative statement than would be appropriate in the circumstances. So there is an implicature ... that he is not in a position to make a stronger statement, and if, in conformity with the second maxim of Quality, the speaker is to be presumed to have evidence for what he says, then the speaker thinks that there are non-truth-functional grounds for accepting A or B. (Grice 1989: 46)

Building on these ideas, one might construct a Gricean account of the fact that someone who says 'I think that P' generally communicates that she does not know, or is not certain, that P. The idea would be that in using evidential expressions such as *I think, I suppose* that P, the speaker suggests that by being more specific, she would violate either the supermaxim of Quality — not trying to make her contribution one that is true — or the second maxim of Quality — making a claim for which she lacks adequate evidence. In using the evidential expression, the speaker is implicating that she is not able to be more informative or more certain than she is.

An account along these lines is sketched by Lyons (1977):

> Taken together, the maxims of quantity and quality can be invoked, ... to account for the fact that, if someone says *I think it's raining* or *It may be raining*, he can be held to have implied that he does not know for certain that it is raining .... The speaker would presumably have said *It is raining*, without qualifying in any way his own commitment to the truth of the proposition "It is raining", if he had known for certain that it was raining. For knowledge that *p* is true constitutes adequate evidence for asserting that *p*. (Lyons 1977: 594–595)

Lyons claims that the evidential *I know* should be treated in a similar way:

> ... also *It must be raining* and *I know it's raining*, involve a weakening of the speaker's commitment to the truth of the proposition "It's raining" ... This too can be explained in terms of the Gricean maxims: if the speaker's evidence is unimpeachable or his commitment to the truth of *p* so firm that there is no doubt at all in his mind that *p* is true, he will not feel obliged to make explicit the fact that this is so. (Lyons 1977:595)

Surely, however, *I know* is often used to communicate the speaker's *strengthened* degree of commitment, as in (10b):

(10) a. I know Bill is coming.
      b. I know for certain that Bill is coming, I saw him this morning.

These utterances, where evidentials indicate an increased degree of certainty, would presumably be treated in terms of the second maxim of Quantity, which says that we should not make our contribution more informative than required. If (10b) is not to be more informative than is required, it must presumably allow the hearer to infer that the speaker's evidence for the claim she makes is stronger than would have been realized without the presence of the evidential.

    Levinson (1983) also accounts for degrees of speaker's commitment in terms of conversational implicatures:

> ... if I use some linguistic expression that fails to commit me to some embedded proposition, in preference to another available stronger expression that would so commit me, then I may be taken to implicate that I am not in the (epistemic) position to make the stronger statement. Thus if I say (127) instead of (128),
>
> > (127) I believe John is away.
> > (128) I know John is away.
>
> I implicate that it is possible, for all I know, that John is in fact not away. (Levinson 1983:136)

According to Levinson, these are Generalized Quantity implicatures: they arise in all normal contexts, and are recognized by reference to the maxims of Quantity. Levinson characterizes a range of linguistic constructions that give rise to implicatures concerning speakers' degrees of commitment in the following way:

> A sentence of the form *p or q* has these implicatures by reference to the availability of other sentences like *p and q* or simply *p* or *q* which are stronger or more informative because they do entail *p* or *q* or both. Similar pairs of 'stronger' and 'weaker' constructions are illustrated in (131):

(131) (a) *stronger form*   (b) *weaker form*   (c) *implicatures of (b)*
        '*p* and *q*'   '*p* or *q*' $\{Pp, P{\sim}p, Pq, P{\sim}q\}$
        'since *p, q*'   'if *p* then *q*' $\{Pp, P{\sim}p, Pq, P{\sim}q\}$
        '*a* knows *p*'   '*a* believes *p*' $\{Pp, P{\sim}p\}$
        '*a* realized *p*'   '*a* thought *p*' $\{Pp, P{\sim}p\}$
        'necessarily *p*'   'possibly *p*' $\{Pp, P{\sim}p\}$

      (Levinson 1983: 137)

So, it is easy in principle to see how a combined Gricean/speech-act theory of evidentials could be developed, in which both decoding and inference could play an appropriate role. This looks like quite a reasonable approach, but there are questions about the adequacy of the Quantity and Quality maxims which play a crucial role in Grice's account. As regards the Quality maxims, and in particular the first maxim of Quality ("Do not say what you believe to be false"), it has been argued by Sperber and Wilson (1985/6) that no such maxims are needed in an adequate pragmatic theory. The existence of loose talk and metaphor, free indirect speech and irony present problems for the Quality maxims which, according to Sperber and Wilson, the Gricean framework has never satisfactorily solved. In the next chapter I will outline these problems, and sketch an alternative framework in which there are no maxims of Quality, and hence a different analysis of evidentials and degrees of speaker commitment must be found.

As regards the Quantity maxims, there is a problem about the notion of "required" information, and about Grice's claim that speakers are expected to give the "required" information regardless of whether it is in their own interests to do so. This claim plays a crucial role in the communication of negative propositional attitudes (as where the speaker who says 'I think that P' implicates that she does not *know* that P, because otherwise she would have said so). It will need more careful investigation in the light of Sperber and Wilson's arguments that speakers have no obligation at all to provide information just because it is "required".

3.3   Grice and non-truth-conditional semantics

As we saw in section 3.1.2 above, Grice thought that not all linguistic meaning was truth-conditional. He introduced the term *conventional implicature* to accommodate non-truth-conditional linguistic meaning. The issue I want to investigate in this section is whether the meaning encoded by evidential expressions can be analysed in terms of Grice's notion of conventional implicature. I will argue that Gricean conventional implicatures are carried by a subset of speech-act indicators as defined in chapter 2, so that Grice's account is not really distinct from the speech-act account of non-truth-conditional meaning. Moreover, evidential expressions do not fall into the subset of speech-act indicators with which Grice was concerned. Hence, the notion of conventional implicature is inadequate for the analysis of evidentials.

Grice's remarks on conventional implicatures were very brief, but entirely consistent with each other. He was concerned with a small class of non-truth-conditional connectives, including *but*, *so* and *moreover*. These connectives, he argued, did not contribute to the truth-conditional content of utterances, or, in his terms, to what was said. Rather, they carried information about a certain type of speech act that the speaker intended to perform.

The following is a sample Gricean analysis. In saying (11), according to Grice, the speaker communicates the following information:

(11) He is an Englishman; he is *therefore* brave.

> *what is said*:   (a) X is an Englishman.
>   (b) X is brave.

> *what is conventionally implicated*: (b) follows from (a).

Here, Grice comments, in saying (11),

> ... I have said that he is an Englishman, and said that he is brave, [but] I do not want to say that I have said (in the favoured sense) that it follows from his being an Englishman that he is brave, though I have certainly indicated, and so implicated that this is so. I do not want to say that my utterance of this sentence would be, *strictly speaking*, false should the consequence in question fail to hold. So *some* implicatures are conventional, ... (Grice 1989:25)

For Grice, then, (12a) and (12b):

(12) a. It's midnight and the pubs are open.
       b. It's midnight *but* the pubs are open.

would be true if and only if (a) the time of the utterance is indeed midnight, and (b) the pubs are open at that time. On this account, (12a) and (12b) express the same proposition. Clearly, though, they differ in meaning, a difference which is attributed to the lexical meaning of *and* and *but*. In Gricean terms, *but* conventionally implicates that there is a contrast between the fact (or statement) that it is midnight and the fact (or statement) that the pubs are open. Hence the connotation of contrast carried by (12b), but not by (12a).

Grice generalizes his claims in the following way: "I would wish to maintain that the semantic function of the word "therefore" is to enable the speaker to *indicate*, though not to *say*, that a certain consequence holds. *Mutatis mutandis*, I would adopt the same position with regard to words like "but" and "moreover"." (ibid.: 121)

Notice that Grice sees these non-truth-conditional constructions as *indicating*, which suggests that he is analysing them in familiar speech-act terms. The question is, what is the relation between Grice's notions of saying and conventionally implicating, on the one hand, and the speech-act distinction between describing and indicating, on the other? Does Grice see expressions like *but, moreover, therefore*, as encoding information about the type of speech act the speaker intends to perform? If so, then Grice's notion of conventional implicature offers no real alternative to the standard speech-act account.

In fact, Grice thought it was possible to distinguish between two types of speech acts: central, or lower-order, speech acts, e.g. saying, telling, asking, and less central, or higher-order speech acts, e.g. adding, contrasting, concluding, which comment on the lower-order ones. Consider (13):

(13)   My brother-in-law lives on a peak in Darien; his great aunt, on the other hand, was a nurse in World War I.

In discussing this example, Grice comments:

> ... speakers may be at one and the same time engaged in performing speech-acts at different but related levels. One part of what the cited speaker in example two ["My brother-in-law lives on a peak in Darien; his great aunt, on the other hand, was a nurse in World War I"] is doing is making what might be called ground-floor statements about the brother-in-law and the great aunt, but at the same time as he is performing these speech acts he is also performing a higher-order speech act of commenting in a certain way on the lower-order speech acts. He is contrasting in some way the performance of some of these lower-order-acts with others, and he signals his performance of this higher-order speech act in his use of the embedded enclitic phrase, "on the other hand". The truth or falsity and so the dictive content of his words is determined by the relation of his ground-floor speech acts to the world; consequently, while a certain kind of misperformance of the higher-order speech-act may constitute a semantic offense, it will not touch the truth-value, and so not the dictive content, of the speaker's words. (Grice 1989: 362)

According to Grice, it is the central, or lower-order, speech acts which determine the truth conditions of utterances. These speech acts are (at least in part) linguistically encoded by means of mood indicators (ibid.: 118–119). Higher-order speech acts, by contrast, do not affect truth conditions, and it is these that are treated in terms of conventional implicatures.

In Grice's view, the performance of a less central speech act is dependent on the performance of a more central speech act. For example: "... the meaning of "moreover" would be linked with the speech act of adding, the performance of which would require the performance of one or another of the central speech-acts." (Grice 1989: 122) One cannot *add* something, or *contrast*, *conclude* and so on, without first *asserting, ordering* or *asking* something. On this account, then, the speaker simultaneously performs speech acts on two levels, as illustrated in (11).

This account suggests that Grice indeed viewed discourse connectives as a subset of speech-act indicators in the sense discussed in chapter 2. For example, the function of *moreover, on the other hand, therefore* and *so* above is to indicate that the higher-order speech acts of *adding, contrasting, concluding* and *explaining* are being performed. Conventional implicatures express such additional comments on more basic speech acts being performed.

Notice that this type of information is often encoded by parenthetical comments or adverbials. Thus, the functions of *moreover, on the other hand* and *therefore* above run parallel to the function of the parentheticals in (14a), (15a), (16a) and the adverbials in (14b), (15b) and (16b):

(14) a. Her husband — *to add to that* — lost his job.
     b. *In addition*, her husband lost his job.

(15) a. Her sister — *and this contrasts with what I've just said* — got married.
     b. *By contrast*, her sister got married.

(16) a. He is — *I conclude* — brave.
     b. *Consequently*, he is brave.

This suggests at least the possibility that evidential adverbials (*clearly, obviously*) and parentheticals (*I guess, I conclude*) might be analysable as carrying conventional implicatures, i.e. as non-truth-conditional indicators of non-central speech-acts commenting on more basic speech-acts performed.

However, it seems pretty clear that evidential adverbials and parentheticals do not, in fact, perform higher-order, less basic, speech acts. Speech acts such as *asserting, guessing, concluding, confirming*, are analysed by Griceans, e.g. Bach and Harnish (1979, chapter 4), as basic speech acts. Thus, evidential adverbials and parentheticals are, if anything, indicators of such basic, lower-order, speech acts, and Grice's notion of conventional implicature is not suitable for the analysis of evidentials.

To conclude, Grice distinguished between what is said, the truth-conditional content of an utterance, and conventional implicatures carried by non-truth-conditional indicators. Examples of such indicators are various discourse connectives. However, evidentials do not seem to be analysable as carrying conventional implicatures. Hence the standard speech-act account is the only one available so far. The question I want to consider in subsequent chapters is whether there is any alternative to this standard speech-act approach.

3.4   Grice and the explicit/implicit distinction

As suggested in the previous chapter, Grice appears to see the distinction between *explicit* and *implicit* communication as coinciding roughly with the saying/implicating distinction. However, as we saw in section 3.3 above, this distinction is not exhaustive. Certain types of speech-act and propositional-attitude information communicated by an utterance appear to fit into neither side of the dichotomy. In this section, I shall pursue the question of where they fit in.

Grice's main concern was with the implicit aspect of communication. He used the term 'implicature' for everything communicated by an utterance other than 'what is said'. He comments: "'Implicature' is a blanket word to avoid having to make choices between words like 'imply', 'suggest', 'indicate' and 'mean'." (Grice 1989:86)

As we have seen, implicatures can be either conventional or nonconventional (Grice 1989:24–26, 118). *Conventionally* implicated meaning is semantic, but non-truth-conditional. By contrast, nonconventionally implicated meaning is pragmatic or social, i.e. it is inferred on the basis of pragmatic or social principles, including the CP and maxims (for examples and discussion, see sections 3.1.2, 3.3; Neale 1992:520–526).

Notice here that Grice differs from standard speech-act theorists in that he regards at least some indicators, i.e. the discourse connectives, as falling on the *implicit* rather than the explicit side, even though they carry linguistically encoded meaning; and the fact that he regards 'indicating' as a sub-type of 'implicating' seems to suggest that he might want to treat other indicators as falling on the implicit side, although new categories would have to be added to handle them, as we have seen.

As we have seen, by 'what is said', Grice meant the truth-conditional content of an utterance (Grice 1989: Logic and conversation, Essays 2, 6; Levinson 1983: 97; Neale 1992: 520, 556). He comments: "In the sense in which I am using the word *say*, I intend what someone has said to be closely related to the conventional meaning of the words (the sentence) he has uttered." (Grice 1989: 25)

However in his framework, recovering what is said involves not only knowing the meaning of the words used but disambiguation and reference assignment too. With regard to the utterance 'He is in the grip of a vice', he comments:

> ... for a full identification of what the speaker had said, one would need to know (a) the identity of *x*, (b) the time of utterance, and (c) the meaning, on the particular occasion of utterance, of the phrase *in the grip of a vice* [a decision between (1) *x* was unable to rid himself of a certain kind of bad character trait and (2) some part of *x*'s person was caught in a certain kind of tool or instrument]. (Grice 1989: 25)

Thus, the speaker of (17):

(17)   He went to the bank.

might have *said* that *John Smith* went to the *financial institution* (see Katz 1972: 444; Sperber and Wilson 1986/95: 183; Carston 1988: 155; Neale 1992: 520). Hence, if what is said is part of what is explicitly communicated, then explicit communication involves pragmatic processes too.

In Grice's framework, then, truth-conditional meaning falls under explicit communication, whereas non-truth-conditional meaning falls under implicit communication. As I have already established, though, the distinction is not exhaustive. In particular, basic, central speech-act information falls into neither the category of what is said nor any of the existing categories of what is implicated; and the fact that a speaker, in saying P, communicates that she believes that P, also appears to fall outside Grice's saying/implicating distinction.

In fact, there is a whole range of non-truth-conditional expressions which Grice does not explicitly deal with, and which need to be fitted into his framework. These include a variety of sentence adverbials and parentheticals, and various sorts of discourse and illocutionary particle. Since this class of expressions includes most of the evidentials that I am concerned with in this book, I will consider them briefly here.

Let us start by considering mood indicators — a type of non-truth-conditional expression Grice does not discuss in relation to the saying-implicating distinction. Grice links mood indicators to a range of central, basic (ground-floor) speech acts such as asserting, telling, asking. Thus, the speaker of (18a–c) would be seen as performing the central, basic speech acts in (19a–c):

(18) a. Bill runs.
      b. Does Bill run?
      c. Run, Bill.

(19) a. The speaker is asserting that Bill runs.
      b. The speaker is asking whether Bill runs.
      c. The speaker is telling Bill to run.

In this framework, (18a–c) would communicate the speech-act information in (19a–c). But is this information explicitly or implicitly communicated? Clearly, it cannot be conventionally implicated, since as we have seen, Grice links conventional implicatures to a range of non-basic, non-central speech-acts such as *adding, contrasting, explaining.*

Grice seems to treat mood indicators as contributing to what is *said* (1989: 118–122). On his account, someone who utters 'Go home' says '!You go home', where what is *said* includes the mood indicator for imperative ("!"), and someone who utters 'He went home' says '⊢John went home', where what is *said* includes the mood indicator for indicative ("⊢") (Grice 1989: 121).

The best way of reconciling these remarks with Grice's suggestion that indicating falls on the implicit side appears to be as follows. First, Grice claims that there are three basic types of proposition, distinguished by the presence of "⊢", "!" and "?", with three different modes of satisfaction: say, truth conditions for "⊢P", compliance conditions for "!P" and answerhood conditions for "?P". Thus, what is *said* (i.e. explicitly communicated) by (18a–c) differs because of the difference in satisfaction conditions. Second, Grice claims that the mood indicators, in addition to altering the satisfaction conditions of their associated proposition, carry speech-act information that is *not* part of what is said. For (18a–c), this is the information given in (19a–c). However, Grice does not regard (19a–c) themselves as part of what is said. On this account, the speaker of (18a) asserts (or says) that ⊢P, but merely indicates (or implicates) that he is asserting that ⊢P. As we have seen, although this 'implicature' is encoded by the mood indicator, it cannot be a conventional implicature according to Grice's definition, and there appears to be no place for it in the framework.

Similar remarks apply to various types of propositional-attitude information conveyed by utterances. Thus, (20a–b) might communicate the information in (21a–b):

(20) a. *Mary* (sincerely): Bill is coming.
      b. *Mary* (happily): Bill is coming.

(21) a. Mary believes that Bill is coming.
      b. Mary is happy that Bill is coming.

As noted above, it follows from the maxim of truthfulness that the speaker of (20a) will communicate (21a); but Grice specifically states that (21a) is not a conversational implicature of (20a) because it follows too directly from the maxims. Grice does not deal with (21b) at all. Clearly, neither (21a) nor (21b) is part of what is said; so these types of communicated information do not fit into Grice's framework.

It follows from the above discussion that evidentials do not fit straightforwardly into Grice's account either. Pragmatically inferred evidential information falls into a similar category to the information conveyed by (20) above. Consider the following examples:

(22) a. *Mary* (firmly): Bill will be here.
      b. *Mary* (hesitantly): Bill will be here.

(23) a. Mary firmly believes that Bill will be here.
      b. Mary has some evidence that Bill will be here.

(23a–b) appear to follow as directly from the maxims of quality (perhaps with help from the manner maxims) as does (21a). Hence they can not be regarded as conversational implicatures. But the evidential information in (23a–b) cannot be part of what is said either: the speaker of (22a) *says* (or confirms) that Bill will be here; she does not *say* that she firmly believes that Bill will be here. The speaker of (23b) *says* that Bill will be here; she does not say that she has some evidence that Bill will be here. Thus, pragmatically inferred evidentials do not fit straightforwardly into Grice's framework. Similar remarks apply to the speech-act information carried by a combination of mood indicators and contextual information (e.g. *speculate, confirm, guess,* etc.). These are central, or lower-order, speech acts, like *ask* and *say,* and present the same problems of categorization for Grice.

As for linguistically encoded evidentials, it is not really any clearer where they would fit in. Consider (24) and (25):

(24) a.   John is, *I guarantee*, a bright student.
      b.   John is, *I guess*, a bright student.

(25) a.   *Evidently*, John is a bright student.
      b.   *Obviously*, John is a bright student.

As we have seen, Grice's distinction between *saying* and *conventionally implicating* roughly parallels the speech-act distinction between *describing* and *indicating*. The question is whether Grice saw the parentheticals as contributing to truth conditions or not. If he did, then they would, of course, contribute to what was said. If not, then it appears that the parentheticals might be analysable in his framework along the same lines as mood indicators — as indicating what type of central, lower-order speech act is being performed. However, this would leave the parentheticals as unclassifiable as the mood indicators, which, as we have already seen, have no obvious place within Grice's saying/implicating distinction.

In the next chapter, I will show how Sperber and Wilson have introduced a category of *explicit communication*, or *explicature*, parallel to Grice's notion of *implicit communication*, or *implicature*, to deal with the types of communicated information that Grice's saying/implicating distinction ignores.

CHAPTER 4

Relevance theory

4.1 Introduction

Relevance theory developed out of Grice's pragmatic theory, but differs from it in many respects. Although still at an early stage of development, it has provided a useful framework for a considerable variety of research (for representative collections, see *Lingua* 1992, 1993; Rouchota and Jucker (eds) 1998; Carston and Uchida (eds) 1998; see also *Behavioural and Brain Sciences* 1987, 1996 and references in Sperber and Wilson 1986/95). In this chapter, I will present a brief sketch of the theory, with emphasis on those of its features which bear on the study of evidentials, and in particular on the three central issues raised in the Introduction.

As pointed out in previous chapters, evidential information is partly linguistically encoded and partly pragmatically inferred; I will be considering what light relevance theory might shed on the role of pragmatic inference in evidentials. Relevance theorists have also thrown new light on the distinction between explicit and implicit communication; I will be considering on which side of the distinction evidentials might fall. Finally, relevance theorists have proposed new analyses of non-truth-conditional expressions such as *but, so, moreover,* within the framework of a broader distinction between conceptual and procedural meaning; I will be investigating what light the relevance-theoretic approach might shed on the semantics of evidentials. This discussion will lay the groundwork for a detailed consideration of the truth-conditional status of evidentials, to be offered in later chapters.

4.1.1 Relevance and communication

Relevance theory (Sperber and Wilson 1986/95) builds on Grice's fundamental assumptions that (a) the primary domain of pragmatic theory is *overt* intentional communication and (b) utterance interpretation is a non-demonstrative inference process, where hearers *infer* the intended interpretation using contextual assumptions and general principles of communication. A few words of explanation about each of these points.

As noted above, overt intentional communication differs from accidental information transmission or covert communication in that the speaker wants to convey a certain message, is actively helping the hearer to recover it, and would acknowledge it if asked. If Peter points at one of my shelves and asks me to lend him the red book, he wants me to recognize his intention to pick out a particular red book; if I do not, communication will fail. While relevance theory has much to say about accidental information transmission and covert forms of communication, it follows Grice in claiming that overt intentional communication forms a natural theoretical domain, with its own theoretical principles and generalizations. In what follows, I shall use 'communication' to mean 'overt intentional communication', and 'understanding an utterance' to mean recovering the overtly intended interpretation, or speaker's meaning.

Like most pragmatists, Sperber and Wilson emphasize that understanding an utterance is not simply a matter of linguistic decoding. It involves identifying (a) what the speaker intended to say, (b) what the speaker intended to imply, (c) the speaker's intended attitude to what was said and implied, and (d) the intended context (Wilson 1994). Thus, the intended interpretation of an utterance is the intended combination of explicit content, contextual assumptions and implications, and the speaker's intended attitude to these (ibid.). To illustrate, consider the following examples:

(1) Sarah's book sold very little.

(2) A: Would you like an ice-cream?
      B: I am on a diet.

(3) A: What will happen to the economy?
      B: Bill will be the new President.

For the possessive phrase in (1) there are several linguistically possible interpretations: it could mean the book Sarah owns, the book Sarah wrote, the book Sarah is holding, etc. In order to decide what the speaker intended to say, i.e. what proposition she intended to express, the hearer needs to resolve this semantic vagueness: he may also have to disambiguate ambiguous expressions, assign reference to referentially ambivalent expressions, or recover ellipsed material. Thus, identifying what the speaker intended to say is not simply a matter of linguistic decoding.

As Grice has shown, often what a speaker intends to communicate goes beyond what was said. Thus, it is clear that in (2) B does not simply intend to communicate that he is on a diet. On the assumption that ice-cream is excluded from the menu of those who are dieting, B implies, and A will infer, that she does not want any ice-cream. The recovery of this intended implication, or implicature, is essential to the understanding of (2B), and cannot be identified by linguistic decoding alone.

As we have seen in previous chapters, it is often important to know the speaker's attitude towards the propositions expressed and implied. The same proposition can be entertained as a belief or a desire, as a certainty, a specula-tion, a suggestion, a fantasy, and so on. Thus, in (3) B may be expressing a belief, and in doing so he may communicate a prediction, a promise, a warning, a confirmation, and so on. As Wilson observes:

> In deciding on the speaker's intended attitude to the propositions expressed and implied, the audience has to answer the following sorts of question. Is she endorsing these propositions or dissociating herself from them; is she asserting that they are true, wondering whether they are true, perhaps wishing or hoping that someone will make them true? To a certain extent, these attitudes can be linguistically encoded (e.g. by declarative, interrogative or imperative syntax), but ... what is communicated generally goes well beyond what is linguistically encoded. (Wilson 1994).

It is obvious that in recovering the speaker's meaning, context plays an import-ant role. Here, context is not just the preceding linguistic text, or the spatiotemporal setting in which the utterance takes place. It includes any assumptions used to arrive at the intended interpretation, which may be drawn from the immediate linguistic and physical environment, but also from scien-tific, cultural, or common-sense knowledge, or any type of public or individual information that the hearer has access to at the time. Accessing the appropriate contextual assumptions is crucial for the understanding of (1)–(3) above.

The role of context in communication and understanding has not been studied in detail in Gricean approaches to pragmatics. Relevance theory makes it a central concern, raising fundamental questions such as: How is the appro-priate context selected? How is it that from the huge range of assumptions available at the time of utterance, hearers restrict themselves to the intended ones? To illustrate, consider the following example:

(4)   He will be the Chomsky of the next generation.

For linguists at least, the intended interpretation of this utterance will be immediately obvious. The audience is intended to use the contextual assump-tion that Chomsky revolutionised work in Linguistics, and draw the conclusion that the linguist in question is a potentially outstanding figure in linguistics. The question is why this is so. Surely, most linguists will have much more information than this retrievable for 'Chomsky'. For example, they might know that Chomsky is a Professor at M. I. T., that he is actively involved in politics as well as linguistics, that he has a bad back, and so on. Why don't hearers consider these assumptions, either instead of, or as well as, the obvious one?

In *Relevance* (1986/95), Sperber and Wilson developed a unitary answer to all these questions, based on the assumption that communication, like cognition, is relevance-oriented. The central ideas of relevance theory are contained in a definition of relevance and two principles (Sperber and Wilson 1998a), to which I will now turn.

4.1.2   The principles of relevance

Sperber and Wilson's inferential account of communication is based on a fundamental assumption about cognition. As Wilson and Sperber (1987:27) put it, humans pay attention to some phenomena rather than others; they represent these phenomena to themselves in one way rather than another; they process these representations in one context rather than another. Wilson and Sperber suggest that these choices are governed by a Cognitive principle of relevance:

Cognitive principle of relevance: Human cognition tends to be geared to the maximisation of relevance.

The suggestion is that humans tend to pay attention to the most relevant phenomena available; that they tend to construct the most relevant possible representations of these phenomena, and to process them in a context that maximizes their relevance. In other words, human cognition is relevance-oriented: we pay attention to information that seems relevant to us.

This assumption has an immediate consequence for the theory of communication. The very act of claiming an audience's attention encourages the audience to believe that the information offered will be relevant enough to be worth their attention. In other words, every act of communication creates an expectation of relevance. This fact, Sperber and Wilson call the Communicative principle of relevance.

Communicative principle of relevance: Every utterance communicates a presumption of its own optimal relevance.

It is around the idea that communicated information creates a presumption of relevance that Sperber and Wilson's account of comprehension is built.

The communicative principle of relevance differs from other principles, maxims or conventions proposed in modern pragmatics in that it is not something that people have to know, let alone learn, in order to communicate successfully. It is not a norm speakers can obey or disobey; it does not even assume that communication is necessarily co-operative in Grice's sense (i.e. that speaker and hearer should share a common purpose beyond that of understanding and being understood). It is a generalization about human communicative behaviour, expressing the idea that what is fundamental to communication — because it is fundamental to cognition — is the pursuit of relevance (Wilson and Matsui 1998).

Sperber and Wilson define relevance in terms of cognitive effect and processing effort.

Relevance
a.   The greater the cognitive effects, the greater the relevance;
b.   The smaller the effort needed to achieve those effects, the greater the relevance.

Information achieves relevance for someone by interacting with and modifying their existing assumptions about the world. Sperber and Wilson distinguish three ways in which newly presented information may interact with a context of existing assumptions, and hence achieve relevance:

Cognitive effects
a.   Strengthening an existing assumption
b.   Contradicting and eliminating an existing assumption
c.   Combining with the context to yield contextual implications.

Cognitive effects cost some mental effort to derive. The processing effort needed to derive the cognitive effects of an utterance is determined by factors such as: (a) the linguistic complexity of the utterance; (b) the accessibility of the context; (c) the logical complexity of the utterance; (d) the size of the context (e) recency of use; (f) frequency of use; and (g) the inferential effort needed to compute the cognitive effects of the utterance in the chosen context.

To illustrate these ideas, suppose that Mary is buying a ticket for the next train to Cambridge. On handing over the ticket, the ticket assistant may say one of the following:

(5)   a.   The ticket costs £14.35,
      b.   The ticket costs a bit less than £15,
      c.   The ticket costs 65 pence less than £15.

Which statement would be most relevant to Mary? Answer: (5a). It is more relevant than (5b) for reasons of effect: it implies everything that (5b) does and more besides. It is also more relevant than (5c), this time for reasons of effort. Since '65 pence less than £15' is in fact £14.35, (5c) has the same cognitive effects as (5a), but more processing effort is required to derive them.

There are thus two factors that determine the relevance of newly presented information: (a) cognitive effects — the greater the effects, the greater the relevance; and (b) the processing effort needed to recover those cognitive effects — the smaller the effort, the greater the relevance (Sperber and Wilson 1998a: 192).

How much relevance is the hearer of an utterance entitled to expect? In their book *Relevance*, Sperber and Wilson define a notion of optimal relevance, which is designed to spell out what the hearer is entitled to look for in terms of effort and effect:

Optimal relevance
An utterance is optimally relevant to an addressee if and only if:
a.   it is relevant enough to be worth the hearer's processing effort;
b.   it is the most relevant one compatible with the speaker's abilities and preferences.

According to clause (a), the very fact of requesting the hearer's attention by means of an utterance entitles the hearer to expect enough effects to make the utterance worth processing. Clause (a) then sets a minimal degree of relevance that the hearer is encouraged to expect. But is the hearer entitled to expect more relevance than this?

According to clause (b), if it is compatible with her preferences (goal pursued in communicating or rules of style or etiquette she wishes to follow) and abilities (information available and capacity to employ it effectively) the speaker should go beyond the minimally necessary degree of relevance. It is in her interest to do so, because the smaller the effort and the greater the effect, the greater the relevance, and the more relevant the utterance, the more likely the hearer will be to attend it and understand it correctly (Wilson 1998; Wilson and Sperber 2000)

A speaker aiming at optimal relevance should try to formulate her utterance in such a way as to spare the hearer gratuitous processing effort, so that the first acceptable interpretation to occur to the hearer is the one she intended to convey. This in turn suggests a comprehension procedure which according to Sperber and Wilson, hearers spontaneously follow in utterance interpretation:

Relevance-theoretic comprehension procedure
a. consider cognitive effects in their order of accessibility (i.e. follow a path of least effort);
b. stop when the expected level of relevance is achieved.

The expectation of relevance may be more or less sophisticated. Most adults, on most occasions, allow for the possibility that optimal relevance may be aimed at but not necessarily achieved. As a result, they do not automatically accept any interpretation that *happens* to be optimally relevant to them but look instead for an interpretation that the speaker might have *thought* would be optimally relevant to them (Sperber 1994; Wilson 2000). I would like to end this section by looking at two cases in which actual relevance and attempted relevance come apart in this way. Both occur because of a mismatch between the context the speaker expected the hearer to have immediately accessible and the context the hearer does in fact have immediately accessible. The first is a case of accidental irrelevance. Suppose Ann knows that Bill watches all Rossini's opera performances. She sees *The Barber of Seville* advertised in the Royal Opera House, and tells him excitedly:

(6)   *The Barber of Seville* is being put on at the ROH.

In fact, Bill has already seen the advertisement, so the proposition Ann has expressed is not relevant to him. Thus, there will be no interpretation on which this utterance is optimally relevant to Bill. Nonetheless, it is easy for him to see how Ann might reasonably have *expected* it to be optimally relevant to him, and he will interpret the utterance accordingly. This is a case where the expectation of relevance is revised in the course of the interpretation process, becoming an expectation of optimal relevance *attempted* rather than optimal relevance *achieved*.

The second type of example is a case of accidental relevance, where the hearer, because of a mismatch between expected and actual contexts, finds an interpretation that happens to seem optimally relevant to him, but is not one the speaker could have intended to convey. Suppose Mary plays handball for the local women's team. Normally, when they have to compete outside their region, they use their own means of transport due to insufficient financial resources. This time, because of an unexpected windfall, a bus has been hired, a fact which has been briefly mentioned, but which Mary has not fully taken in. So when Paul, the team administrator, says to Mary and her team-mates:

(7)   The coach will be here tomorrow morning at 9.00.

the first interpretation to occur to Mary is that their trainer will meet them at the gymnasium at 9.00. The utterance, on this interpretation, may seem optimally relevant to Mary given the long-standing arrangements that are very familiar to her. However, on recalling (or being reminded of) the new travelling arrangements, she should be able to reject this interpretation in favour of the one on which Paul is telling the team that a bus will pick them up at 9.00 outside the local gymnasium. This is a case where an interpretation that seemed optimally relevant does not satisfy an expectation of relevance that the speaker could have plausibly have foreseen.

Notice here a crucial consequence of the relevance-theoretic comprehension procedure: in every aspect of interpretation — i.e. in deciding (a) what the speaker intended to say, (b) what the speaker intended to imply and (c) what is the speaker's attitude to what was said and implied — the *first* interpretation that satisfies the hearer's expectation of relevance is the only one he can legitimately choose. To illustrate, consider again example (8), first discussed in chapter 3 as (4):

(8) Bill Clinton is a crook.

When the speaker of (8) is prosecuted for libelling the president of the USA, his defence lawyer argues that he was not referring to the President but to a local shopkeeper who had cheated him. As Katz argues (1972:450), such a defence is likely to fail because the audience was entitled to assume that the speaker was referring to their President. How does this follow from the Relevance-theoretic comprehension procedure? According to this procedure, the hearer is entitled to accept the first interpretation that satisfies his expectation of relevance, that is, the first interpretation that the speaker might reasonably have expected to achieve adequate cognitive effects for no gratuitous effort. But if the speaker of (8) intended to refer to someone other than the President of USA, he *would* have put his audience to some gratuitous effort, since the first plausible interpretation to occur to them would have been the one on which he was referring to the President of USA, and this would have to be rejected if successful comprehension was to occur. It follows from the relevance-theoretic comprehension procedure that if, in the circumstances, an utterance has an immediately accessible interpretation which the speaker might reasonably have intended to satisfy the hearer's expectation of relevance, that is the only one the hearer is entitled to choose.

The pragmatic framework just outlined differs from Grice's framework in one important respect. Its central principle is one of relevance: it contains no maxims of truthfulness, informativeness or clarity. Yet Grice's Quality maxims played a central role in accounting for the interpretation of evidentials, and more generally, of speaker commitments. In the rest of this chapter, I propose to show how a pragmatic theory based on a single communicative principle of relevance might help with the analysis of evidentials.

4.2 Pragmatic inference and evidentials

My aim in this section is to examine how relevance theory would answer one of the questions raised in this book: how are degrees of speaker commitment pragmatically inferred? Notice that these are degrees of commitment to what is said, the proposition explicitly expressed. As pointed out in the previous chapter, relevance theory acknowledges the role of pragmatic principles at this level in a way that Gricean pragmatists often have not. On the other hand, by specifically rejecting Grice's maxims of Quality, it may appear that relevance theorists have deprived themselves of some essential tools for explaining how speaker commitment is communicated at all. I shall look first at this fundamental question of how commitment is communicated in a framework without the maxims of Quality, and then turn to the question of how specific degrees of commitment are inferred.

4.2.1 Problems with the maxims of Quality

Grice's maxims of Quality are formulated as follows:

> *Quality*
> Supermaxim: Try to make your contribution one that is true.
> Maxims: (1) Do not say what you believe to be false.
>   (2) Do not say that for which you lack adequate evidence.
> (Grice 1989:27)

These maxims were central to his theory. Indeed, he saw the first maxim of Quality (which, following Sperber and Wilson, I shall call the maxim of truthfulness) as the most important of all. He comments:

> ... the observance of some ... maxims is a matter of less urgency than is the observance of others; a man who has expressed himself with undue prolixity

would, in general, be open to milder comment than would a man who has said something he believes to be false. Indeed, it might be felt that the importance of at least the first maxim of Quality is such that it should not be included in a scheme of the kind I am constructing; other maxims come into operation only on the assumption that the maxim of Quality is satisfied. (Grice 1989:27)

The maxim of Quality is highlighted again later on:

The maxims do not seem to be coordinate. The maxim of Quality, enjoining the provision of contributions which are genuine rather than spurious (truthful rather than mendacious), does not seem to be just one among a number of recipes for producing contributions; it seems rather to spell out the difference between something's being, and ... failing to be, any kind of contribution at all. False information is not an inferior kind of information; it just is not information. (Grice 1989:371)

By contrast, Sperber and Wilson have argued that the maxims of Quality create more problems than they solve, and are better dispensed with (Sperber and Wilson 1985/6; Wilson 1995; Wilson and Sperber 2000).

One problem is that Grice is forced to treat all figurative language as involving a violation of the maxim of truthfulness, and hence a deviation from the norm. Thus, he treats metaphor, irony and hyperbole as blatant violations of the maxim of truthfulness, designed to implicate some related true proposition. Consider the following examples:

(9) a. Bill is a fox.
     b. Bill is like a fox.

(10) *He*: It's a lovely day for a picnic.
      [They go for a picnic and it rains]
      She (sarcastically): It IS a lovely day for a picnic.

(11) a. This walk is a marathon.
      b. This walk is very long.

According to Grice, in the case of the metaphor in (9a), the hearer should infer from the fact that the speaker has blatantly violated the maxim of truthfulness, that she must have implicated the related proposition in (9b). In (10), the ironist deliberately flouts the maxim of truthfulness in order to implicate the opposite of what was literally said. The hyperbole in (11a) also involves a deliberate violation of the maxim of truthfulness with the intention of communicating something weaker than what was said, e.g. (11b). All three figures are seen as implicating some related proposition — in irony the opposite of what is said, in metaphor a related simile, and in hyperbole a related weaker proposition — by means of a deliberate violation of the maxim of truthfulness.

Sperber and Wilson (1985/6, 1986/95: chapter 4, sections 8, 9) argue against both the general claim that figurative language is deviant, and Grice's attempt to analyse figurative interpretations as implicatures created by deliberate violation of the maxim of truthfulness. In fact, figurative language seems to be universal and natural, to arise spontaneously without being taught or learned (Sperber and Wilson 1985/6: 169–170).

> ... the possibility of expressing oneself metaphorically or ironically and being understood as doing so follows from very general mechanisms of verbal communication ... metaphor and irony involve no departure from a norm, no transgression of a rule, convention or maxim.
> (Sperber and Wilson 1986/95: 242)

Another problem with Grice's account is that not all metaphors express propositions that are literally false. Consider (15):

(12) a. Susan is no angel.
      b. No man is an island.

The problem with (12a) and (12b) is that what the speaker has said is not patently false, but patently true. Thus, the connection Grice wanted to establish between metaphor and deliberate violation of the maxim of truthfulness breaks down.

Sperber and Wilson further observe that Grice's framework offers no explanation for why a speaker who wanted to communicate (9b) or (11b) did not simply say (9b) or (11b) instead of putting her hearer to the extra effort of processing the indirect utterances in (9a) and (11a) respectively. In relevance-theoretic terms, (9a) and (11a) could not be optimally relevant if they were only intended to communicate (19) and (11b) (Sperber and Wilson 1985/6: 166–167, 1986/95: 236–237).

Sperber and Wilson also point out that hyperbole is more closely related to metaphor than it is to irony (Sperber and Wilson: 1985/6: 166, 1986/95: 235). In fact, with utterances such as (13), it is hard to say whether metaphor or hyperbole is involved:

(13)

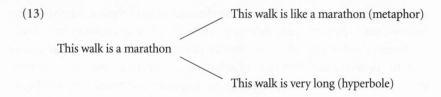

This walk is a marathon

This walk is like a marathon (metaphor)

This walk is very long (hyperbole)

For Grice, though, there would be two entirely different analyses depending on whether (13) is construed as metaphor or hyperbole: communication of a related simile for metaphor, communication of a weaker proposition for hyperbole. On the relevance-theoretic account, both figures of speech are treated along the same lines, and Grice's distinction is seen as artificial.

A problem more closely connected with issues of evidentiality arises when we look at loose talk and rough approximations. Consider (14)–(16):

(14)   Thessaloniki is north of Athens.

(15)   I live 10 minutes from Darwin College.

(16)   The lake is circular.

There are circumstances where the terms 'north', '10 minutes' and 'circular' would be strictly and literally intended, but in many cases, they would be intended and understood as mere approximations to the truth. Here, there is no question of a deliberate and blatant violation of the maxims of Quality; yet if strictly and literally interpreted, these utterances would be false. The problem is that Grice's framework appears to offer no account at all of how loose talk should be understood. Are (14)–(16), when understood as rough approximations, true or false, deviant or not? Whatever the problems they create for Grice's framework, it is clear that hearers have no problem understanding them, and we need some explanation of how this is so (Sperber and Wilson 1985/6: 162–165, 1986/95: 233–235, 1998a; Wilson and Sperber 2000).

A further problem with both figurative language and loose talk arises from Grice's claim that the strictly literal interpetation should be tried first, and only abandoned if it fails to satisfy the maxims. For him, a figure of speech necessarily involves a flouting of the maxims, which is essential to their recognition.

Sperber and Wilson have argued that, on the contrary, with utterances like (14)–(16), in many circumstances the loose interpretation is the first to be tested, and will only be abandoned if it fails to satisfy the hearer's expectation of relevance. As they claim "... the hearer should take an utterance as fully literal only when nothing less than full literality will confirm the presumption of relevance.

In general, some looseness of expression is to be expected" (Sperber and Wilson 1986/95: 234). Thus, when I say:

(17)   I will be there in 10 minutes,

the natural understanding is that I will be there in *roughly 10 minutes*: the loose interpretation is preferred even though there is nothing obviously unsatisfactory about the strictly literal one.

But the main problem that Sperber and Wilson find with the maxims of Quality is that they have no obvious cognitive basis. As we have seen, the communicative principle of relevance follows from fundamental assumptions about human cognition. Grice argues that the maxims of Quality have a basis in rationality: that if we are interested in communication at all, it will be rational to adopt the maxim of Quality among others. He also seems to feel that the maxim of truthfulness has a moral content which his other major categories of maxims lack (Grice 1989: 27, 371).

Sperber and Wilson challenge these assumptions. They claim that:

> ... the hearer is not invariably entitled to expect a literal interpretation of the speaker's thought, nor is such an interpretation always necessary for successful communication to take place. A less-than-literal interpretation ... may be good enough: may indeed be better on some occasions than a strictly literal one. (Sperber and Wilson 1985/6: 158)

Sperber and Wilson argue that in a framework with a communicative principle of relevance but without Grice's Quality maxims, a better account of rational communication will result (Sperber and Wilson 1985/6: 170, 1986/95: 230–231, 1998a; Wilson and Sperber 2000).

4.2.2   Dispensing with the maxims of Quality

The main function of the Quality maxims is to explain how a speaker who utters (18) can communicate the information in (19a) and (19b):

(18)   The sun is shining.

(19)   a.   The speaker believes the sun is shining.
        b.   The speaker has adequate evidence that the sun is shining.

In other words, the function of these maxims is to explain how the speaker *presents* herself (either honestly or dishonestly) as telling the truth.

The fact that speakers often commit themselves to the truth not only of what they say, but also of what they imply, is dealt with in Grice's framework by the supermaxim of Quality, "Try to make your contribution one that is true". Here "contribution" is presumably intended to refer *both* to what was said *and* to what was implicated, whereas the Quality maxims themselves refer only to what is said. The question is, how can these commitments be accounted for in a framework without either maxims or supermaxims of Quality?

Notice first what follows from the definition of optimal relevance. A speaker aiming at optimal relevance must intend to achieve adequate cognitive effects for no unjustifiable effort. Cognitive effects, as we have seen, are of three sorts: (a) strengthening existing assumptions; (b) contradicting and eliminating existing assumptions; and (c) combining with existing assumptions to yield contextual implications. The greater the cognitive effects, the greater the relevance. As Sperber and Wilson point out (1986/95: chapter 2, sections 3, 7) the cognitive effects of an utterance, and hence its relevance, will increase depending on the *number* of assumptions affected, and the *degree* to which they are strengthened or weakened.

> When all the premises actually used in the derivation of a particular conclusion are certain, the conclusion is also certain. When all the premises but one are certain, the conclusion inherits the strength of the less-than-certain premise. When more than one premise is less than certain, then the conclusion is weaker than the weakest premise. Conclusions derived from several weak premises inherit a value that is very weak and vague. However, inherited degrees of strength are lower limits: generally speaking, conclusions are more likely to be true than the conjunction of the premises from which they are deduced. (Sperber and Wilson 1986/95: 111)

Sperber and Wilson provide a more formal statement of how these alterations in contextualization are achieved as following:

> Let C be a context and P a set of new premises. Let *Conclusions of* P be the set of conclusions deducible from P alone, *Conclusions of* C the set of conclusions deducible from C alone, and *Conclusions of* P∪C the set of conclusions deducible from the union of P and C. Let two assumptions with the same content but with different strengths count as two different assumptions. Then the contextualization of P in C has no contextual effect if and only if the two following conditions are met:
>
> i   *Conclusions of* C is a subset of *Conclusions of* P ∪C;
> ii   the complement of *Conclusions of* C with respect to *Conclusions of* P ∪C is a subset of *Conclusions of* P.

> If conditions (i) and (ii) are not both met, then the contextualization of P in C
> has some contextual effect. (Sperber and Wilson 1986/95: 286, footnote 26)

It is the connection between relevance, strength of assumptions and speaker commitment that I want to consider here.

The idea that assumptions may vary in their strength is put forward in *Relevance*, chapter 2, section 3. For Sperber and Wilson, the strength of an assumption for an individual is equated, roughly, with his degree of confidence in it. This will be affected by the source and subsequent processing history of the assumption: an assumption derived by direct observation will be very strong; the strength of an assumption derived by inference will depend on the strength of the premises used to derive it; the strength of an assumption communicated to us by someone else will depend, first, on how strongly we are *intended* to take it, and, second, on how much we trust the communicator (Sperber and Wilson 1986/95: 77).

Within this framework, an utterance can achieve optimal relevance only by altering the hearer's existing assumptions, e.g. by strengthening them, or by contradicting them and being strong enough to overturn them. For Sperber and Wilson, a totally groundless speculation, i.e. an assumption which can be formulated but for which the individual has no evidence, has no intrinsic relevance. It follows that a speaker aiming at optimal relevance must intend to communicate a set of assumptions that are strong enough to make her utterance worth the hearer's attention. In other words, it follows that some subset of the propositions potentially expressed and implied by the utterance must be being put forward as true, or probably true.

In this way, relevance theory predicts something quite similar to what is predicted by Grice's supermaxim of Quality, "Try to make your contribution one that is true", but with two important differences. In the first place, these predictions follow from considerations of relevance alone, without additional stipulation, and with no appeal to a supermaxim of Quality. In the second place, it is quite possible within this framework for an utterance to satisfy the hearer's expectation of relevance even though the proposition explicitly expressed is false, as long as enough of its potential implications are put forward as true, or likely to be true.

This is how Sperber and Wilson propose to analyse metaphor and loose talk. Both are cases in which the proposition strictly and literally expressed is false, but gives access to a range of contextual implications which the speaker does want to put forward as true, or probably true. In Sperber and Wilson's framework, such utterances can achieve optimal relevance as long as there was no alternative utterance which would have communicated these implications more economically. In this framework, which contains no maxims of Quality, metaphor and loose talk need not be seen as violations of a pragmatic principle, or deviations from a norm. They are merely alternative ways of achieving optimal relevance (For a recent account of the relation between loose and literal talk, see Sperber and Wilson 1998a; Wilson and Sperber 2000).

4.2.3 Inferring degrees of speaker commitment

Relevance theorists (Blakemore 1987, 1992; Carston 1988, 1998; Wilson and Sperber 1981, 1993; Sperber and Wilson 1998a) have drawn attention to the linguistic under-determination of the proposition expressed by an utterance. They argue that this proposition "is obtained by inferential enrichment of the linguistically encoded logical form" (Wilson and Sperber 1993:9). Consider the following examples:

(20) It will take us some time to get there.
(21) He ran to the edge of the cliff and jumped.
(22) Susan's performance isn't good enough.
(23) At home.
      (Carston 1988:164, 167; Blakemore 1992:60)

For (20), by linguistic decoding alone the hearer will recover the trivially true proposition that it takes a certain amount of time to get to the intended destination. Surely this is not the proposition the speaker intended to communicate, and not the one the hearer will recover. The hearer by using contextual information, should recover a richer, more specific proposition, along the lines of (24):

(24) It will take us more time to get there than you might otherwise assume.

For (21), the hearer will understand in appropriate circumstances that the jumping was over the cliff, although there is no linguistic indication that this is so. For (22) the hearer must answer the question, not good enough for what? And for (23) the answers to still further questions must be supplied.

This inferential process of filling in partially specified semantic representations is generally known as *enrichment*. What guides the hearer in this inferential process is his expectation of relevance. In interpreting an utterance, the hearer looks for an interpretation which satisfies his expectation of relevance, i.e. which a rational communicator might have expected to be optimally relevant to the addressee. And the first interpretation which satisfies the hearer's expectation of relevance is the only one he is justified in accepting.

As suggested in section 4.1.1, identifying the speaker's intended attitude to what she said is as important as identifying what she said. In fact, the main relevance of an utterance may depend on correct identification of this attitude. For example, if, after repeatedly denying allegations that he handled forged currency, the accused says finally:

(25)   I did it.

the proposition expressed, i.e. 'The speaker handled forged currency' may not be very relevant to the prosecutor, who is already firmly convinced that this is so. For him, the main relevance of (25) may lie not in the proposition expressed but in the higher-level speech-act description in (26):

(26)   The speaker is admitting that he handled forged currency.

Recovering the speaker's intended attitude to the proposition expressed by the utterance is a fundamental task of the hearer. According to Sperber and Wilson:

> The same sentence, used to express the same thought, may sometimes be used to present this thought as true, sometimes to suggest that it is not, sometimes to wonder whether it is true, sometimes to ask the hearer to make it true, and so on. Utterances are used not only to convey thoughts but to reveal the speaker's attitude to, or relation to, the thought expressed; in other words they express 'propositional attitudes' ... It makes a difference to the interpretation of (4) [You're leaving] whether the speaker is informing the hearer of a decision that he is to leave, making a guess and asking him to confirm or deny it, or expressing outrage at the fact that he is leaving. ... Often the linguistic structure of the utterance suggests a particular attitude, as, for example, interrogative form most naturally suggests that the utterance is a request for information. However, as examples (4)–(5) show, the hearer is generally left a certain latitude, which he must make up on the basis of non-linguistic information. (Sperber and Wilson 1986/95: 10–11)

As to how propositional attitudes are recovered, they add "One of the hearer's sub-tasks, again an inferential one, is to identify this propositional attitude." (Sperber and Wilson 1986/95: 180)

On the approach just outlined, then, the process of enrichment involved in utterance interpretation goes beyond the recovery of the proposition expressed; it includes identifying the speaker's *attitude* towards the proposition expressed. Thus, the speaker of (27) may intend to communicate not only the proposition expressed but also the propositional-attitude information in (28):

(27)   Susan won the elections.

(28)   a.   The speaker believes that Susan won the elections.
       b.   The speaker regrets that Susan won the elections.
       c.   The speaker feels sad that Susan won the elections.

By the same token, the speaker of (27) may also want to communicate the speech-act information in (29):

(29)   a.   The speaker is asserting that Susan won the elections.
       b.   The speaker is admitting that Susan won the elections.
       c.   The speaker is bemoaning that Susan won the elections.

Here it is clear that a given utterance, e.g. (27), may grossly underdetermine the speech-act and propositional-attitude information that the speaker intends to communicate. Which of all the possible interpretations is the hearer justified in choosing? The answer follows from the relevance-theoretic comprehension procedure: he is justified in choosing only the first, i.e. most accessible, interpretation which satisfies his expectation of relevance, e.g. which yields adequate effects for no unjustifiable effort in a way the speaker could manifestly have foreseen. Thus, speech-act and propositional-attitude information is identified by the same considerations that guide the identification of the proposition expressed.

The particular attitude conveyed on a given occasion may or may be not indicated by the linguistic form of the utterance. In cases such as (25) and (27), para-linguistic features, e.g. tone of voice or facial expression, may help to make certain interpretations more accessible. In other cases the speaker may provide explicit linguistic clues, in the form of illocutionary-force indicators. In later sections, I will consider how the speaker decides when to use such linguistic clues. In the remainder of this section, I will look at how different degrees of speaker commitment are pragmatically inferred when no specific linguistic guidance is given.

Consider an example used in a previous chapter:

(30)   There are 2,716 beans in the bag.

I noted there that when offered as a guess in a fairground competition, this would be understood as carrying a lower degree of commitment (or strength) than when used to announce the results of the competition. In each case, the circumstances of utterance provide clues to the intended degree of commitment: could the speaker *know* how many beans there are, is she participating in a guessing game; if she knows, is she willing to reveal her knowledge, and so on. When the circumstances make highly accessible a particular hypothesis about the speaker's degree of commitment, and when that hypothesis leads us to a manifestly satisfactory interpretation, then this is the only interpretation the hearer is justified in choosing, and all other interpretations are disallowed.

Suppose, now, that in the circumstances there is no single highly accessible hypothesis. Then considerations of optimal relevance dictate that additional linguistic clues — say, in the form of illocutionary-force indicators, should be given. Or suppose that the circumstances make highly accessible a certain hypothesis that the speaker does *not* want the hearer to use. Then again considerations of relevance dictate the use of a linguistic indicator. Thus, suppose one of the organizers of the fairground competition is accidentally asked to buy a ticket and make a guess. In these circumstances, the utterance of (30) would be interpreted as a guess, and in order to communicate her knowledge, she would have to say 'I know there are 2,716 beans in the bag'.

Notice here the importance of the relevance-theoretic assumption that the first interpretation that satisfies the hearer's expectation of relevance is the only one he is justified in choosing. In the case of pragmatically inferred degrees of speaker commitment, if there is a salient, i.e. immediately accessible interpretation which the speaker could have intended, this is the one she *should* have intended. This is the only interpretation the speaker can rationally intend to communicate. Recall that according to clause (b) of the definition of optimal relevance, the speaker should put the hearer to no unjustifiable effort in achieving the intended effects. If, in the circumstances, an utterance has a manifestly satisfactory and immediately accessible interpretation which the speaker does not intend to communicate, she would put her hearer to the unjustifiable effort of first recovering, processing and accepting the wrong interpretation, then wondering whether this was, indeed, the intended one, entertaining alternative ones, and trying by further inference to choose between the interpretations currently available. In these circumstances, the speaker could have saved her audience a lot of unnecessary effort by reformulating her utterance — e.g. by using an explicit evidential construction, to eliminate the unintended interpretation. Hence, the first interpretation that satisfies the hearer's expectation of relevance is the only one he can legitimately choose.

4.3   Relevance and the explicit/implicit distinction

In *Relevance*, Sperber and Wilson introduce a notion of explicature which is meant to parallel Grice's notion of implicature. In this section I will explore the consequences of this for a problem raised in previous chapters: do illocutionary-force indicators (many of which are evidentials) contribute to the explicit or the implicit side of communication? My conclusion will be that they are best treated as falling on the explicit side.

Sperber and Wilson define the notion of explicitness as follows: "An assumption communicated by an utterance U is explicit if and only if it is a development of a logical form encoded by U" (Sperber and Wilson 1986/95:182)

The logical form of the utterance is the semantic representation assigned to it by the grammar and recovered by an automatic process of decoding. To illustrate, the sentence in (34) might encode something like the incomplete semantic representation in (35):

(31)   He saw it.
(32)   x SAW y AT t.

(32) can be enriched by pragmatic inference to yield the proposition expressed by (31), i.e. something like (33):

(33)   Peter Smith saw 'Tosca' at 7.30 on May 6, 1999.

Generally, the logical form encoded by an utterance is not fully propositional, and the hearer needs to enrich it on the basis of contextually inferred information to obtain the fully propositional form the speaker intended to express. The amount of enrichment needed will vary from utterance to utterance. To illustrate, consider the following examples:

(34)   a.   Neil Smith will be in UCL at 9.00 am on October 6 1993.
       b.   The carpenter made a bolt for the door.
       c.   The talk was too long.
       d.   He saw it.
       e.   Telephone.

The propositional form of (34a) is substantially determined by the linguistic form of the utterance, and the amount of inference required to derive it from the linguistically encoded logical form is relatively small. Understanding (34b–e) require various types and amounts of enrichment, including disambiguation, as in (34b), resolution of semantic vagueness, as in (34c), reference assignment, as in (34d), and completion where ellipsed material has to be supplied, as in (34e) (for detailed discussion, see Carston 1988, 1998). Sperber and Wilson say that a proposition communicated by an utterance is explicit if and only if it is a *development* of a logical form encoded by U. The enrichment processes just described are examples of what they mean by 'development'. The result is (a hypothesis about) the proposition the speaker intended to express. A second type of development process consists in optionally embedding this proposition under a speech-act or propositional-attitude description, such as 'X thinks that', 'X admits that', etc. The result is (a hypothesis about) the speaker's intended attitude to the proposition expressed, or the speech act she intended to perform. Notice that in this framework, unlike Grice's, there is only a single basic type of proposition, corresponding to Grice's "⊢", whose satisfaction conditions are truth conditions, and which is expressed by imperatives and interrogatives as well as declaratives.

According to Sperber and Wilson, the set of communicated propositions resulting from these two types of development process are the *explicatures* of the utterance: "On the analogy of "implicature", we will call an explicitly communicated assumption an *explicature*. Any assumption communicated, but not explicitly so, is implicitly communicated: it is an *implicature*." (Sperber and Wilson 1986/95: 183)

As we have seen, the recovery of explicatures may involve a greater or lesser element of decoding, and a greater or lesser element of inference. Sperber and Wilson introduce a notion of *degrees* of explicitness based on the relative contributions of decoding and inference: the greater the element of decoding involved in explicit communication, the greater the explicitness (Sperber and Wilson 1986/95: 182). Notice that this captures our intuition, discussed in an earlier chapter, that increases in linguistic encoding make an utterance more explicit. To illustrate, compare (38) with (39):

(35) a. *Peter*: Is Bill awake?
     b. *Mary*: He is.

(36) a. *Peter*: Is Bill awake?
     b. *Mary*: Bill is awake.

In chapter 2.4, when the examples were first discussed, the intuition was that (35b) was less explicit than (36b). Sperber and Wilson's definition of degrees of explicitness explains this intuition: both (35b) and (36b) will communicate identical explicatures; nevertheless, the information that Bill is awake will be *more* explicitly communicated by (36b) than by (35b) because the relative amount of linguistic decoding involved is greater in (36b) than in (35b). Similarly, compare (37) and (38):

(37)   *Mary* (sadly): Susan lost the election.

(38)   *Mary*: Sadly, Susan lost the election.

Both these utterances will explicitly communicate the information that Mary is sad that Susan lost the election. However, because of the presence of 'sadly' in (38), and hence the greater element of linguistic decoding, the information will be *more* explicitly communicated by (38) than by (37).

Explicatures, then, are obtained by a combination of decoding and inference. In order to recover the explicatures of an utterance, the hearer needs not only to disambiguate, assign reference and resolve various types of semantic indeterminacies; he also needs to retrieve information about the speaker's attitude to the proposition expressed — is she speaking literally or metaphorically, seriously or jokingly — or about the speech act she intends to perform — is the utterance an admission or warning, a promise or a prediction?

To illustrate, the utterance in (39) might communicate the following explicatures:

(39)   *Mary* (crossly): You've stained my shirt.

(40)   a.   Mrs Smith has stained Mary's shirt.
       b.   Mary is saying that Mrs Smith has stained her shirt.
       c.   Mary is saying crossly that Mrs Smith has stained her shirt.
       d.   Mary is cross that Mrs Smith has stained her shirt.
       e.   Mary believes that Mrs Smith has stained her shirt.
       f.   Mary is blaming Mrs Smith for staining her shirt.

Thus, an utterance may communicate a whole range of explicatures, some of which are more explicit than others depending on the amount of decoding involved.

In more technical terms, the most deeply embedded explicature of (39) is the *proposition expressed* by (39), and (40b–f) are *higher-level explicatures* of (39). According to Sperber and Wilson, the truth conditions of (39) will depend solely on (40a), the proposition expressed, whereas the higher-level explicatures (40b–f) will be explicitly communicated but make no contribution to the truth conditions of the utterance (Wilson and Sperber 1993: 5–6, 16). These notions will be taken up in the next section, and their implications for the analysis of evidentials will be discussed in later chapters.

Having distinguished the proposition expressed by an utterance from its higher-level explicatures, let us see in more detail how the latter are obtained. Higher-level explicatures, like the proposition expressed, are recovered by a combination of decoding and inference. To obtain (40a), the hearer must not only decode the logical form of the utterance but make an inference about the intended referent of 'you'; to obtain the remaining explicatures (40b–f), he must make additional inferences about Mary's attitude to the proposition she is expressing, and the type of speech-act she intends to perform. As we have seen, the utterance may offer the hearer more or less linguistic guidance as to what explicatures are intended. Within this framework, illocutionary-force indicators may be analysed as encoding information about higher-level explicatures. Some such indicators appear to be obligatory: for example, the declarative, imperative and interrogative mood indicators in English. Thus, (41a–c) are widely regarded as expressing the same proposition, (42), but as encoding different information about speaker's attitude to this proposition, or the illocutionary act she is intending to perform:

(41) a. You write novels.
      b. Write novels.
      c. Do you write novels?

(42) *Peter Smith writes novels.*

In the speech-act framework, mood indicators are analysed in speech-act terms: declaratives are seen as semantically connected with the speech act of *saying* (or asserting), imperatives with the speech act of *telling to*, and interrogatives with the speech act of *asking whether*. Thus, the information communicated by (41a–c) would be along the lines of (43a–c):

(43) a. Mary is saying that Peter writes novels.
      b. Mary is telling Peter to write novels.
      c. Mary is asking Peter whether Peter writes novels.

As we have seen, in the framework of relevance theory, (43a–c) are higher-level explicatures of (41a–c), and if this analysis of mood indicators is correct, then the mood indicators would encode information about a certain type of higher-level explicature.

In fact, many relevance theorists reject the speech-act account of the semantics of mood indicators. Instead, Wilson and Sperber (1988) propose a propositional-attitude account, on which mood indicators are seen as encoding information about the propositional attitude the speaker intends to express.

Here too the mood indicators are seen as encoding information about higher-level explicatures, and hence as falling on the explicit side of communication. On this account, declarative mood is connected with the propositional attitude of belief, and imperative mood is connected with the propositional attitude of desire. Hence, the choice of declarative syntax is seen as guiding the hearer towards a certain hypothesis about the speaker's propositional attitude, which may be narrowed down on the basis of further linguistic or contextual clues.

Turning to evidentials, it should be clear that they contribute to the explicit aspect of communication in a similar way by conveying information about the speaker's propositional attitude. On this analysis, pragmatically inferred evidential information contributes to higher-level explicatures. Thus, (44a–b) might communicate (45a–b):

(44)   a.   *Mary* (firmly): John is qualified.
     b.   *Mary* (hesitantly): John is qualified.

(45)   a.   Mary strongly believes that John is qualified.
     b.   Mary thinks that John is qualified.

And evidentials themselves might be analysed along similar lines, with (46a–b) communicating the higher-level explicatures in (47a–b). These ideas will be taken up in later sections.

(46)   a.   *Mary: Clearly*, John is qualified.
     b.   *Mary*: John is, *I think*, qualified.

(47)   a.   Mary strongly believes that John is qualified.
     b.   Mary thinks that John is qualified.

Thus, Sperber and Wilson's notion of explicit communication includes, but goes beyond, Grice's notion of what is said. Grice's notion of what is said largely coincides with the relevance-theoretic notion of the proposition expressed. The notion of higher-level explicature captures propositional-attitude and speech-act information, as well as information about mood indicators, all of which are types of communicated information that apparently fail to fit into Grice's framework.

To conclude, explicitly communicated information is obtained by recovering the proposition expressed by the utterance and optionally embedding it under a speech-act or propositional-attitude description. Everything that it is not explicitly communicated is implicitly communicated. Thus, the distinction between explicit and implicit communication, unlike Grice's distinction between saying and implicating, appears to be exhaustive. Evidentials should be analysed in this framework as encoding information about the explicatures of the utterance. The question I want to raise in later chapters is: do they contribute to the proposition expressed or to higher-level explicatures? To the extent that these constructions are non-truth-conditional, the information they encode will contribute to higher-level explicatures rather than to the proposition expressed. The truth-conditional status of evidentials will be examined in detail in chapters 5 and 6. The next section contains a brief preliminary survey of some relevant background material.

4.4   Relevance and non-truth-conditional meaning

Most linguistic semanticists observe that not all linguistically encoded meaning is truth-conditional: not every linguistic construction affects the *truth conditions* of utterances in which it occurs. Relevance theorists have proposed new analyses of some of the constructions that are generally seen as non-truth-conditional, e.g. mood indicators, various types of sentence adverbials, parentheticals, and so-called 'discourse' or 'pragmatic' particles and connectives (Blakemore 1987, 1992; Blass 1990; Clark 1991; Gutt 1991; Rouchota 1994; Wilson and Sperber 1988, 1993; Wilson 1998). These constructions are illustrated in (48)–(53):

Mood indicators

(48)   a.   Bill writes novels.
       b.   Does Bill write novels?
       c.   Bill, write novels!

Sentence adverbials

(49)   a.   *Frankly*, Bill doesn't like fish.
       b.   *Seriously*, Bill went to Moscow.

(50)   a.   *Unfortunately*, Susan lost the election.
       b.   *Sadly*, you have to come back tomorrow.

Parentheticals

(51)   a.   John is, *I think*, the best candidate.
       b.   John, *I guess*, is the best candidate.
       c.   John is the best candidate, *I suppose*.

'Discourse' particles and interjections

(52) a. Susan lost the election, *alas.*
      b. I'll beat him, *huh!*
      c. *Oh,* you are late.
      d. I'm making too much noise, *eh?*

'Discourse' or 'pragmatic' connectives

(53) a. It's Sunday *but* the shops are open.
      b. Susan lives in Hampstead. *After all,* she's got a rich father.
      c. Susan's got a rich father, *so* she lives in Hampstead.
      d. I talked to John. *However,* he didn't change his mind.

One fundamental question raised by relevance theorists is whether all non-truth-conditional meaning is of the same type, so that it should all be analysed in the same way. This seems to be the assumption behind the two main alternative approaches that have dealt with the above constructions, i.e. speech-act theory and Grice's theory of conversation. As noted in chapter 2, the linguistic constructions in (48)–(53) have been analysed by speech-act theorists as non-truth-conditional illocutionary-force indicators. As noted in chapter 3, Grice treats these constructions as conveying conventional implicatures, i.e. non-truth-conditional but implicit aspects of linguistically encoded meaning.

Relevance theorists have argued against the hypothesis that all non-truth-conditional meaning is cut to the same pattern. It has been claimed within this framework that linguistically encoded meaning can fall into four distinct categories,

> defined by an interaction between two independently necessary distinctions: between explicit and implicit communication, and between conceptual and procedural ... meaning. When faced with a particular non-truth-conditional construction, we thus need to ask ourselves two questions: first, does it contribute to the explicit content of an utterance or to its implicatures; and second, is its meaning conceptual or procedural, i.e. does it encode an element of a conceptual representation or a constraint on processing? (Wilson 1991)

Within this framework, the distinction between conceptual and procedural meaning was first drawn by Blakemore (1987) and has been developed by Wilson and Sperber (1993), among others. In the following sections, I shall outline the distinction; its application to evidentials will be discussed in later chapters.

4.4.1   Conceptual meaning

The distinction between conceptual and procedural meaning is based on a fundamental distinction drawn by modern theories of mind between *representation* and *computation* (Chomsky 1980; Fodor 1983; Pylyshyn 1984; Sperber and Wilson 1986/95). For example, utterance interpretation is seen as involving a variety of representations (phonetic, phonological, syntactic and semantic) linked by a variety of rules or computations (phonetic, phonological, syntactic or semantic). Representations are distinguished by their formal properties: for example, a phonetic representation is a string of segments in the form of feature matrixes. Computations are also distinguished by their formal properties: for example, a phonological rule (e.g. the vowel length rule) may take as input a phonological representation and yield as output its corresponding phonetic representation. Thus, for *cab*, applications of the aspiration and vowel length rules to the phonological representation /kæb/ yield the phonetic representation [kʰæːb].

On Fodor's modular approach to cognition (Fodor 1983), the mind is seen as consisting of a variety of specialized representational/computational systems. These are *input* systems, which process perceptual information (visual, auditory, linguistic etc.), converting sensory representations into *conceptual* representations, and *central* systems, which process these conceptual representations further (see Sperber and Wilson 1986/95, chapter 2, sections 1, 2). Conceptual representations have logical and semantic properties: they can represent states of affairs in the world, they are capable of being true or false, they can imply or contradict other conceptual representations, they act as the input to inference rules (Sperber and Wilson 1986/95: 72; Wilson and Sperber 1993: 10).

Within this framework, most words in a language, including the vast majority of those that contribute to the truth conditions of utterances in which they occur, are seen as encoding *concepts*, constituents of conceptual representations. The noun 'boy', for example, encodes the concept BOY, the verb 'play' encodes the concept PLAY and so on. In more formal terms, concepts consist of labels, or conceptual addresses, which (a) serve as headings for the storage and retrieval of various types of information and (b) are constituents of conceptual representations to which deductive rules may apply (Sperber and Wilson 1986/95: 86). Concepts are seen as providing access to three main types of information, stored in associated *encyclopaedic*, *logical* and *lexical* entries. According to Sperber and Wilson, the *encyclopaedic* entry for a concept "contains information about the extension and/or denotation of the concept: that is, about the objects, events and/or properties that instantiate it." (Sperber and Wilson 1986/95: 86)

For example, the encyclopaedic entry for BOY contains information about boys, the encyclopaedic entry for PLAY contains information about playing, and so on. The *logical* entry for a concept "consists of a set of deductive rules which apply to logical forms of which that concept is a constituent." (ibid.)

For example, the logical entry for BOY might contain a rule enabling the hearer to deduce, from the premise that *X is a boy*, the conclusion that *X is male*, and so on. Finally, the *lexical* entry for a concept contains information about the word whose meaning is the concept: for example, that BOY is realized in English as the noun 'boy', and so on. On this approach, the encyclopaedic entries for concepts make accessible contextual assumptions (conceptual representations) that can be used in processing propositions containing the associated conceptual address. Logical entries supply inference rules (computations) that apply to these propositions to yield various conclusions. In other words, the information in encyclopaedic entries is representational, whereas the information in logical entries is computational (Sperber and Wilson 1986/95: 89).

Conceptual representations may be either complete propositional forms or incomplete logical forms. Incomplete logical forms are incapable of being true or false. Thus, the sentence in (54) encodes an incomplete logical form along the lines of (55):

(54)   He performed at the Royal Opera House.

(55)   x performed at the ROH at t.

Given that 'He' in (54) does not encode a determinate concept, but simply marks the point at which such a concept must be supplied, sentence (54) is neither true or false. However, despite the fact that it is not fully propositional, (54) has logical properties: it implies (56), which is also non-propositional, and contradicts (57), which is (perhaps) fully propositional:

(56)   He was in the ROH.

(57)   No one ever performed at the ROH.

On this approach, both explicatures and implicatures are conceptual representations, and can be recovered by decoding, by inference, or a mixture of both decoding and inference. Thus, (55) can be enriched by pragmatic inference procedures to yield the proposition expressed by (54), which might be:

(58)   Thomas Hampson performed at the ROH at 7.30 on March 2, 1999.

As suggested in section 4.3, the proposition expressed by an utterance can be optionally embedded under a speech-act or propositional-attitude description to yield a higher-level explicature such as (59) or (60):

(59)   A. Stewart says Thomas Hampson performed at the ROH at 7.30 ...

(60)   A. Stewart believes Thomas Hampson performed at the ROH at 7.30 ...

In other words, both the proposition expressed by an utterance and its higher-level explicatures are *conceptual representations* which are recovered partly by decoding and partly by inference. Thus, (58), as well as (59) and (60), contain the concepts 'ROH' and 'performed', which, as we have seen, are encoded by the words *Royal Opera House* and *performed*. However, they also contain the concepts 'Thomas Hampson' and '7.30 on March 2, 1999', which are not encoded, but must be pragmatically inferred. Similarly, every utterance communicates various implicatures, which, like explicatures, are conceptual representations, but which are recovered *entirely* by pragmatic inference rather than decoding.

4.4.2   Procedural meaning

Within relevance theory, not all word meaning is analysed in conceptual terms. Brockway 1983 (see also Blakemore 1987) was the first to argue that certain discourse connectives might be treated in this framework as encoding information about *computations*, rather than representations: that is about how utterances containing these expressions should be processed. On this approach, the meaning of a word or other linguistic construction is *procedural* if it constrains the inferential phase of comprehension by indicating the type of inference process that the hearer is expected to go through in order to satisfy his expectation of relevance (Wilson and Sperber 1993).

Blakemore (1987) analysed a variety of discourse connectives in procedural terms. She saw expressions such as *after all, so, but, however*, not as encoding concepts, or contributing to the truth conditions of utterances, but as indicating to the hearer what type of inference process he is in. Blakemore proposed a non-unitary theory of linguistic semantics.

> On the one hand, there is the essentially *conceptual* theory that deals with the way in which elements of linguistic structure map onto concepts ... On the other, there is the essentially *procedural* theory that deals with the way in which elements of linguistic structure map directly onto computations ... (Blakemore 1987: 144)

To illustrate, consider the procedural analysis for *so* and *after all* in (61) and (62):

(61)   Susan's got a rich father, *so* she lives in Hampstead.

(62)   Susan lives in Hampstead; *after all*, she's got a rich father.

According to Blakemore, *so* in (61) 'instructs' the hearer to identify the proposition it introduces as a contextual implication of the preceding segment; *after all* in (62) 'instructs' the hearer to identify the proposition it introduces as providing justification for the proposition expressed in the previous segment (Blakemore 1987: 85–90, 1992: 139–140). For Blakemore, discourse connectives are constraints on *implicatures*, i.e. intended context and cognitive effects, because they encourage the hearer to supply the appropriate contextual assumptions and conclusions in interpreting an utterance.

Blakemore provides an alternative to Grice's notion of conventional implicature by suggesting a procedural rather than a conceptual approach. Although Grice does not use a conceptual/procedural distinction, he appears to treat conventional implicatures as linguistically encoded *conceptual* representations which do not contribute to the truth conditions of the utterances that carry them. As Wilson and Sperber observe:

> ... he [Grice] seems to have thought of the conventional implicatures carried by discourse connectives such as "but", "moreover", "so" and "on the other hand" in conceptual rather than procedural terms. For one thing, his choice of the term "implicature" suggests that he thought of conventional implicatures, like conversational implicatures, as distinct propositions with their own truth conditions and truth values. Moreover, he talks in almost identical terms of what was conventionally implicated and what was said, noting, for instance, that items or situations are "picked out by", or "fall under", both what was conventionally implicated and what was said. (Wilson and Sperber 1993: 12)

It might be possible to choose between the two approaches on the basis of the following considerations. First, conceptual expressions should be able to contribute to truth conditions in at least some utterances in which they occur, whereas procedural expressions never do. Thus, no one would deny that the word 'boy' contributes to the truth conditions of the utterance in (63):

(63)   A boy cried.

This can be explained on the assumption that it encodes a concept. By contrast, it is difficult to think of *any* utterance in which 'but' contributes to truth conditions; hence, there is no reason to think of it as encoding a concept. Second, the meanings of discourse connectives, e.g. *but, so, well*, are hard to bring to consciousness in the way that conceptual meanings are, e.g. 'cat', 'walk', 'clever'. This is explained on the assumption that their meanings are procedural, because computations in general (grammatical rules, inference rules) are not easily accessible to consciousness (Wilson and Sperber 1993:16).

If these arguments are correct, then we might be tempted to conclude that all truth-conditional meaning is conceptual and all non-truth-conditional meaning is procedural. In fact, I shall argue that the situation is more complicated. These issues will be pursued in chapters 5 and 6.

Sperber and Wilson (1986/95) argue that apart from the discourse connectives discussed by Blakemore, the mood indicators might also be best approached in procedural terms. In *Relevance*, they claim that: "illocutionary force indicators such as declarative or imperative mood or interrogative word order make manifest a rather abstract property of the speaker's informative intention; the direction in which relevance is to be sought." (Sperber and Wilson 1986/95:254)

Their view (developed in Wilson and Sperber 1988, 1993), is that mood indicators, like discourse connectives, act as constraints on the inferential phase of comprehension. Unlike the discourse connectives, which are constraints on implicatures, Sperber and Wilson argue that the mood indicators are constraints on explicatures, guiding the hearer towards the intended propositional attitude, which is recovered in the form of a higher-level explicature.

In this framework, the declarative mood indicator is associated with the attitude of belief (Sperber and Wilson 1986/95:180, 248–249). To illustrate, consider the sentence in (64):

(64)   The sun is shining.

As we have seen, the declarative mood indicator suggests to the hearer that the appropriate attitude to adopt towards the proposition expressed by (64) is one of belief. Hence, one of the higher-level explicatures communicated by (64) might be (65):

(65)   Mary believes that the sun is shining.

As we have also seen, this is not part of the truth conditions of the utterance in (64), but in appropriate circumstances it would be communicated, and would therefore fit Sperber and Wilson's definition of higher-level explicature.

To the extent that 'discourse' or 'pragmatic' particles are fully grammaticalized, it might be possible to develop a similar procedural approach. Thus, consider (66a–b):

(66)   a.   Susan lost the election, *alas.*

      b.   Susan lost the election, *eh?*

Alas is used to communicate disappointment and sorrow, and it might be argued that it encourages the construction of a higher-level explicature along the lines of (67):

(67)   The speaker is sad that Susan lost the election.

Similarly, *eh*, together with rising intonation, is one way of asking a question, and it might be argued that it encourages the construction of a higher-level explicature along the lines of (68):

(68)   The speaker is requesting confirmation of (or wondering about the truth of) the statement that Susan lost the election.

4.5   Relevance and the descriptive/interpretive distinction

A further distinction that will be central to the arguments in this book is Sperber and Wilson's distinction between descriptive and interpretive use of language and thought. Descriptive use is the use of an utterance or thought to represent a state of affairs in an actual or possible world: that state of affairs which would make it true. Interpretive use is the use of an utterance or thought to represent some other utterance or thought which it resembles in content — i.e. with which it shares logical or contextual implications. Sperber and Wilson claim that utterances are used in the first instance as interpretations of the speaker's thoughts, and that these interpretations may be more or less faithful to the original. A fully faithful (or literal) interpretation is one which reproduces the thought it represents. According to Sperber and Wilson, however, a speaker aiming at optimal relevance often has good reasons to produce a less than fully faithful interpretation, that is, an utterance expressing a proposition which merely *resembles* the thoughts she wants to convey. Metaphor, hyperbole and loose talk (see above, section 4.2.1) are cases in point.

4.5.1   Interpretive resemblance

In introducing the idea that utterances may be more or less faithful interpretations of the thoughts they represent, Sperber and Wilson point out that communication often involves the exploitation of resemblances. Natural or artificial phenomena can be used to represent other phenomena which they resemble.

Welcoming you at the door I can indicate that a common friend is inside by mimicking one of her most typical grimaces. If you ask me what is the shape of Italy, I can point to a boot, or if I want to indicate how bored I feel during a lecture, I can yawn ostentatiously.

Sperber and Wilson argue that verbal communication also involves the exploitation of resemblances. Sometimes — as in direct quotation — an utterance is used not to describe a state of affairs in the world, but to represent another utterance or thought which it resembles. As noted above, in the framework of relevance theory, a proposition can be *descriptively* used to represent a state of affairs which makes it true, and *interpretively* used to represent some representation — for example a thought — which it resembles in content (Sperber and Wilson 1985/6: 157).

Descriptive representation is a relation between a proposition and a state of affairs, and has already been extensively discussed in truth-conditional semantics. Interpretive representation is a relation between representations which resemble each other in content, and, being a central relevance-theoretic notion, needs further introduction.

Notice first that when I point to a boot in order to give you an idea of what Italy looks like on the map, you are meant to assume that it shares some but not all of Italy's actual or imaginary properties; you are meant to assume that this is how the outline of Italy more or less goes; you are not meant to assume, and indeed you will not assume, that this is the actual scale of Italy, for example. When you ask me how I spend my Tuesday evenings, I might act out a few ballet steps. If you already know that I attend ballet classes and if my 'performance' has been good enough, you will notice its resemblance to the act of ballet dancing, assume that this resemblance was intentional, and come to the reasonable conclusion that on Tuesday evenings I have a ballet class. You are not meant to conclude that I normally perform a ballet piece with no music and in jeans.

These examples should illustrate the fact that when representation by resemblance is involved, the relation between representation and original is not normally one of full identity. Clearly, the observer is not meant to assume that every property of the representation carries over to the original. Reasonable assumptions have to be made about which assumptions carry over to the original and which do not. Sperber and Wilson argue that the exploitation of resemblances in content, i.e. interpretive resemblance, is subject to the same constraint. In particular, when an utterance is used to represent a thought, all the hearer is entitled to assume is that the content of the utterance resembles the content of the represented thought to some degree — i.e. that some degree of faithfulness has been attempted. Seen from this perspective, a requirement that the proposition expressed by an utterance should *reproduce* a thought of the speaker's — which is what Grice's maxim of truthfulness demands — is too strong.

What does it mean to say that the content of an utterance must resemble the content of the thought it represents? According to Sperber and Wilson (1985/6: 157–158, 1986/95: 233–234), two representations interpretively *resemble* each other if and only if they share logical and contextual implications; and the more implications they share, the more they interpretively resemble each other. For example, on the assumption that foxes are cunning, the thought that Bill is a fox and the thought that Bill is very cunning will resemble each other in content, because they both share the implication that Bill is cunning. Hence, on the assumption that utterances may be used to represent thoughts that they merely resemble in content, the utterance in (69)

(69)   Bill is a fox.

might be used as an interpretive representation of the thought in (70)

(70)   Bill is cunning.

Interpretive resemblance, on this account, is a comparative notion with two extremes: no resemblance at all, i.e. no shared implications, at one end, and full propositional identity at the other. If an utterance and the thought it represents have the same propositional content, they will share all their logical and contextual implications in every context. When this happens, Sperber and Wilson say that the utterance is a literal (i.e. fully faithful) interpretation of the thought it represents. On this account, literalness is just a limiting case of interpretive resemblance.

Against this background, Sperber and Wilson question the fundamental assumption made by any framework with a maxim of truthfulness: that every utterance must be a fully literal interpretation of the speaker's thought. Where representation by resemblance, or interpretive use, is involved, all the audience is entitled to expect is that *some* degree of faithfulness — *some* degree of resemblance — has been attempted. There is no more reason to expect an utterance to be a fully literal interpretation of the speaker's thought than there is to expect a map of Italy to be life-size.

4.5.2   Attributive interpretive use

So far, I have been tacitly assuming, with Grice, that the proposition expressed by an utterance is invariably an interpretation of a thought of the speaker's own.

But, as Sperber and Wilson point out, this assumption is mistaken. Often, an utterance is put forward as an interpretation of a thought that the speaker attributes to someone other than herself. In this case, Sperber and Wilson talk of *attributive* interpretive use.

In introducing this notion, it might be helpful to consider the fact that an utterance is often used to represent an *utterance* of someone other than the speaker, and here too the notion of degrees of faithfulness applies.

Direct quotation is an obvious example where an utterance is used, in the first instance, to represent another utterance which it resembles. Consider the possible answers (71b–d) to the question in (71a):

(71) a. *He*: What did Mary say?
      b. *She*: I don't care.
      c. *She*: 'I don't care'.
      d. *She*: She didn't care.

The speaker of (71b) says that she doesn't care what Mary said; the speaker of (71c) directly quotes Mary's claim that she doesn't care. A misunderstanding would occur if the hearer failed to make the correct assumption about what these utterances were intended to represent. (71d) has two possible interpretations: the speaker is either indirectly reporting Mary's claim that she doesn't care, or she is drawing the conclusion, on her own initiative, that Mary doesn't care: Mary herself might have said nothing at all. Again, when processing this utterance, the hearer must make some assumption about whose beliefs or claims the speaker intends it to represent. Sperber and Wilson argue that the only interpretation the hearer is justified in accepting satisfies his expectation of relevance, e.g. the first interpretation to yield adequate effects for no unjustifiable effort in a way the speaker could manifestly have foreseen. A speaker who thought there would be any difficulty about arriving at the correct interpretation should make her intentions more explicit, for example by adding 'she said' to (71c) or (71d).

Direct quotation, as in (71c), involves resemblance in linguistic properties. Indirect quotation, as in (71d), involves interpretive resemblance, i.e. resemblance in content. Consider (72):

(72) a. She said 'Make sure you come home before 11 o'clock'.
      b. She told me to make sure that I come home before 11 o'clock.
      c. She told me that I should be home early tonight.
      d. She said I shouldn't be late tonight.

Direct quotation, as in (72a), must resemble the original in linguistic structure. In the case of indirect quotation, as in (72b–d), the demands are much weaker. What is reported is merely the *content* of the original. As Sperber and Wilson show, indirect quotation differs from direct quotation in that the required resemblances are purely logical. A speech in one language can be as adequately reported in the same or a different language: it is only the logical properties of the original that need to be preserved. Moreover, as (72b–d) indicate, indirect reports may be more or less detailed, more or less of a summary. In other words, an indirect report can be less than fully faithful, i.e. a less than fully literal interpretation of the original. Full identity of content between report and original is not required.

Having shown that an utterance may interpretively represent either a thought of the speaker's or a thought attributed by the speaker to someone else, Sperber and Wilson define a proposition as *descriptively* used when the thought it interprets is a current thought of the speaker's which is itself entertained as a description of a state of affairs, and as *interpretively* used when the thought it interprets is attributed to someone other than the speaker (or to the speaker herself at another time) (see also Gutt 1991).[1]

Reporting actual *speech*, as illustrated in (71c) or (72b), is the best-known type of attributive interpretive use of utterances. Another case of attributive interpretive use involves the attribution not of utterances but of *thoughts* (Sperber and Wilson 1986/95:229). Consider (73):

(73) *Susan*: John is very lucky to have got a fellowship in Oxford, Peter thinks, and I agree with him.

Here, the first part of Susan's utterance reports a thought which she explicitly attributes to Peter.

Sometimes, the speaker may communicate not only what someone else said or thought but her *attitude* or reaction to what was said or thought. In these cases, the interpretations are called *echoic* (Sperber and Wilson 1986/95:238; Wilson and Sperber 1992:59). Echoic utterances are used to express a wide variety of attitudes, as the following examples show:

(74) *Mary* (to Peter): I won the race.
      Peter (to Mary) (happily): You won the race!

(75) *Mary*: It's a lovely day for a picnic.
      [They go for a picnic and it rains]
      Peter: It's a lovely day for a picnic, indeed.

In (74), Peter echoes Mary's utterance and indicates his own attitude towards its content: he is delighted that she won the race. In (75), Peter echoes Mary's utterance and again indicates his own attitude towards it: this time, however, he is dissociating himself from it, and his attitude is mocking or critical. Notice that (75) is a case of verbal irony, which is analysed in the framework of relevance theory in terms of the notion of dissociative echoic use: in ironical utterances, the speaker echoes an attributed thought which she rejects with mockery or scorn (for detailed discussion, see Sperber and Wilson 1986/95: 237–243, 1998b; Wilson and Sperber 1992: 53–76).

In this section, I have introduced a distinction between descriptive and interpretive use, which will be used in later chapters when I come to analyse a variety of evidential constructions. A crucial point to notice is that descriptive use of a proposition carries some degree of speaker commitment, whereas attributive interpretive use suspends the speaker's commitment by indicating that the views being represented are not the speaker's own. We would thus expect descriptively and interpretively used propositions to differ in truth-conditional status, and this is what we will find.

4.6 Conclusion to chapter 4

We now have three distinctions: between truth-conditional and non-truth-conditional meaning, between conceptual and procedural meaning, and between explicit and implicit communication. Having shown how pragmatically inferred evidential information would be dealt with in the framework of relevance theory, I will now turn to linguistically encoded evidential information, and try to show on which side of these three related distinctions a variety of evidential items fall. I will focus in particular on the claim made by many speech-act theorists that evidentials are illocutionary-force indicators, and are therefore non-truth-conditional. I will argue that, on closer investigation, this claim turns out to be false. In chapter 5, I will therefore compare the behaviour of a variety of adverbials that have been treated by speech-act theorists as illocutionary-force indicators. The arguments will be developed and applied to a variety of parenthetical expressions in chapter 6.

CHAPTER 5

Sentence adverbials

5.1 Introduction

In this chapter, I will be concerned with four types of sentence adverbial: illocutionary, attitudinal, evidential and hearsay adverbials. All are standardly treated in non-truth-conditional terms, as contributing not to the proposition expressed by the utterance, its truth-conditional content, but to indicating the type of speech-act performed. I shall survey some standard speech-act analyses, and then raise an obvious question: are these adverbials really non-truth-conditional, as speech-act theorists have claimed? I shall show that by the standard tests for truth-conditionality, these classes of adverbial behave quite differently from each other: some are clearly truth-conditional, whereas others are not. This raises two further questions: how can these facts be described, and how can they be explained? Using the framework of relevance theory outlined in previous chapters, I shall sketch the lines on which answers to these questions might be found.[1]

5.2 Types of sentence adverbial

Illocutionary adverbials are those, like *frankly, confidentially, honestly, seriously*, that are understood as modifying an implicit illocutionary verb (Sadock 1974:36; Bach and Harnish 1979:219–228; Vanderveken 1990:16, 119). Examples are given in (1a–c), which would be understood as communicating (2a–c):

(1) a. *Frankly*, I'm bored.
     b. Mary has, *confidentially*, failed the exam.
     c. *Seriously*, your argument is fallacious.

(2) a. I tell you frankly that I'm bored.
     b. I inform you confidentially that Mary has failed the exam.
     c. I tell you seriously that your argument is fallacious.

Attitudinal adverbials are those, like *unfortunately, happily, sadly, luckily,* which do not name a speech act but indicate the speaker's attitude to the statement she makes (Urmson 1963:228; Strawson 1973:57–58; Recanati 1987:50; Vanderveken 1990:116–117). Examples are given in (3a–c), which are understood as communicating (4a–c), not (5a–c):

(3) a. *Unfortunately,* Mary has missed the deadline.
     b. *Sadly,* Paul's car was stolen.
     c. *Happily,* Bill was in time for the interview.

(4) a. It is unfortunate that Mary has missed the deadline.
     b. It is sad that Paul's car was stolen.
     c. It is happily true that Bill was in time for the interview.

(5) a. I tell you unfortunately that Mary has missed the deadline.
     b. I tell you sadly that Paul's car was stolen.
     c. I tell you happily that Bill was in time for the interview.

Evidential adverbials are those that indicate the source or the strength of the speaker's evidence (Urmson 1963:228; Palmer 1986:45–46, 64; Chafe 1986: 261–272). This class includes adverbials such as *evidently, obviously, clearly.* Examples are given in (6a–c), which are understood as communicating (7a–c):

(6) a. *Evidently,* Bill has cheated in the exam.
     b. *Obviously,* the ball as over the line.
     c. *Clearly,* you are responsible for the damage.

(7) a. It is evident (evidently true) that Bill has cheated in the exam.
     b. It is obvious (obviously true) that the ball was over the line.
     c. It is clear (clearly true) that you are responsible for the damage.

Hearsay adverbials, such as *allegedly* and *reportedly,* are generally treated as a type of evidential (Palmer 1986:73; Chafe 1986:268), because they indicate that the source of knowledge is not the speaker herself but someone else. They are typically used to report actual speech. Examples are given in (8a–b), which are understood as communicating (9a–b):

(8) a. *Allegedly,* the cook has poisoned the soup.
     b. *Reportedly,* the ball was over the line.

(9) a. It is alleged that the cook has poisoned the soup.
     b. It is reported that the ball was over the line.

These four classes of adverbial are interesting because they have traditionally been treated as providing evidence for a speech-act semantics and against a truth-conditional account of at least some lexical items. In the next section, I shall consider some speech-act accounts.

5.3 Speech-act accounts of sentence adverbials

As noted in chapter 2, speech-act theorists assign particular importance to linguistic devices that enable the speaker to make the force of her utterance explicit. Austin claims that an illocutionary act can be performed only if there is a conventional means of performing it — a 'formula' or 'indicator' whose only function is to indicate the performance of the act. Performative verbs are the illocutionary force markers *par excellence* simply because they explicitly name the act to be performed (Austin 1962). Parenthetical constructions have also been treated as indicators, signalling the force of the utterance to which they are attached (Austin 1962; Urmson 1963; Strawson 1971).

All such indicators have been traditionally treated as non-truth-conditional, i.e. as not contributing to the truth conditions of the *utterance* in which they occur, or to the proposition expressed by the utterance. Speech-act theorists repeatedly assert that their function is not to describe but to indicate the illocutionary force of the utterance a request for information, an order, a promise, a warning, an assertion, a guess.

Certain types of sentence adverbials seem to fit naturally into this framework. Although speech-act theorists have not dealt extensively with adverbials, the following should give an idea of how the speech-act approach would go.

The salient features of the speech-act approach to adverbials are:

a.   illocutionary, attitudinal, evidential and hearsay adverbials are standardly treated as non-truth-conditional and

b.   non-truth-conditional expressions are treated as *indicating* a speech act or propositional attitude rather than *describing* a state of affairs.

These claims are linked because, as we have seen, the crucial feature of an indicator, in this framework, is that it does not contribute to the proposition expressed, i.e. to the truth conditions of the utterance.

Illocutionary adverbials will be the first to be discussed, being the most promising candidates for speech-act analysis. According to the speech-act view the adverbials *frankly, confidentially, seriously* in (1a–c)

(1)   a.   *Frankly*, I'm bored.
      b.   Mary has, *confidentially*, failed the exam.
      c.   *Seriously*, your argument is fallacious.

do not modify anything in the proposition that follows them, they make no contribution to the truth conditions of these utterances; they do not *describe* anything, but merely *indicate* what type of speech-act is being performed (Sadock 1974: 36, 66–71; Bach and Harnish 1979: 220). Here is how Sadock presents this view:

> (68)   *For the last time, I don't like liver.*
>
> It is obvious ... that the adverbial phrase *for the last time* is not understood as modifying the sentence in the same way that it does in one interpretation of (69).
>
> (69)   *For the last time, Ussorssuaq beheld his native land.*
>
> In fact, *for the last time* cannot modify the propositional content of sentence (68), as is shown by (70):
>
> (70)   **I don't like liver for the last time.*
>
> ...
>
> (72)   I tell you for the last time that I don't like liver.
>
> Sentence (72) is a fairly close paraphrase of sentence (68), ... thus ... the distribution of the adverbial is explained by the abstract-performative hypothesis. (Sadock 1974: 36)[2]

Sadock claims that a large class of adverbials such as *frankly, finally, in conclusion*, have the same function, i.e. "modify the abstract performative." (ibid.) Similarly, Bach and Harnish observe that:

> ... the prefatory adverbial is not used to modify the main clause of the sentence (it may not even contribute to the locutionary act). Rather it is used to characterize, in one way or another, the *utterance* of the main clause. In (30) [Frankly, you bore me] "frankly" describes *S*'s act of stating that *H* bores *S*. (Bach and Harnish 1979: 220)

This analysis treats *frankly* in (1a) as indicating that the speech act performed is one of saying frankly/telling the hearer frankly/admitting frankly/informing the hearer frankly that the speaker is bored.

One advantage of this proposal is that it provides an explanation for the ambiguity of utterances like (10):

(10)   Seriously, is she coming?

Here, *seriously* can have two possible interpretations: (a) the speaker is asking a serious question or (b) the speaker is asking for a serious answer.

(10) a'. I ask you seriously to tell me whether she is coming.

(10) b'. I ask you to tell me seriously whether she is coming. (Bach and Harnish 1979:221)

This is perhaps the strongest confirmation of the speech-act analysis of illocutionary adverbials (Wilson 1991).

Similarly, the speech-act account treats attitudinal adverbials as indicating the propositional attitude the speaker intends to convey. It is Urmson who provides us with the most extensive speech-act account of these adverbials (1963:227–229), in the course of a discussion of parenthetical verbs (ibid.:220–240) which will be considered in more detail in chapter 6. He refers to adverbs such as *luckily, happily, unfortunately,* as being "loosely attached to sentences as are parenthetical verbs" (ibid.:228), and notes that their position in the sentence can vary "as in the case of parenthetical verbs". These adverbs, he claims, modify the whole statement to which they are attached "*by giving a warning how they are to be understood*" (emphasis added). Thus, attitudinal adverbials are considered as non-truth-conditional indicators, semantically external to the proposition expressed by the utterances that carry them.

Strawson (1973:57–58) and Recanati (1987) express the same view. This is how Recanati summarizes the point in relation to the attitudinal adverb 'happily':

> Deleting the adverb would not change the proposition expressed by the sentence when interpreted in this manner, because the modification introduced by the adverb is external to the proposition and concerns the speaker's emotional attitude toward the latter. This attitude is not "stated" nor "described", but only "indicated". (Recanati 1987:50)

Evidential adverbials are treated by speech-act theorists as indicators of the kind or amount of evidence the speaker has for what she is saying. Urmson (1963:228) and Chafe (1986:264) consider evidential adverbials such as *certainly, probably, possibly, definitely, undoubtedly* as indicators of the extent to which the speaker's statement is reliable. For Urmson, "... *certainly, probably* and *possibly,* among others, show how much reliability is to be ascribed to the statement." (Urmson 1963:228) and for Chafe,

> ... one way in which knowledge may be qualified is with an expression indicating the speaker's assessment of its degree of reliability, the likelihood of its being a fact.
> ...

(9s) But I'm _probably_ not going to do it any more.

(10s) He's quite nice, and _certainly_ very cheery.

...

(13w) _The positive and negative decisions in the Johnson-Laird et al. (1978) study may have allowed equal elaboration, but _possibly_ not._

(14w) _The answer _undoubtedly_ varies from one situation to another._

(15w) _Then this limitation will _surely_ play a part in determining the nature of the "rules" for reference in any language._ (Chafe 1986: 264–265)

Evidential adverbials are also considered as indicators of the speaker's degree of commitment (Palmer 1986: 64) or as an alternative device to the explicit performative for making clear the force of utterances (Austin 1962: 74–77). According to Austin: "... when we say "I shall" we can make it clear that we are forecasting by adding the adverbs "undoubtedly" or "probably", that we are expressing an intention by adding the adverbs "certainly" or "definitely"..." (Austin 1962: 77).

Similar analyses have been proposed for the hearsay adverbials _apparently, allegedly, reportedly._ These are usually treated as a type of evidential (Palmer 1986: 7, 9, 51, 56–57, 71, 73; Chafe 1986: 268–269), and hence speech-act theorists analyse them as indicating a diminished speaker commitment.

The main point to be emphasized in these accounts is that speech-act theorists have indiscriminately treated the different types of sentence adverbials as being consistently _non-truth-conditional_. In the next section, I will try to show that this treatment is inadequate. By applying some standard tests for truth-conditionality, I will try to show that different classes of sentence adverbial behave in very different ways. In later sections, I will ask why this is so.

5.4   Testing for truth-conditionality

There is a standard test for distinguishing truth-conditional from non-truth-conditional meaning, which I am going to apply to the four classes of adverbial illustrated above. Its core mechanism consists in embedding the item to be tested into the antecedent of a conditional and seeing if it falls within the scope of the 'if'. If it does, the item is truth-conditional, if it does not, it is non-truth-conditional.

The way the test works and the results it yields are best illustrated by using it to show that _but_ is non-truth-conditional (Wilson 1998–9). Consider _but_ in (11):

(11)   Mary is here but Sue isn't.

The question is whether the suggestion of contrast carried by *but* is truth-conditional or not. In other words, are the truth conditions of (11) correctly given in (12a–b) or (13a–c)?

(12) a. Mary is here.
      b. Sue isn't here.

(13) a. Mary is here.
      b. Sue isn't here.
      c. There is a contrast between the fact that Mary is here and the fact that Sue isn't.

It is easier to answer this question when we embed (11) into a conditional, as in (14):

(14) If Mary is here but Sue isn't, we can't vote.

The question now is: under what circumstances is the speaker of (14) claiming that we can't vote? Is she saying that we can't vote if (12a–b) are true, or is she saying that we can't vote if (13a–c) are true? In other words, does (13c) contribute to the truth conditions of (14), or does it remain outside the scope of the 'if … then' connective?

It should be clear that (13c) does not contribute to the truth conditions of the utterance in (11). Thus, *but* is non-truth-conditional, as most analysts who deal with *but* have assumed.

Let us examine how the test applies to each group of adverbials in turn. The attitudinal adverbials *unfortunately* and *sadly* will be the first to be tested, since they are, along with hearsay adverbials, the clearest cases. Consider (3a–b):

(3) a. *Unfortunately*, Mary has missed the deadline.
     b. *Sadly*, Paul's car was stolen.

Intuitively, as speech-act theorists have claimed, the adverbials in (3) do not make any contribution to the proposition expressed, hence to the truth conditions of the utterances in question. (3a) would be true if and only if Mary missed the deadline, (3b) would be true if and only if Paul's car was stolen. However, it will be interesting to see if our intuitions are confirmed by the test illustrated above.

Regarding (3a), the issue is whether its truth conditions are (15) or (16):

(15) Mary has missed the deadline.

(16) It is unfortunate that Mary has missed the deadline.

To apply the test, we embed (3a) into a conditional. Note that since (3a) sounds odd when embedded as it stands, the synonymous (17) will be used.[3]

(17)   Mary has unfortunately missed the deadline.

(18)   If Mary has unfortunately missed the deadline, she can reapply in May.

The question is: under what circumstances is the speaker of (18) claiming that Mary should reapply in May? Is she saying that Mary should reapply in May if (15) is true, or is she saying that Mary should reapply in May if (16) is true? Clearly, she is saying the former, not the latter. Hence, (16) does not contribute to the truth conditions of the utterance, and the attitudinal adverbial *unfortunately* is non-truth-conditional.

Exactly parallel arguments apply to *sadly* in (3b). Regarding (3b), the issue is whether its truth conditions are (19) or (20):

(19)   Paul's car was stolen.

(20)   It is sad that Paul's car was stolen.

Since (3b) again sounds odd when embedded as it stands, the synonymous (21) will be used.

(21)   Paul's car was, sadly, stolen.

(22)   If Paul's car was, sadly, stolen, he will start using the underground.

The question is: under what circumstances is the speaker of (22) claiming that Paul will start using the underground? Is she saying that Paul will start using the underground if (19) is true, or is she saying that Paul will start using the underground if (20) is true? Again, it is clear that (20) does not contribute to the truth conditions of the utterance, and hence the non-truth-conditional status of attitudinal adverbials is confirmed. Notice that these results are exactly as the speech-act theorists predict.

I will next examine the hearsay adverbials *allegedly* and *reportedly*. These also yield uncontroversial results, but results which go in quite the opposite direction from those obtained with attitudinal adverbials. Consider again (8a–b):

(8)   a.   *Allegedly*, the cook has poisoned the soup.
      b.   *Reportedly*, the ball was over the line.

In the case of (8a), the question is whether its truth conditions are (23) or (24):

(23)   The cook has poisoned the soup.

(24)   It is alleged that the cook has poisoned the soup.

To test (8a) we embed the synonymous (25)

(25)   The cook has allegedly poisoned the soup.

into a conditional, as in (26):

(26)   If the cook has allegedly poisoned the soup, the police should make
        an inquiry.

The question is: under what circumstances is the speaker of (26) claiming that
the police should make an inquiry into the case? Is she saying that the police
ought to make an inquiry if (23) is true, or is she saying that the police ought to
make an inquiry if (24) is true?

    Interestingly, in this case the results obtained are quite different. (24) *does*
contribute to the truth conditions of the utterance. Hence, the hearsay
adverbial *allegedly* is truth-conditional, contrary to what is claimed on the
speech-act account.

    Similarly, in the case of (8b), we want to know whether its truth conditions
are those in (27) or (28):

(27)   The ball was over the line.

(28)   It is reported that the ball was over the line.

Assuming that (8b) is synonymous with (29),

(29)   The ball was reportedly over the line

we embed (29) into a conditional as in (30):

(30)   If the ball was reportedly over the line, the matter should be
        investigated further.

Under what circumstances is the speaker of (30) claiming that the matter
should be investigated further? Is she saying that the matter should be investigated further if (27) is true, or is she saying that the matter should be investigated further if (28) is true? It is clear again that (28) contributes to the truth
conditions of the utterance. Hence, the truth-conditional status of hearsay
adverbials is confirmed.

    Note that the testing of hearsay adverbials yields results that go exactly
against the speech-act predictions. Thus, we have one clear argument against
the speech-act approach, and one clear problem: why do these two types of
adverbial behave differently?

    Turning to illocutionary and evidential adverbials, a number of problems
arise in applying the tests.

a.   First, when we embed illocutionary adverbials under 'if', they often seem to take not the embedded clause but the whole utterance in their scope. For example, (31) would often be understood as communicating (32a) rather than (32b):

(31)   If Mary, frankly, is unqualified, we should not give her the post.

(32)   a.   I tell you frankly that if Mary is unqualified, we should not give her the post.
        b.   If I tell you frankly that Mary is unqualified, we should not give her the post.

These adverbials cannot easily be interpreted as taking merely the embedded antecedent in their scope. A similar point applies to disjunctions. Just as (31) would often be understood as communicating (32a), so (33) would often be understood as communicating (34a) rather than (34b):

(33)   Either Mary, frankly, isn't as qualified as you say she is, or she is inefficient.

(34)   a.   I tell you frankly that either Mary isn't as qualified as you say she is, or she is inefficient.
        b.   Either I tell you frankly that Mary isn't as qualified as you say she is, or she is inefficient.

b.   Second, when we embed at least some illocutionary adverbials, they often seem to take only the embedded VP in their scope. For example, (35) can be understood as communicating (36):

(35)   If John is frankly annoyed, we should drop the subject.

(36)   If John is honestly/openly showing his annoyance, we should drop the subject.

Notice, moreover, that this interpretation is possible even without embedding. (37) can be understood as communicating (38):

(37)   John is frankly annoyed.

(38)   John is honestly/openly showing his annoyance.

However, this is not the interpretation we are interested in. We are looking for an interpretation on which 'frankly' modifies an implicit illocutionary verb, i.e. an interpretation of (35) which would be equivalent not to (36) but to (39):

(39)   If I tell you frankly that John is annoyed...

The question is whether both these possibilities of interpretation can be eliminated in order to show whether these adverbials are truth-conditional in the sense we are interested in.

The second problem seems to arise with evidentials too. Here, the possible confusion is over cases where the evidential can be understood as a manner adverbial modifying the embedded VP. For example, (40) can be understood as communicating (41a) or (41b):

(40) The cook obviously poisoned the soup.

(41) a. The cook poisoned the soup in an obvious way.
      b. It is obvious that the cook poisoned the soup.

There are also cases parallel to (35) and (36) above, i.e. where (42) is understood as communicating (43):

(42) If John is evidently annoyed, we should drop the subject.

(43) If John is showing his annoyance in an evident way, we should drop the subject.

The issue is whether there is a way of dealing with points (a) and (b) for both illocutionary and evidential adverbials.

On point (a), notice that 'if...then' and 'either...or' are, as it were, non-factive connectives: they do not commit the speaker to the truth of the propositions embedded under them. With factive connectives such as *although, since* and *because*, which commit the speaker to the truth of the propositions embedded under them, the scope facts are quite different. Thus (44a) is equivalent to (44b) and (45a) is equivalent to (45b):

(44) a. Mary shouldn't get the post, because she frankly isn't qualified enough.
      b. Mary shouldn't get the post, because (I tell you frankly that) she isn't qualified enough.

(45) a. Mary might get the post, although she frankly isn't qualified enough.
      b. Mary might get the post, although (I tell you frankly that) she isn't qualified enough.

In these examples, we have an interpretation of the sort we are interested in testing for truth-conditional status. I have put the embedded illocutionary clause in parentheses, to indicate that we have not yet decided whether, in this position, it is fully truth-conditional or not. These examples suggest that we should be able to avoid problem (a) by constructing test sentences based on factive rather than non-factive connectives. I will return to this point below.

On point (b), the manner-adverbial interpretation can be eliminated in the case of evidentials on the basis of the following syntactic/semantic arguments. (i) Manner adverbs must be semantically compatible with the verbal construction they modify (Hartvigson 1969:172). The manner adverb *clearly*, for example, requires a verb that denotes 'actions' which can be performed in a more or less clear way or manner. Thus the manner adverbial *clearly* co-occurs with verbs like *see, explain, write* but not a verb like *die*. The evidential *clearly*, however, can modify any verbal construction. (ii) In American English, manner adverbs do not occur before aspect or modals (Jackendoff 1972:75). Hence the un-acceptability of manner-adverbial interpretations of (A):

(A)   *The driver clearly has seen the pedestrian.
       *The cook obviously has poisoned the soup.
       *The cook clearly is poisoning the soup.
       *The cook clearly will poison the soup.

Compare with the same utterances interpreted as evidentials, which are perfectly acceptable in American English:

(B)   The driver, clearly, has seen the pedestrian.
       The cook, obviously, has poisoned the soup.
       The cook, clearly, is poisoning the soup.
       The cook, evidently, will poison the soup.

Some of these examples sound strange in British English, which prefers to put the adverbial after the auxiliary, but the same point can be made with the negative counterparts of (A). Thus, in British English 'The driver clearly hasn't seen the pedestrian' etc. can only have an evidential interpretation.

Let us, then, use the following examples, which by the arguments given above have only an evidential interpretation, to test for truth-conditionality of evidentials:

(46)   a.   The driver clearly hasn't died.
       b.   The cook obviously won't poison the soup.

The issue is whether the truth conditions of (46a) are (47) or (48).

(47)   The driver hasn't died.

(48)   It is clear that the driver hasn't died.

To sharpen our intuitions, we embed (46a) into a conditional, as in (49):

(49)   If the driver clearly hasn't died, you must hurry for an ambulance.

The question is: under what circumstances is the speaker of (49) claiming that they must hurry for an ambulance? Is she saying that they must hurry for an ambulance if (47) is true, or is she saying that they must hurry for an ambulance if (48) is true? In other words, is (48) contributing to the truth conditions of the utterance as a whole or does it remain outside the scope of the conditional? Here, (48) does seem to contribute to the truth conditions of the utterance. This suggests that the evidential adverbial *clearly* is truth-conditional.[4]

The results are even sharper for (46b). We need, again, to decide whether its truth conditions are (50) or (51):

(50)   The cook won't poison the soup.

(51)   It is obvious that the cook won't poison the soup.

To sharpen our intuitions we embed (46b) into a conditional, as in (52):

(52)   If the cook obviously won't poison the soup, we can eat the meal without worrying.

The question is: under what circumstances is the speaker of (52) claiming that they can eat the meal without worrying? Is she saying that they needn't worry if (50) is true, or is she saying that they needn't worry if (51) is true? Clearly, (51) does contribute to the truth conditions of (46b). Hence the truth conditional status of evidential adverbials is confirmed.

With illocutionary adverbials, the manner-adverbial interpretation can be eliminated by choosing VPs that do not take human subjects, as in (53):

(53)   John's book has frankly sold very little.

or by using *confidentially* or some other adverbial instead,[5] as in (54):

(54)   Mary has, confidentially, failed the exam.

Let us examine how the test applies to *frankly* first. We want to know whether the truth conditions of (53) are (55) or (56):

(55)   John's book has sold very little.

(56)   I tell you frankly that John's book has sold very little.

To sharpen our intuitions, we embed (53) into a conditional, as in (57):

(57)   If John's book has frankly sold very little, you shouldn't be surprised.

The question is: under what circumstances is the speaker of (57) claiming that the hearer shouldn't be surprised? Is she saying that he shouldn't be surprised if (55) is true, i.e. if the book has sold very little, or is she saying that he shouldn't be surprised if (56) is true, i.e. if the speaker tells him frankly that the book has sold very little? Clearly, the former interpretation is correct. Hence, (56) does not contribute to the truth conditions of the utterance as a whole, and the illocutionary adverbial *frankly* is non-truth-conditional.

Similar arguments apply to (54). When testing (54), the question is whether its truth conditions are (58) or (59):

(58)   Mary has failed the exam.

(59)   I inform you confidentially that Mary has failed the exam.

To sharpen our intuitions, we embed (54) into a conditional, as in (60):

(60)   If Mary has, confidentially, failed the exam, you mustn't be upset.

The question is: under what circumstances is the speaker of (60) claiming that the hearer mustn't be upset? Is she saying that he mustn't be upset if (58) is true, or is she saying that he mustn't be upset if (59) is true? Clearly, the former interpretation is correct. Hence, (59) does not contribute to the truth conditions of the utterance as a whole, and the non-truth-conditional status of illocutionary adverbials is confirmed.

This last example returns us to an important issue raised above, about the scope of sentence adverbials embedded in subordinate clauses. Although, as we have just seen, *confidentially* does not appear to contribute to the truth conditions of (60), it still has two natural scope possibilities, brought out by the paraphrases in (61) and (62):

(61)   I tell you this confidentially: if Mary has failed the exam, you
       mustn't be upset.

(62)   If Mary has failed the exam — and I am telling you in confidence
       that she has — you mustn't be upset.

In (61), the speaker is not conceding that Mary has failed her exam; in (62) it seems that she is. Notice that in (62), the parenthetical clause 'and I am telling you that she has' does not fall semantically within the scope of the connective 'if', despite its syntactic position: it is not part of the conditions under which the speaker is telling the hearer that he mustn't be upset. This, on the one hand, confirms the non-truth-conditional status of the illocutionary adverbial 'confidentially' in (60), and, on the other hand, suggests that a closer study of parentheticals might shed more light on sentence adverbials too. This topic will be pursued in the next chapter.

Meanwhile, let us pursue this matter one stage further by looking at the behaviour of illocutionary and evidential adverbials embedded under factive connectives, which eliminate the possibility of an interpretation along the lines of (61) above. Notice first that the use of factive connectives such as *because* and *although* eliminates a syntactic problem encountered above. In order to embed the sentence adverbials felicitously under 'if' and 'or', we had to move them from sentence-initial position to mid-sentence, relying on the synonymy between 'Fortunately, he has left' and 'He has fortunately left': utterances such as 'If, fortunately, John left, we can celebrate' are either ungrammatical or infelicitous. With factive connectives, i.e. connectives which entail the truth of their constituent clauses, this problem does not arise. Thus, consider (63) and (64):

(63) a. John's here, although unfortunately his train was late.
     b. Susan's lucky, because frankly she should have lost the election.

(64) a. John's here, although allegedly his train was late.
     b. Susan's lucky, because obviously she should have lost the election.

Here, there is no need to move the adverbial from sentence-initial position to obtain a fully acceptable result. In these examples, the speaker is clearly committed to the following:

(65) a. Unfortunately, his train was late.
     b. Frankly, she should have lost the election.
     c. Allegedly, his train was late.
     d. Obviously, she should have lost the election.

The question is, though, whether these adverbials fall within the scope of *because* and *although*, as they would if they were genuinely truth-conditional.

In the case of (63a) and (63b), it seems clear that the results are as before. These adverbials remain outside the scope of the connectives. The facts being contrasted in (63a) are (a) that John is here and (b) that his train was late. What makes the speaker conclude that Susan is lucky in (63b) is the fact that Susan ought to have lost the election rather than the fact that this information is being given frankly. This confirms the non-truth-conditional status of attitudinal and illocutionary adverbials.

With (64), by contrast, things seem less clear cut. There appears to be both a truth-conditional and a non-truth-conditional reading: *obviously* and *allegedly* can fall both inside and outside the scope of *although* and *because*. That is, (64a) might be equivalent to 'although it is alleged that his train was late', or to 'although his train was late', and similarly for (64b). This suggests that the truth-conditional status of evidential and hearsay adverbials is even more complicated than either pure truth-conditional theorists or pure speech-act theorists have thought. These points will be taken up in the next chapter.

In this section, I have tried to show that illocutionary, attitudinal, evidential and hearsay adverbials behave very differently from each other, both semantically and pragmatically, and present a variety of descriptive problems that are entirely unexpected on the standard speech-act account. Hence, we need a new descriptive and explanatory framework in which to analyse them. In the next section, I shall start to analyse them in the framework of relevance theory.

5.5   Relevance theory and sentence adverbials: possibilities for description

Relevance theory provides a rich enough framework for describing the facts about sentence adverbials that have been presented above. The basic assumptions I shall develop are the following:

1. Sentence adverbials encode elements of *conceptual representations*, which may be true or false in their own right, even if they do not contribute to the truth conditions of the utterances in which they occur.
2. Sentence adverbials contribute to the *explicatures* of an utterance, rather than its implicatures.
3. Where they do not contribute to the proposition expressed, they contribute to what Wilson and Sperber (1993) call *higher-level explicatures* of the utterance, where higher-level explicatures by definition do not contribute to the truth conditions of the utterances, though they may be true or false in their own right.

5.5.1   Conceptual versus procedural

The distinction between conceptual and procedural meaning was introduced in chapter 4. The assumption is that most ordinary nouns, verbs, adjectives and adverbs which contribute to truth conditions do so by encoding concepts. Hence, since we have seen that evidential, including hearsay, adverbials appear to be truth-conditional, they should be treated as encoding concepts.

Blakemore (1987) argues that non-truth-conditional discourse connectives such as *after all, so, but,* etc., encode procedural rather than conceptual meaning, indicating to the hearer what type of inference process he is in.

The question is, are all non-truth-conditional expressions to be analysed in procedural terms? In particular, do the non-truth-conditional adverbials, i.e. the illocutionary and the attitudinal adverbials, also encode procedural rather than conceptual meaning? I shall argue, following Wilson and Sperber (1993), that they do not.

Note first that a speaker who uses the illocutionary adverbials in (66)–(68) and the attitudinal adverbials in (69)–(70) can lay herself open to charges of untruthfulness in their use:

(66) a. *Peter*: *Frankly*, this party is boring.
      b. *Mary*: That's not true. You're not being frank. I've just seen you dancing with the blonde beauty in blue.

(67) a. *Bill*: *Confidentially*, Peter broke up with Jane.
      b. *Ann*: Liar. You're not being confidential, you've told everybody in the College.

(68) a. *Peter*: *Honestly*, I don't care.
      b. *Mary*: That's not true. You're not being honest! I know you have sent her another Valentine card this year.

(69) a. *Peter*: *Unfortunately*, John lost his job.
      b. *Mary*: That's not true. It's not unfortunate! He got a fellowship in Oxford instead!

(70) a. *Peter*: *Sadly*, she missed the deadline.
      b. *Mary*: That's not true, no-one's sad about it!

This can be explained on the assumption that the adverbials in (66)–(70) encode elements of conceptual representations which can be true or false in their own right, though not contributing to the truth conditions of the utterance in which they occur.

More importantly, illocutionary and attitudinal adverbials have synonymous manner-adverbial counterparts which are clearly truth conditional, and should therefore, on standard assumptions, be treated as encoding concepts (Wilson and Sperber 1993). Thus, consider (71) and (72):

(71) Peter spoke *frankly*.

(72) It's *unfortunately* true that John lost his job.

The manner adverbials *frankly* and *unfortunately* make a contribution to the truth conditions of the utterances in (71) and in (72): (71) is true if and only if Peter spoke *frankly* and (72) is true if and only if it is unfortunately true that

John lost his job. By the above arguments, the two adverbials must be treated as encoding concepts.

But the only difference between these truth-conditional manner adverbials and their non-truth-conditional illocutionary and attitudinal counterparts is that the truth-conditional adverbials modify *explicit* illocutionary and attitudinal predicates, whereas the non-truth-conditional ones must be seen as modifying *implicit* illocutionary and attitudinal predicates. Thus, compare (73) and (74):

(73)   *Frankly*, this party is boring.

(74)   I'm telling you *frankly* that this party is boring.

and (75) and (76):

(75)   *Unfortunately*, John lost his job.

(76)   It is *unfortunately* true that John lost his job.

The sense of *frankly* in (73) and (74) and of *unfortunately* in (75) and (76) seems to be the same, the only difference being that in (74) and (76) the adverbs contribute to the truth conditions of the utterances whereas in (73) and (75) they do not. The simplest way to account for these facts is to assume that the two adverbs encode the same concepts in both cases, but that in (74) and (76) these concepts contribute to the proposition expressed by the utterance, and hence to its truth conditions, whereas in (73) and (75) they do not.

A further argument for the view that illocutionary and attitudinal adverbials encode concepts is based on *compositionality* (Wilson and Sperber 1993). These adverbials can have a quite complex syntactic and semantic structure. Consider (77a–d):

(77)   a.   *Quite frankly*, he is a fool.
       b.   *In strictest confidence*, he is a fool.
       c.   *Very sadly and regrettably*, your fête will be rained off.
       d.   *Not surprisingly*, he didn't win.

These more complex adverbials are easily analysable on the assumption that they encode concepts in the same way as regular, truth-conditional expressions, with the sole exception that the concepts they encode do not contribute to the truth conditions of utterances in which they occur.

Notice that, as Wilson and Sperber (1993) point out, none of these arguments carries over to discourse connectives such as *but*, *however*, etc., which we have seen are analysed within the relevance-theoretic framework as encoding procedural rather than conceptual meaning. Thus, *but* and *however* appear to have no synonymous truth-conditional counterparts, which was one of the strongest reasons for assigning conceptual status to sentence adverbs such as *frankly, unfortunately,* etc. Nor do they appear to occur in complex connectives corresponding to the complex adverbials in (77) above. Moreover, as Wilson and Sperber (1993) also point out, the meanings of discourse connectives such as *but, so, well,* etc., are hard to bring to consciousness and to analyse in conceptual terms:

> Conceptual representations can be brought to consciousness: procedures cannot. We have direct access neither to grammatical computations nor to inferential computations used in comprehension. A procedural analysis of discourse connectives would explain our lack of direct access to the information they encode. (Wilson and Sperber 1993: 16)

Clearly, the meaning of all the adverbials dealt with here *are* easy to bring to consciousness and to analyse in conceptual terms. Notice, too, that in the last section I showed that evidential and hearsay adverbials seemed to vacillate between truth-conditional and non-truth-conditional status. Surely they do not also vacillate between conceptual and procedural status: they are conceptual throughout.

5.5.2   Explicatures versus implicatures

I shall now argue (following Wilson and Sperber 1993) that there is a second important difference between Blakemore's pragmatic connectives and the non-truth-conditional adverbials we are dealing with here. Blakemore analyses her connectives as encoding constraints on implicatures, i.e. as contributing to the implicit aspect of communication. Illocutionary and attitudinal adverbials, by contrast, appear to contribute to what Sperber and Wilson call the *explicatures* of an utterance: i.e. to the explicit aspect of communication.

As we have seen, Sperber and Wilson define *explicatures* as explicitly communicated assumptions. The explicatures of an utterance will typically include:

a.   the proposition expressed by the utterance
b.   higher-level descriptions obtained by optionally embedding this
     proposition under a speech-act verb or a propositional-attitude verb.

Thus, the explicatures of the utterance in (78) might include the propositions in (79):

(78)   *Mary* (frankly): I lied.

(79) a. *Mary lied.*
   b. Mary is saying that she lied.
   c. Mary is saying frankly that she lied.
   d. Mary is telling Peter that she lied.
   e. Mary believes that she lied.
   f. Mary is admitting that she lied.

As we have seen, Mary's utterance in (78) is true if and only if Mary lied, i.e. if and only if the explicature in (79a) is true. The remaining explicatures (79b–f) may be true or false in their own right but make no contribution to the truth conditions of Mary's utterance. In more technical terms, the most deeply embedded explicature of (78) is the *proposition expressed* by (78) and (79b–f) are *higher-level explicatures* of (78). The truth conditions of (78) will depend solely on (79a), the proposition expressed, whereas the higher-level explicatures (79b–f) will be explicitly communicated, but make no contribution to the truth conditions of (78).

As noted in chapter 4, higher-level explicatures, like logical forms and fully propositional forms, are recovered by a combination of decoding and inference (Wilson and Sperber 1993:11). To obtain (79a) the hearer must not only decode the semantic representation of the utterance but make an inference about the intended referent of 'I'; to obtain the remaining explicatures (79b–f) he must make additional inferences about Mary's attitude to the proposition she is expressing, and the type of speech act she is intending to perform. On this approach, higher-level explicatures are conceptual representations, which can entail and contradict each other and represent determinate states of affairs. Although they are true or false in their own right, they do not contribute to the truth conditions of the utterances in which they occur (ibid.:16). Within this framework, then, both the fact that illocutionary and attitudinal adverbials encode concepts, and the fact that they are nonetheless non-truth-conditional, can be described.

Evidential and hearsay adverbials, as we have seen, encode concepts too, and in many cases these concepts appear to contribute to the truth conditions of utterances in the regular way. Thus, consider (80a–b):

(80) a. *Evidently*, Bill has cheated in the exams.
   b. *Allegedly*, Bill has cheated in the exams.

According to the tests described above, (80a) and (80b) communicate the explicatures in (81) and (82) respectively, but these constitute the truth conditions of (80a) and (80b):

(81) It is evident that Bill has cheated in the exams.

(82) It is alleged that Bill has cheated in the exams.

Within this framework, these facts can be described by saying that the evidential (*evidently*) and hearsay (*allegedly*) adverbials in (80a) and (80b) contribute to the proposition expressed; in other words, (81) and (82) constitute the truth-conditional content of the utterance rather than its higher-level explicatures. A description, of course, is not an explanation. The four classes of adverbial we have been considering are syntactically very similar: why is it that two appear to contribute to the truth conditions of utterances, and two do not? In this chapter, I shall not attempt a full explanation, but merely indicate the lines along which I think an explanation might be sought. The matter will be taken up in later chapters.

5.6 Relevance theory and sentence adverbials: possibilities for explanation

The questions that have been raised in this chapter are:

a. are all the adverbials we have been discussing really non-truth-conditional?
b. if so, how do we establish this? If not, what tests for truth-conditionality can we use?
c. for non-truth-conditional adverbials, why are they non-truth-conditional?
d. do they encode conceptual or procedural information?
e. do they contribute to the implicit or the explicit aspect of communication?
f. if there is a difference between truth-conditional and non-truth-conditional adverbials, how can this difference be explained?

It has been shown by the standard test for truth-conditionality that evidential and hearsay adverbials are (generally) truth-conditional, whereas attitudinal and illocutionary adverbials are non-truth-conditional. The distinction between proposition expressed and higher-level explicatures makes it possible to describe the facts in a natural way: truth-conditional adverbials contribute to the proposition expressed whereas the non-truth-conditional ones contribute to higher-level explicatures. It has also been shown that all these adverbials, whether truth-conditional or non-truth-conditional, encode conceptual information and contribute to the explicit aspect of communication.

However, it still remains to provide an explanation for these facts, i.e. to answer questions (c) and (f) above. I suggest that an answer to question (c) might be sought along the following lines. The comma intonation separating off sentence adverbials and their position in the sentence (initial, mid or final) seems to suggest that they should be treated along with parentheticals. In the literature, parenthetical constructions have been classed with appositive clauses (e.g. 'Mary's car, and it is an expensive one, is blue') (Emonds 1979), nonrestrictive relative clauses (NRR) (e.g. 'I talked to Mary, who is nice') (Fabb 1990) or disjunct constituents (Espinal 1991; for discussion within a traditional framework see Meyer 1992).

The general claim is that all these constructions are phonologically, syntactically and semantically independent of their host clauses (Emonds 1979; McCawley 1982; Fabb 1990; Haegeman 1991; Espinal 1991). This might be taken to suggest that there is not one single utterance involved, with a single set of truth conditions. Instead, there might be two separate syntactic and discourse units or two separate utterances involved, each with their own truth conditions, which might make different contributions to overall relevance. This would connect up with suggestions traditionally made by speech-act theorists along similar lines (Recanati 1987:36–40). If such speculations prove to be correct, one might further speculate that intuitions about the truth conditions of the utterance as a whole will be intuitions about the sub-part of it which makes the major contribution to overall relevance.

In order to pursue these ideas further I must first investigate the nature of parentheticals, and examine their truth-conditional status. As we will see, an important subclass of parentheticals perform an evidential function, and are generally treated by speech-act theorists as non-truth-conditional. The next chapter will therefore look at the truth-conditional status of parentheticals in general, and of evidential parentheticals in particular, and discuss how they function in pragmatic terms.

CHAPTER 6

Parentheticals

6.1 Introduction

At the start of this book, I raised three main questions about the nature of evidentials:

a. what is the role of pragmatic inference in the interpretation of evidential utterances?
b. do overt evidential expressions contribute to the explicit or the implicit aspect of communication?

and

c. do these expressions contribute to the truth conditions of utterances in which they occur?

I have now offered partial answers to all three questions, within the framework of relevance theory, outlined in chapter 4.

These answers might be summarised as follows. Utterance comprehension involves the formation and evaluation of hypotheses about the speaker's intended interpretation, i.e. the intended combination of contextual assumptions, propositions expressed and implied, and attitudinal or speech-act information. Evidential utterances typically communicate attitudinal or speech-act information — about degree of speaker commitment or source of information — which may be either linguistically encoded or pragmatically inferred. In chapter 4, I showed how inferences about degree of speaker commitment were constrained by considerations of optimal relevance: the first hypothesis which leads to an overall interpretation consistent with the principle of relevance is the one the hearer should choose. I have not yet considered how relevance theory can account for the effect on pragmatic interpretation of overt evidential expressions such as *I think*, or *I know* — an effect described in speech-act terms as that of weakened speaker commitment. Such an account will be provided towards the end of this chapter.

As regards the interpretation of overt evidential expressions, we have seen that they typically encode attitudinal or speech-act information, and as such contribute to the explicatures of an utterance rather than its implicatures. Evidential adverbials do this by encoding conceptual rather than procedural information. In a later section of this chapter, I will show briefly that parenthetical expressions such as *I think* and *I know* also encode conceptual rather than procedural information, and contribute to the explicit rather than the implicit aspect of communication. This opens the way for a unified treatment of evidential adverbials and parentheticals.

By the standard tests for truth-conditional status, evidential and hearsay adverbials seem to contribute to the truth-conditional content of utterances on at least some occasions, whereas illocutionary and attitudinal adverbials seem always to contribute to non-truth-conditional content. I have shown that these facts can be described within the framework of relevance theory by saying that evidentials and hearsay adverbials can contribute to the proposition expressed, whereas illocutionary and attitudinal adverbials invariably contribute to higher-level explicatures. I have as yet offered no explanation for why this should be so. Such an explanation will be sketched in a later section of this chapter.

In testing for truth-conditional status, I also came across a variety of puzzling scope facts that I felt would be illuminated by a study of parentheticals. Parenthetical utterances have often been analysed as performing two separate speech acts, one commenting on the other, and I suggested that this might provide a key to explaining the differences in truth-conditional status between evidential and hearsay adverbials, on the one hand, and illocutionary and attitudinal adverbials, on the other. It is to the study of parentheticals that I now turn.[1]

6.2   Speech-act accounts of parentheticals

The philosopher Urmson, in a famous paper (1963), treated *think, know, believe, suppose,* as parenthetical verbs. Such verbs can appear in main-clause or syntactically parenthetical position, as illustrated in (1):

(1)   a.   *I suppose* that your house is very old.
      b.   Your house is, *I suppose*, very old.
      c.   Your house is very old, *I suppose*.
           (Urmson 1963:221)

Regardless of their syntactic position, Urmson saw parenthetical verbs as contributing not to the proposition expressed by the utterance but to indicating the type of speech act performed — often indicating, in particular, the speaker's degree of commitment to the proposition expressed. On this account, (1a–c) would be mere stylistic variants. Further examples are given in (2):

(2) a. *I believe* that he is at home.
     b. He is, *I hear*, ill in bed.
     c. He is, *I fear*, too old.
     d. You intend to refuse, *I gather*.
     e. Jones was the murderer, *I conclude*.

The parenthetical expressions in (1a–c), (2a–e), are interesting because they have been treated as providing evidence for a speech-act semantics and against a truth-conditional account of at least some lexical items. In this respect, they resemble a more famous class of lexical items, the so-called performative verbs. In this section, I will compare and contrast the speech-act approaches to these two classes of items.

As we have seen, speech-act theorists attached particular importance to linguistic devices which enable the speaker to make the illocutionary force of her utterance explicit. Austin's theory of illocutionary acts relies heavily on the idea that an illocutionary act can be performed only if there is a conventional means of performing it — a "formula" or "indicator" whose only function is to indicate the performance of the act. Performative verbs are the illocutionary force markers *par excellence* simply because they explicitly name the act to be performed (Austin 1962). However, "parenthetical" constructions, such as those in (1) and (2), have also been treated as illocutionary force indicators even though, unlike performatives, they do not name any speech act (Austin 1979 [1946]; Urmson 1963; Strawson 1971).

Speech-act theorists tend to treat all illocutionary force indicators as non-truth-conditional, i.e. as not contributing to the proposition expressed by the *utterance* in which they occur. Thus, according to traditional speech-act accounts (Austin 1979 [1946]; Urmson 1963; Strawson 1971) both performatives and parentheticals lack any descriptive meaning and do not contribute to the proposition expressed by the utterance. And there are further similarities in the behaviour of these two classes, as illustrated by the parentheticals in (1) above and the performatives in (3):

(3) a. *I warn you* that Jill is there.
     b. Jill, *I warn you*, is there.
     c. Jill is there, *I warn you*.
         (Holdcroft 1978:64)

In both cases, the claim of many speech-act theorists has been that the examples in (a)–(c) are stylistic variants of each other, which reinforces my point about the close connections between performative and parenthetical verbs.[2] And a careful examination of the speech-act literature indicates that these two classes have never really been treated independently of each other. Speech-act theorists rarely miss the opportunity of drawing parallels between them (see, for example, Austin 1979 [1946], 1962; Strawson 1971; Urmson 1963, 1977).

Performative verbs are verbs that name illocutionary acts. Austin, in his paper "Other Minds" (1979 [1946]: 103), discusses uses of expressions such as *I warn, I ask, I define, other* than the familiar performative ones. When they are used performatively, the speaker is not describing an action, but performing it. In their non-performative uses, he thought, these expressions functioned as signals or indicators of how the utterance is to be understood: as a warning, a promise, an assertion, a guess. As he puts it, they function like *tone* and *expression*, or like *punctuation* and *mood*, signalling the force of the utterance. One question I want to consider in this chapter is whether it is really right to classify parenthetical constructions along with mood, intonation or punctuation: are they non-truth-conditional in the way mood, tone or punctuation are?

Urmson, in his papers "Parenthetical Verbs" (1963) and "Performative Utterances" (1977), developed Austin's observation concerning the non-performative use of expressions such as *I warn, I ask, I define,* into a technical notion of parenthetical use. Like Austin, he considers parenthetical verbs as non-descriptive and hence as non-truth-conditional. He too sees them as functioning in a similar way to intonation, choice of words, manner of expression, etc.: they signal how the associated statements are to be taken; they *show*, rather than state, the speaker's attitude to the proposition expressed, the logical relevance and the reliability of the associated statements.

According to Urmson, "parenthetical" expressions can function as evidentials indicating the type of evidence ("good", "moderate", "poor") the speaker has for the assertion being made. On the standard speech-act account, the pragmatic effect of employing an expression such as *I think* is to weaken the strength of the assertion. When it is used "The claim to truth need not be very strong, … the whole point of some parenthetical verbs is to modify or to weaken the claim to truth which would be implied by a simple assertion *p*." (Urmson 1963:-224–225)

Thus, our assertions may come with varying degrees of strength, as illustrated below:

(4) a.   John is in Berlin.   *stronger*
     b.   *I think* John is in Berlin.   *weaker*
     c.   John is, *I think*, in Berlin. *weaker*
     d.   John is in Berlin, *I think*.   *weaker*

In an earlier chapter, we have considered some Gricean accounts of how these degrees of commitment are conveyed by the use of overt parenthetical expressions. In a later section of this chapter, I will sketch a relevance-theoretic account.

Regarding the relation between performative and parenthetical verbs, Urmson claims that "parenthetical and performatory verbs have much in common as against ordinary descriptive verbs" (Urmson 1963:233). As we have seen, he also distinguishes between performative and parenthetical verbs on the basis of their function, or force: "doing" (e.g. *I guarantee, I bet*) is one thing, and "orientating the hearer" (e.g. 'He'll come to a bad end, *I guarantee*'; 'He'll forget to come, *I bet*') is another (Urmson 1963:238, 1977:263). Blakemore (1990/1) points out that:

> As Urmson has observed, it is possible to use many so-called performative verbs parenthetically. Consider, for example, the utterances in (15) and (16):
>
> (15)   It is, I admit, difficult.
> (16)   He'll forget to come, I bet.
>
> However, Urmson also points out that in these uses the performative verbs have a rather different force:
>
>> "To ask for odds or cry 'Taken' when someone says 'He'll forget to come, I bet', has, as Aristotle would say, the mark of an uneducated man (1966:210)" (Blakemore 1990/1:202–203)

There is a further, more important, difference between performative and parenthetical verbs that Urmson seems to be drawing. Parenthetical verbs are seen as comments *loosely attached* to the sentences they accompany. They give rise to complex speech acts, one part of which comments on the other (Urmson 1963:227, 233). As Urmson notes:

> They are not part of the statement made, nor additional statements, but function with regard to a statement made rather as "READ WITH CARE" functions in relation to a subjoined notice, … They help the understanding and assessment of what is said rather than being a part of what is said. (Urmson 1963:239–240)

With genuine performatives, by contrast, only a single speech act is performed. For, Urmson, then, the two types of construction are parallel, but distinct.

Strawson (1971:159–161) also linked performative verbs to expressions attached to the utterance to make the "character" or "intention" of the latter clear (ibid.:160). Adopting the standard speech-act view, he treats the explicit performative as the primary linguistic means for indicating the illocutionary force of the utterance. Parenthetical comments are also a means of signalling illocutionary force. Examples are phrases such as *This is only a suggestion, I'm only making a suggestion,* or *That was a warning, I'm warning you* (ibid.). Strawson goes on to note that from such parenthetical comments to the explicitly performative formula the step is only a short one. In other words, the function of both *parenthetical comment* and *explicit performative formula* is very much the same. Like Urmson, however, he draws a fundamental distinction between the two types of construction in terms of a two-utterance effect. For Strawson, the use of a performative verb subtracts the effect of having two utterances, one a comment on the other, which is created by the use of parenthetical comments. Instead, we have a "single utterance in which the first-person performative verb *manifestly*" (ibid.) indicates the illocutionary force of the utterance. Thus, the speech-act analysis of performatives is, or ought to be, quite different from the analysis of parentheticals. In particular, if parenthetical constructions involve two utterances, or a complex utterance, presumably each one, or part of one, could have its own truth conditions. After all, a *comment* ought to have truth conditions too. This is rather different from claiming that parentheticals are devoid of any descriptive content (see also Blakemore 1990/1:206–207).

There are a few points to be emphasized in these accounts. Firstly, the claim that performative verbs are non-truth-conditional has been seriously challenged (Lemmon 1962; Hedenius 1963; Lewis 1970; Warnock 1971; Wiggins 1971; Bach 1975; Ginet 1979; Cresswell 1979; Bach and Harnish 1979; Recanati 1987). If this claim is false, might not the treatment of parenthetical expressions as non-truth-conditional be invalid too? Secondly, speech-act theorists do not generally distinguish between genuine (i.e. syntactic) parentheticals, and their main-clause counterparts. Thirdly, they do not operate with a distinction between conceptual and procedural meaning. In a framework which makes use of such a distinction — the framework of relevance theory, for example — it would be instructive to consider on which side of this distinction genuine parentheticals fall. In the next section, I will consider the truth-conditional question, arguing that there are clear differences in the truth-conditional status of genuine parentheticals and their main-clause counterparts.

6.3   Testing for truth-conditionality

Before applying the standard test for truth-conditional status, I would like to emphasize an important syntactic difference between main-clause constructions like (1a) and genuine parentheticals like (1b–c). This difference is best brought out by looking not at declaratives such as (1a–c), but at non-declaratives. On many speech-act accounts, (5a–c):

(5)   a.   *I beg you* to come with me to Paris.
      b.   Come with me, *I beg you*, to Paris.
      c.   Come with me to Paris, *I beg you*.

and (6a–c):

(6)   a.   *I wonder* whether he's coming.
      b.   Is he, *I wonder*, coming?
      c.   Is he coming, *I wonder*?

are stylistic variants. Yet in (5a) 'I beg you' is the main clause and 'come with me' is a subordinate clause, whereas in (5b) and (5c), 'come with me' is not an embedded clause at all.

This is shown in (5) by the fact that imperative morphology in English is found only in main clauses. The infinitival 'come' in (5a) indicates the presence of a subordinate clause, embedded under a main verb 'I need'. By contrast, 'come with me' is a main clause in (5b) and (5c). Similarly, English yes-no interrogatives exhibit subject-aux inversion only in main clauses. The non-inverted 'whether he's coming' in (6a) indicates a subordinate interrogative clause embedded under a main verb 'I wonder', whereas 'is he coming?' in (6b) and (6c) is a main clause.

In fact, there is a genuine parenthetical counterpart of (5b–c) and (6b–c) with the parenthetical comment in fronted position, but it is not (5a–6a) but (7a–b):

(7)   a.   *I beg you*, come with me.
      b.   *I wonder*, is he coming?

Thus, if we are looking for stylistic variants, we should really be considering (8a–c) and (9a–c):

(8)   a.   *I beg you*, come with me to Paris.
      b.   Come with me, *I beg you*, to Paris.
      c.   Come with me to Paris, *I beg you*.

(9) a. *I wonder*, is he coming?
     b. Is he, *I wonder*, coming?
     c. Is he coming, *I wonder*?

These facts reinforce the claim sometimes made in the recent philosophical literature that in a main-clause utterance like (5a) or (6a) it is the matrix, speech-act clause that is the bearer of illocutionary force, whereas in genuine (syntactic) parentheticals, the propositional-content clause has its own illocutionary force (see for example Hand 1993). I will return to this issue later. Meanwhile, given these facts, the results of our tests for truth-conditionality, which show a marked difference between genuine parentheticals and their main-clause counterparts, should not be too surprising.

As shown in chapter 5, the core mechanism of the test consists in embedding into a conditional the sentence which includes the expression to be tested, and seeing if this expression falls within the scope of the 'if'. If it does, it is truth-conditional; if it does not, it is non-truth-conditional. Let us examine how the test applies to main-clause "parentheticals" first:

(10) If *I think* that John is abroad, he will not come to the meeting.

The question is, under what circumstances is the speaker claiming that John will not come to the meeting? If *I think* makes no contribution to truth conditions, then (10) should be synonymous with (11):

(11) If John is abroad, he will not come to the meeting.

Clearly, the two utterances are not synonymous; *I think* does fall within the scope of 'if' in (10) and is therefore truth-conditional. The results generalize quite straightforwardly to other main clause "parenthetical" verbs, such as *believe* and *suppose*.

The results of applying the embedding test to genuine parentheticals are quite different. These can indeed be embedded into a conditional:

(12) If John is, *I think*, abroad he will not come to the meeting.

(13) If John is abroad, *I think*, he will not come to the meeting.

However, there is an important difference between (10), the embedded main-clause construction, and (12)–(13), the embedded genuine parentheticals. The preferred interpretations of (12) and (13) are not synonymous with (10). Semantically, the embedded parentheticals in (12) and (13) take the whole utterance in their scope. The preferred interpretations of these utterances are thus equivalent to (14):

(14)   *I think* that if John is abroad he will not come to the meeting.

The same point applies to disjunctions. Just as (12) is synonymous with (14), so (15):

(15)   Either John is, *I think*, abroad, or he will be there soon.

is normally synonymous with (16):

(16)   *I think* that either John is abroad or he will be there soon.

This scope effect becomes even clearer if we substitute *I think* with a third person parenthetical, as in (17):

(17)   a.   This is, *the catalogue says*, a Tintoretto.
        b.   If this is, *the catalogue says*, a Tintoretto, it is the most valuable painting in the museum.
        c.   *The catalogue says* that if this is a Tintoretto, it is the most valuable painting in the museum.

In other words, genuine parentheticals take wide scope even when embedded into the antecedent of conditionals. Their main-clause counterparts do not. These main-clause counterparts are clearly truth-conditional. In the case of genuine parentheticals, the issue is not so clear-cut. One might argue that (17c) correctly states the truth conditions of (17b), or one might agree with the speech-act theorist that what is being asserted is merely the embedded conditional, with 'the catalogue says' functioning merely as a comment on this assertion. Things may become clearer if we consider some further examples.

If ... then and *either ... or ...* are 'non-factive' connectives, which do not commit the speaker to the truth of the propositions embedded under them. With factive connectives such as *because, since* and *although*, which automatically commit the speaker to the truth of the propositions embedded under them, we have seen that the scope facts are quite different. Thus consider (18a) and (18b):

(18)   a.   John's here, although his train, *I think*, was late.
        b.   Susan's lucky, because she should, *I think*, have lost the election.[3]

Here, the speaker is clearly committed to the following:

(19)   a.   I think his train was late.
        b.   I think she should have lost the election.

In other words, the parenthetical has a narrower scope than it did in (14) and (15). The question is, though, whether the parenthetical expressions fall within the scope of, and therefore interact with, *because* and *although*, as they would if they were genuinely truth-conditional. For (18a) and (18b) the results are relatively clear: the parentheticals seem to remain outside the scope of the connectives. The facts being contrasted in (18a) are (a) that John is here and (b) that his train was late, rather than the fact that the speaker thinks his train was late.[4] What makes the speaker conclude that Susan is lucky in (18b) is the fact that Susan ought to have lost the election, rather than the fact that the speaker *thinks* she should have lost. Hence the parenthetical *I think* seems to have non-truth-conditional status even when it takes narrow scope.

Actually, the scope facts are even more complicated than these examples suggest. From the discussion so far, we would expect a 'main-clause' *I think* to fall within the scope of connectives such as *because* and *although*, as it does when embedded under *if*. But consider the following examples:

(20) a. John's here, although *I think* his train was late.
      b. Susan's lucky, because *I think* she should have lost the election.

Here, as we saw with evidential adverbials in chapter 5, there seem to be two possibilities of interpretation, one in which *I think* does contribute to truth conditions by falling within the scope of the connectives, and one in which it behaves like a parenthetical, and remains outside the scope of the connectives. In other words, when embedded under factive connectives (though not under *if*), it behaves pragmatically very much as it does in main clauses: sometimes confirming the belief that it functions purely truth-conditionally, and sometimes confirming the speech-act view that its occurrence is not essential to the truth conditions of utterances in which it occurs. This vacillation has yet to be explained. I will return to this point in a later section.

In this section, I have tried to show that main-clause "parentheticals", as in (1a), and genuine parentheticals, as in (1b–c), behave very differently from each other, both syntactically and semantically: only the main-clause construction is truth-conditional, and moreover, under embedding, main-clause constructions and genuine parentheticals exhibit important differences in scope. At the same time, genuine parentheticals present a variety of descriptive problems that are entirely unexpected on the standard speech-act account. Hence, we need a new descriptive and explanatory framework in which to analyse them. In the next section I shall start to analyse them in the framework of relevance theory.

6.4   Relevance theory and parentheticals: Possibilities for description

As we have seen with sentence adverbials, relevance theory provides a rich enough framework for describing the facts about parentheticals that have been presented above. Here I will show very briefly that parentheticals pattern like sentence adverbials in two important respects:

1.   Parenthetical constructions encode elements of *conceptual representations*, which may be true or false in their own right, even if they do not contribute to the truth conditions of the utterances in which they occur.

2.   Parenthetical constructions contribute to explicit, rather than implicit, communication. To the extent that they are non-truth-conditional, they contribute not to the proposition expressed, but to *higher-level explicatures*. As we have seen, higher-level explicatures do not contribute to the truth conditions of the utterances which communicate them, though they may be true or false in their own right.

I shall argue, first, that genuine parentheticals encode concepts in just the same way as their main-clause counterparts. If this is so, they are clearly quite different from tone, expression and mood, which are all non-conceptual in nature.

Notice first that main-clause "parentheticals" should be treated as encoding concepts because, as we have seen, they are truth-conditional. The assumption is that most ordinary nouns, verbs, adverbs and adjectives which contribute to truth conditions do so by encoding concepts (Wilson 1998–9). The simplest semantics would then treat the genuine parentheticals as encoding exactly the same concepts, and there are several further arguments for this.

First, the speaker who uses such a parenthetical can lay herself open to charges of untruthfulness in their use:

(21)   *Peter:* John is waiting at the airport, *I think.*
       Mary: That's not true; you don't think anything of the sort.

This can be explained on the assumption that parenthetical comments encode conceptual representations, which, though not contributing to the truth conditions of the utterance which incorporates them, can be true or false in their own right.

Second, parenthetical constructions exhibit a high degree of *compositionality* (Wilson 1998–9). Parentheticals often have a complex syntactic and semantic structure. Consider (22)–(23):

(22) John is, *I increasingly tend to think,* a fool.

(23) This is, *I strongly suspect, despite all indications to the contrary,* a Tintoretto.

These complex parentheticals can be easily understood on the assumption that they encode concepts, which are capable of undergoing the regular compositional semantic rules. It is not clear how they could be analysed in procedural terms.

Having shown that parentheticals, like adverbials, encode conceptual rather than procedural information, I shall now show briefly that, like adverbials, they contribute to the explicit rather than the implicit aspect of communication.

Recall that, according to Sperber and Wilson "an assumption communicated by an utterance *U* is *explicit* if and only if it is a development of a logical form encoded by *U*" (1986: 182), where 'development' is a process of enriching a linguistically encoded logical form. As we have seen, the explicatures of an utterance will typically include:

a. the proposition expressed by the utterance
b. higher-level explicatures obtained by optionally embedding this proposition under a speech-act verb or a propositional-attitude verb.

The truth conditions of the utterance depend only on the proposition expressed, whereas the higher-level explicatures of an utterance make no contribution to its truth conditions, though they may be true or false in their own right. Thus, the explicatures of the utterance in (24) might include the propositions in (25):

(24) *Mary:* John is at the airport.

(25) a. *John is at the airport.*
    b. Mary is saying that John is at the airport.
    c. Mary is asserting that John is at the airport.
    d. Mary thinks that John is at the airport.

Mary's utterance in (24) is true if and only if John is at the airport, i.e. if and only if the explicature in (25a) is true. The remaining explicatures (25b–d) may be true or false in their own right but make no contribution to the truth conditions of Mary's utterance.

Higher-level explicatures, like logical forms and fully propositional forms, are conceptual representations recovered by a combination of decoding and inference (Wilson and Sperber 1993: 11). To obtain (25a) the hearer must not only decode the semantic representation of the utterance but make an inference

about the intended referent of 'I'; to obtain the higher-level explicatures
(25b–d) he must make additional inferences about Mary's attitude to the
proposition she is expressing, and the type of speech act she is intending to
perform. According to Sperber and Wilson, the greater the degree of decoding
involved, the more explicit the communication. Thus, explicitness is a matter
of degree. Within this framework both the fact that genuine parentheticals
encode concepts, and the fact that they are nonetheless non-truth-conditional,
can be described. Consider (26):

(26) John is, *I think*, at the airport.

If the parenthetical *I think* is genuinely non-truth-conditional, it can be
analysed as providing the hearer with explicit guidance as to the intended
higher-level explicature, namely (27):

(27) Mary thinks John is at the airport.

This higher-level explicature is identical to the one in (25d) above: the difference lies merely in the greater degree of decoding involved in obtaining it from
(26) as opposed to the less explicit (24).

    Main-clause "parentheticals", as we have seen, encode concepts too, and
these appear to contribute to the truth conditions of utterances in the regular
way. Thus, consider (28a–b):

(28) a. *I think* that Bill has cheated in the exams.
      b. *I believe* that Bill has cheated in the exams.

These would communicate the information in (29) and (30), respectively:

(29) Mary thinks that Bill has cheated in the exams.

(30) Mary believes that Bill has cheated in the exams.

In this case, though, the information in (29) and (30) would constitute the
proposition expressed by (28a) and (28b), thus accounting for their contribution to truth conditions.

    A description, of course, is not an explanation. Why is it that some genuine
parenthetical constructions appear not to contribute to the truth conditions of
utterances, whereas their main-clause counterparts do? Moreover, why do we
feel that the addition of a parenthetical verb, pre-fixed, inserted or utterance-
final, weakens (*I think*) or strengthens (*I know*) our assertions? It is to these
questions that I shall now turn.

6.5   Relevance theory and parentheticals: Possibilities for explanation

The questions that have been raised in this chapter are:

a. are the utterances in (1a–c) really stylistic variants of each other, i.e. syntactically, semantically and pragmatically equivalent?
b. are genuine parentheticals and their main-clause counterparts really non-truth-conditional, as speech-act theorists claim?
c. do these expressions encode conceptual or procedural information?
d. do they contribute to the implicit or the explicit aspect of communication?
e. if parentheticals weaken the associated assertions, why should this be so?

Earlier in this chapter, I argued that utterances such as (1a–c), (3a–c), (5a–c) and (6a–c) are not stylistic variants of each other, as many speech-act theorists have claimed. In the first place, in the main clause (a) versions, the speech-act or propositional-attitude clause contributes to the truth conditions of the utterance in the regular way, whereas in the genuine parenthetical (b) and (c) versions, it does not. In the second place, if Urmson is right, explicit performative uses can occur only in matrix position, as in (3a); the (b) and (c) versions would have a double speech-act structure, with one speech act being used to comment on another. This is an idea I would like to pursue.

6.5.1   Parentheticals and the double-speech-act analysis

Several recent syntactic/semantic analyses seem to confirm the double-speech-act approach. Thus a variety of writers (Mittwoch 1977, 1979, 1985; Fabb 1990; Haegeman 1984, 1991; Espinal 1991; Burton-Roberts 1999) have argued that genuine parenthetical constructions are phonologically, syntactically and semantically independent of their host clauses. Here I shall take the work of Espinal (1991: 726–762) as illustration.

Espinal analyses parentheticals as a type of Disjunct Constituent. Disjunct constituents include:

a. Sentences: Peter will get married next Sunday, *I guess.*
b. Appositive relatives: John, *who is living on a small income,* is still a bachelor.
c. Adjectival phrases: The secretary, *well mannered as anybody,* will present an apology.
d. Adverbial clauses: I've just received the expected letter, *if that makes you feel any better.*

e. Adverbial phrases: *Frankly,* my dear, I don't know how to handle that.
f. Noun phrases: Frankly, *my dear,* I don't know how to handle that.
g. Prepositional phrases: Your brother, behaved, *of course,* like a gentleman.

Notice that genuine parentheticals and sentence adverbials both appear on the list. Espinal groups these disjunct constituents into three main categories:

i.   those that contain a pronominal expression linked to the main verb (appositive relatives)
ii. those that contain a syntactic gap filled conceptually by the main clause (e.g. *I think*)
iii. those that are syntactically self-contained (e.g. *frankly, my dear*)

According to Espinal, all these constituents are syntactically and semantically independent of their host clauses. They thus escape a variety of otherwise well established syntactic and semantic generalizations. For example, they can be inserted into Wh-islands, which are immune to extraction:

(31) a. John buys books which deal with art.
      b. *Which topic does John buy books which deal with?
      c. John buys books which, I think, deal with art.

In VP anaphora, where the antecedent VP contains a parenthetical, this does not function as part of the antecedent for the empty VP:

(32) John came, *I think,* to the meeting, and Peter did too.
      (= Peter came to the meeting too; not = Peter came, I think, to the meeting too.)

Espinal also cites a variety of binding arguments which distinguish appositive (parenthetical) relative clauses from restrictive (non-parenthetical) relative clauses. If these arguments extended to the adverbial and parenthetical constructions we are interested in, this would confirm their syntactic/semantic independence.

Fabb (1990) also argues for the independence of non-restrictive relative (parenthetical) clauses, but at discourse level. For example, if the *wh*-antecedent of an NRR is moved, the NRR remains behind (Fabb 1990: 70):

(33) a. We taught the boys, some of whom were deaf, French.
      b. Who did we teach [*e*], some of whom were deaf, French?
      c. *Who, some of whom were deaf, did we teach [*e*] French?

NRR (parenthetical) clauses cannot have null operators, i.e. non-overt antecedents, whereas restrictive (non-parenthetical) clauses can (ibid.:72).

(34)   a.   *Mary, I saw standing in the corner, is likely to leave early.
       b.   The woman I saw standing in the corner is likely to leave early.

Haegeman (1991) puts forward similar arguments. For example, true parentheticals cannot contain parasitic gaps, i.e. non-overt elements, — e.g. e_1, which depend on the presence of another null element, — e.g. e_2:

(35)   a.   *This is a subject which John studied e_1 in Cambridge while his son will be studying e_2 in Oxford.
       b.   This is the document which John managed to memorize e_1 while he was copying e_2.

In fact, the various analyses of parenthetical constructions differ as to the level of linguistic representation at which they should be dealt with. Parenthetical discontinuity is treated as an S-Structure phenomenon (Emonds 1979; McCawley 1982), an LF' phenomenon (Safir 1986), a discourse phenomenon (Fabb 1990), a PF phenomenon (Haegeman 1991), and a D-structure phenomenon (Espinal 1991). Among these proposals, a distinction can be drawn between those that place parentheticals within the syntactic representation of the sentences with which they coappear (Emonds 1979; McCawley 1982), and those that treat parentheticals as syntactically unattached to the host clause (Fabb 1990; Haegeman 1991; Espinal 1991). In the latter cases, integration occurs at the level of utterance interpretation. Safir's (1986) proposal can be seen as an intermediate case. He, too, thinks that parentheticals are best treated as falling outside the syntactic representation which they modify. Nonetheless, he claims that they need to be attached to some level of structure in accordance with Chomsky's (1986) principle of Full Interpretation.[5] This happens at LF', a syntactic level of representation later than LF, where 'extra' constituents are attached to independently grammatical sentences (Safir 1986:672).

Espinal's conclusion is that parenthetical adverbials, which are syntactically self contained, are not syntactically linked to the host clause in any way; the only syntactic property shared by the two constructions is a surface linear order. By contrast, parenthetical constructions like *I think, I know*, are syntactically incomplete: they have an empty category in verb complement position. According to Espinal, although the host clause and the parenthetical are still syntactically independent, it follows that there must be some level where the semantic argument corresponding to the complement position of the verb is filled by a conceptual entity. She regards this as a postsyntactic process, i.e. one that takes place at the level of utterance interpretation. To illustrate, for (36):

(36)   The manager has gone, *I think*, to another company

the conceptual entity which fills the semantic argument of *think* is that corresponding to 'The manager has gone to another company'. As Espinal claims:

> The linguistic meaning of the host ... is projected into the empty argument position of the verb of the parenthetical — following lexical specifications — in the final process of utterance interpretation. It is also in this process that the referential expression *that* will point out an event accessible from the most immediate context — the propositional content corresponding to the host clause. (Espinal 1991:748)

Thus, for Espinal, a set of syntactic conditions allow the insertion of disjuncts in certain positions only (ibid.:751–754), and a set of conceptual conditions control the mapping of syntactic constituents onto conceptual constituents (ibid.:754–757). Finally, pragmatic principles enable conceptual structures to be fully interpreted by enabling the hearer to infer the conceptual entities for empty argument positions on the basis of the most accessible information (ibid.:756).

As for the truth-conditional status of parentheticals, Espinal makes the following suggestion: "... disjuncts are fully conceptualized if and only if they contribute to some sort of inferential effect, for example if they contribute somehow to the proposition expressed." (Espinal 1991:748)

This last remark might be taken to suggest that disjuncts are 'somehow' truth-conditional. In fact, what Espinal seems to mean is a pragmatic, *inferential* type of contribution to the proposition expressed, whereby parentheticals point to, or indicate, the conceptual entity that fills the argument position of the verb, or the direction where any other relevant information is to be sought. As she claims:

> ... pragmatically, disjunct constituents may connect with the speaker or the addressee ... they may provide information about the attitude attributed to the communicator of the actual or a future speech act ..., they may introduce an additional assumption of the speaker into the discourse ..., and they may also provide information about the context of interpretation ... Disjuncts are units of information linguistically dissociated from the proposition with which they have to be interpreted at the moment of utterance processing, yet they contribute to the final interpretation of the whole utterance. (Espinal 1991:735)

She must, then, be treating disjuncts as non-truth-conditional. As she points out later on: "... the disjunct ... is saturated at a conceptual level of representation ... as a comment on some other conceptual entity which is not linguistically encoded ..." (ibid.: 756) and we have seen that, in the speech-act literature at least, 'comments' are standardly treated as non-truth-conditional indicators, giving rise to a double-utterance effect. In conclusion, Espinal notes that for: "... complex syntactic structures containing disjunct constituents ... a set of association principles and conditions ... will select the sort of metalinguistic COMMENT licensed by particular kinds of disjuncts." (Espinal 1991: 760)

A double speech-act analysis of parentheticals has also been adopted by Mittwoch (1977, 1979, 1985) and Haegeman (1991). Mittwoch views parentheticals as giving rise to two separate sentences, and two separate speech acts. The speech act performed by the parenthetical somehow "corrects", or "reinforces", or "modifies" the speech act performed by the main clause (1979: 405–409). As regards their syntactic status, Mittwoch claims:

> ... an example with a parenthetical, like *John is coming, I think*, is not a syntactic unit, as in Emonds' analysis, but a sequence of two sentences fused into one discourse unit, such that the proposition expressed by its first sentence is interpreted as the object of the second. (Mittwoch 1985: 138, footnote 2)

As to their truth-conditional status, in analysing sentence adverbials such as *frankly, frankly speaking, in all frankness*, she claims that they: "... modify not the propositional content of the sentence to which they are attached but what I shall provisionally call the pragmatics of the speech situation;" (Mittwoch 1977: 177) and that "... this relationship is not one of super-ordination versus subordination, with the rest of the sentence embedded under the performative clause, but one of juxtaposition or parenthesis." (ibid.: 180)

Mittwoch cites parentheticals such as *I think, he claims*, as "the most obvious analogue" to parenthetical adverbials. Her examples are in (20):

(20)   Kangaroos are $\begin{Bmatrix} \text{I think} \\ \text{he claims} \end{Bmatrix}$ herbivorous. (ibid.: 181)

Thus, for her, both types of parenthetical clause appear to be non-truth-conditional.

Haegeman's (1991) views on the double-speech-act analysis of parentheticals are as follows:

In (17b) [He is a real bully, if you don't mind the expression] too, the *if*-clause *if you don't mind the expression* does not modify the propositional content of the adjacent clause (i.e. "he's a bully"). Rather the sentence is a "metalinguistic" condition on the act of saying "he's a bully". The speaker qualifies the speech act.

...

The hearer of (17b) will integrate the conditional in the following schema:

(20) The hearer doesn't mind the expression
→ The speaker says 17b. (Haegeman 1991)

The parenthetical is seen in terms of a speech act which qualifies, or comments upon, the speech act of saying.

Let us then accept the view that genuine parenthetical utterances perform two separate speech acts, one commenting on the other. On this account, (37) would make two assertions, given in (38a) and (38b), and (39) would make two assertions, given in (40a) and (40b):

(37) That painting is, *I think*, the best in the museum.

(38) a. That painting is the best in the museum.
b. The speaker thinks that painting is the best in the museum.

(39) That is John's book, *I think*.

(40) a. That is John's book.
b. The speaker thinks that is John's book.

Each assertion communicates a separate explicature; each explicature makes manifest a range of higher-level explicatures. As noticed by Blakemore (1990/1), building on the speech-act approach, the function of the assertions in (38b) and (40b) is precisely to guide the interpretation of the assertions in (38a) and (40a) by encoding information about the intended higher-level explicatures of these 'ground floor' assertions. As Hand (1993) puts it, the parenthetical comment has a 'fine-tuning' function, narrowing down the interpretation of the speech act to which it is appended.

Similar remarks apply to the analysis of illocutionary and attitudinal adverbials. Thus, (41) makes two assertions, given in (42a) and (42b), and (43) makes two assertions, given in (44a) and (44b):

(41) *Frankly*, I'm not happy in London.

(42) a. The speaker is not happy in London.
b. The speaker is saying frankly that she's not happy in London.

(43) *Unfortunately*, the party is over.

(44)   a.   The party's over.
       b.   It is unfortunate that the party's over.

Each assertion communicates a separate explicature, the one in (b) 'fine tuning' the interpretation of (a) by encoding information about its intended higher-level explicature. Without the parenthetical comment, the content of this higher-level explicature would have had to be pragmatically inferred.

6.5.2   Scope possibilities[6]

In the last section, I accepted a double-speech-act analysis of parenthetical utterances, on which a parenthetical comment attached to a main clause assertion 'fine-tunes' the higher-level explicature of the assertion to which it is attached. However, the positioning of the parenthetical comment in the utterance may vary: it may, for example, occur within an embedded clause, or, in complex utterances, between the two conjuncts, or at the end of either. Its scope possibilities may vary accordingly. In this section, I intend to investigate the scope possibilities for parentheticals, and how these scope possibilities determine the speech act whose higher-level explicatures are 'fine-tuned'.

As regards the scope facts, I shall not attempt a full analysis, but merely suggest the lines on which I think such an analysis might be found. Before doing so, however, it is important to distinguish two quite different scope questions which I have raised in discussing adverbials and parentheticals. The first is to be dealt with in this section: what is the scope of the parenthetical comment — i.e. what is the phrase or clause whose interpretation it modifies? The second will be dealt with in the next section: can the parenthetical comment itself fall within the scope of truth-conditional connectives, and thus contribute to the truth conditions of the utterance as a whole?

As we have seen in the last section, parenthetical comments are sometimes attached to embedded clauses, and when they are, they sometimes take only the embedded clauses in their scope. Thus, consider (45a–d):

(45)   a.   John wrote a book which was published, *I think*, by Faber.
       b.   John wrote a book which has not, *frankly*, sold very well.
       c.   John wrote a book which was published, *unfortunately*, in January.
       d.   John wrote a book which has not, *allegedly*, sold very well.

Here, the parenthetical comment occurs within a relative clause, and in each case it is most naturally interpreted as modifying this relative clause, rather than the utterance as a whole. Thus, the preferred interpretation is as in (46), rather than (47):

(46) a. I think the book was published by Faber.
   b. Frankly, the book has not sold very well.
   c. Unfortunately, the book was published in January.
   d. Allegedly, the book has not sold very well.

(47) a. I think John wrote a book which was ...
   b. Frankly, John wrote a book which was ...
   c. Unfortunately, John wrote a book which was ...
   d. Allegedly, John wrote a book which was ...

Notice here that when I claim that a parenthetical comment takes an embedded clause in its scope, I am not making any commitment as to the truth-conditional status of the resulting interpretation. Indeed, on the double-speech-act account outlined in the last section, the parenthetical comment is seen as constituting a separate speech act, with its own truth-conditional content. The truth-conditional status of adverbials and parentheticals will be taken up in the next section.

Regarding the scope of parenthetical comments in complex utterances, differences in syntactic position do affect interpretation in a way that speech-act theorists did not foresee. For example, when a parenthetical comment appears at the end of a conjoined utterance such as (48a–c), it can take either the whole utterance, or only the second conjunct, in its scope:

(48) a. John left, but not with Susan, *I think.*
   b. John failed, and so did Bill, *I fear.*
   c. Susan is happy, though Mary is not, *I suspect.*

That is, (48a) can be interpreted as meaning either '[John left, but not with Susan], I think', or 'John left, but [not with Susan], I think'. Similarly, when the parenthetical appears at the end of the first conjunct, it can take either the whole utterance, or only the first conjunct, in its scope:

(49) a. John left, *I think,* but not with Susan.
   b. John failed, *I fear,* and so did Bill.
   c. Susan is happy, *I suspect,* though Mary is not.

In (49a–c), the preferred scope is probably the narrower one, i.e. '[John left], I think', but in certain circumstances the broader scope '[John left but not with Susan], I think' might be possible too.

By contrast, when the parenthetical is inside one or other of the conjuncts, narrow scope is strongly preferred:

(50) a. John left, but not, *I think*, with Susan.
      b. John, *I fear*, failed, and so did Bill.
      c. Susan is happy, though Mary, *I suspect*, is not.

If such intuitions are right, then we have an argument against the speech-act view that true parentheticals are mere stylistic variants of each other. Differences in syntactic position lead to different possibilities of interpretation. These can presumably be explained by an interaction between a 'least effort' parsing principle and an interpretation satisfying the hearer's expectation of relevance. For example, the parsing principles might, in certain circumstances, allow for the narrow-scope interpretation. As long as the resulting interpretation is consistent with the principle of relevance, all other interpretations would be disallowed. In other circumstances, the broad and narrow scope interpretations might be roughly equally accessible. In this case, an interpretation would be selected on semantic and pragmatic grounds.

Conjoined utterances have co-ordinate structure, and co-ordinating conjunctions are, of course, factive. Thus, conjoined utterances can be seen as performing two speech-acts of roughly equal status, to either of which a parenthetical comment can be attached. Turning now to subordinating conjunctions, let us consider the factive subordinating conjunction *because*. Two possibilities have to be examined here. In the first, the 'because' clause is separated off by comma intonation; in the second it is not. These differences in intonation affect the scope of a main-clause negation, as shown in (51a–b):

(51) a. John didn't fail because he worked too hard.
      b. John didn't fail, because he worked too hard.

In (51a), the scope of the negation includes the 'because' clause; in (51b) it does not. Their interpretation will be, then, as in (52a–b):

(52) a. It is not the case that [John failed because he worked too hard].
      b. [John didn't fail], and the reason is that he worked too hard.

Bearing these scope possibilities in mind, let us now examine the interpretation of parentheticals in various positions in 'because' clauses.

First, the parenthetical may appear at the end of the whole utterance, as in (53):

(53) a. John will fail because he won't work hard enough, *I fear*.
      b. John will fail, because he won't work hard enough, *I fear*.

The parenthetical in (53a) is most naturally interpreted as taking the whole utterance in its scope, whereas in (53b) it can be interpreted as having either wide or narrow scope. In (54), where the parenthetical occurs at the end of the main clause, it can take either the main clause 'John will fail' (without the adverbial clause), or the whole utterance in its scope.

(54)   John will fail, *I fear*, because he won't work hard enough.

Consider now (55a–b), where the parenthetical is inside the main clause. Here, the presence or absence of comma intonation again affects the scope possibilities.

(55)   a.   John will, *I fear*, fail because he won't work hard enough.
      b.   John will, *I fear*, fail, because he won't work hard enough.

(55a), without comma intonation, is interpreted as making a single (complex) assertion, with the parenthetical comment taking the whole assertion in its scope. (55b), with comma intonation, is interpreted as making two distinct assertions, only the first being modified by the parenthetical comment. Finally, where the parenthetical comment is inside the embedded clause, as in (56), it seems to be interpretable only as having narrow scope, regardless of whether there is comma intonation or not:

(56)   a.   John will fail because he won't, *I fear*, work hard enough.
      b.   John will fail, because he won't, *I fear*, work hard enough.

Thus, for a full analysis of the scope of parentheticals one must consider not only syntactic facts, including the position of the parenthetical and the difference between main clause and subordinate clause, but also intonational facts. It appears that, generally, factivity favours narrow scope.

Finally, let us turn to 'non-factive' connectives such as *or* and *if … then*. *Or* is a co-ordinating conjunction, which should yield results similar to *and*; *if … then* is a subordinating conjunction, which should yield results similar to *because*. Any differences in patterning between *and* and *or*, or between *if* and *because* are presumably due to the presence or absence of factivity. As we have already seen, factivity does seem to affect the scope possibilities of parentheticals such as *I think* or *Bill says*. Consider (57) and (58):

(57)   a.   If the book is good, *I think*, I'll give it to Susan for Christmas.
      b.   If the book is good, I'll give it to Susan for Christmas, *I think*.
(58)   a.   If I go to the cinema, *Bill says*, I won't get my homework done.
      b.   If I go to the cinema, I won't get my homework done, *Bill says*.

In (57a), where the parenthetical appears at the end of the 'if' clause, the wide-scope interpretation is clearly the preferred one, with *I think* modifying the interpretation of the utterance as a whole. In (57b), it has been argued that the wide scope interpretation is the only possible one (see Sperber 1982, who argues that so-called 'conditional assertions' should be reanalysed as assertions of conditionals). This is certainly true for *Bill says* in the same position in (58b).

With disjunctions, there is always the possibility of a wide-scope interpretation. However, depending on the syntactic position, the semantic content of the parenthetical comment and the clause to which it is attached, a narrow-scope interpretation is possible too. Thus, compare (59) and (60):

(59) a. Either you didn't work hard enough, *I think*, or you need some extra tuition.

b. Either you didn't, *I think*, work hard enough, or you need some extra tuition.

(60) a. Either you didn't work hard enough, *Bill says*, or you need some extra tuition.

b. Either you didn't, *Bill says*, work hard enough, or you need some extra tuition.

All four utterances have the wide-scope interpretations in (61):

(61) a. I think that [either you didn't work hard enough or you need some extra tuition].

b. Bill says that [either you didn't work hard enough or you need some extra tuition].

The question is whether they can also have the narrow-scope interpretations in (62):

(62) a. Either [you didn't work hard enough, I think], or you need some extra tuition.

b. Either [you didn't work hard enough, Bill says], or you need some extra tuition.

Here, the intuitions are that, while this is possible for (62a), it is quite impossible for (62b). As will be shown below, the behaviour of sentence adverbials in 'if' clauses reinforces this intuition: depending on the content and position of the adverbial and the host clause, narrow-scope interpretations are sometimes possible and sometimes ruled out. If this is so, we should allow both wide and narrow-scope interpretations to be constructed in all cases, and then filter out the unwanted ones on semantic and pragmatic grounds.

Let us turn, then, to the scope possibilities for the four types of sentence adverbials discussed in chapter 5. In the case of co-ordinating conjunctions, all these adverbials show exactly the same scope possibilities, which are just the same as those outlined above for parentheticals. To illustrate, consider the illocutionary adverbial *frankly*:

(63)   a.   It's been a dull day, and, *frankly*, I'm bored.
        b.   It's been a dull day, *frankly*, and I'm bored.
        c.   It's been a dull day and I'm bored, *frankly*.
        d.   It has, *frankly*, been a dull day, and I'm bored.
        e.   It's been a dull day and I am, *frankly*, bored.
        f.   *Frankly*, it's been a dull day, and I'm bored.

The possibilities of interpretation are as follows. In (63a), with *frankly* positioned before the second conjunct, it can take only this second conjunct in its scope. In (63b), with *frankly* positioned at the end of the first conjunct, it can take either this conjuct or the whole utterance in its scope. In (63c), with *frankly* positioned at the end of the second conjunct, it can take either this conjunct or the whole utterance in its scope. In (63d), where *frankly* is positioned within the first conjunct, it can take only this conjunct in its scope. In (63e), where *frankly* is positioned within the second conjunct, it can take only this conjunct in its scope. Finally, in (63f), with *frankly* in utterance-initial position, it can take either the whole utterance or the first conjunct in its scope.

In 'because' clauses, all four types of adverbials exhibit identical behaviour, with just the possibilities of interpretation we would predict from our analysis of parentheticals above. I will therefore examine the behaviour of adverbials in 'or' and 'if' clauses next. As we have seen, these adverbials appear to behave very differently from each other when it comes to tests of truth-conditional status. However, I will argue that the scope possibilities for adverbials in 'or' and 'if' clauses again run parallel to the scope possibilities for parentheticals, opening the way for a unified analysis.

In 'or' clauses, it seems that any sentence adverbial, regardless of its syntactic position, can take the whole utterance in its scope. This is, in fact, the only possibility when it appears in utterance-initial position before the 'either'. Consider (64):

(64)   a.   *Frankly*, either this is a bad book, or I didn't read it carefully enough.
        b.   *Evidently*, either this is a bad book, or I didn't read it carefully enough.

    c.   *Allegedly*, either this is a bad book, or ...
    d.   *Unfortunately*, either this is ...

When it appears in other positions, wide-scope interpretations are always possible, and often preferred. Nevertheless, given suitable semantic content, narrow-scope interpretations may be possible too. To illustrate, consider (65):

(65) a.   Either you didn't work hard enough, *frankly/unfortunately*, or you need some extra tuition.
      b.   Either you didn't, *frankly/unfortunately*, work hard enough, or you need some extra tuition.
      c.   Either you need some extra tuition or you didn't, *frankly/unfortunately*, work hard enough.

In (65a), for example, the adverbial can take either the whole utterance or only the first disjunct in its scope. As we have seen, the same example with parenthetical *I think* yields exactly the same possibilities of interpretation; with *Bill says*, however, only the wide-scope interpretation is possible. This confirms my earlier suggestion that, for both adverbials and parentheticals occurring in disjunctions, both wide and narrow scope interpretations should be allowed, and then filtered out on semantic and pragmatic grounds.

Finally, let us examine 'if' clauses, which are central to the standard tests for truth-conditional status. As before, an adverbial in utterance-initial position before the 'if' can take only the whole utterance in its scope. This is shown in (66):

(66) a.   *Frankly*, if the Prime Minister has resigned, we must call an election.
      b.   *Evidently*, if the Prime Minister has resigned, we must call an election.
      c.   *Unfortunately*, if the Prime Minister has resigned, we must call an election.
      d.   *Allegedly*, if the Prime Minister has resigned, we must call an election.

As noted earlier, if Sperber's arguments are right, an adverbial in utterance-final position, or within the main clause, must obligatorily take wide scope. This is illustrated in (67):

(67) a.   If you haven't worked hard enough, you will fail, *frankly/evidently/ unfortunately/allegedly*.
      b.   If you haven't worked hard enough, you will, *frankly/evidently/un- fortunately/allegedly*, fail.

A wide-scope interpretation is also possible when the adverbial appears within the 'if' clause. Consider (68):

(68) a. If you haven't, *frankly*, worked hard enough, you can't expect to pass.
      b. If you haven't, *unfortunately*, worked hard enough, you can't expect to pass.
      c. If you haven't, *obviously*, worked hard enough, you can't expect to pass.
      d. If you haven't, *admittedly*, worked hard enough, you can't expect to pass.

In all these cases, the parenthetical comment can be interpreted as modifying the utterance as a whole. However, a narrow-scope interpretation, where the parenthetical modifies the 'if' clause alone, seems to be possible too. Thus, the narrow-scope interpretation of (68b) would be as in (69):

(69) If you haven't worked hard enough — and it is unfortunate that you have not — you can't expect to pass.

Notice that a narrow-scope interpretation of a parenthetical does not necessarily affect its truth-conditional status. In (69), it functions as a separate assertion, rather than contributing to the truth conditions of the utterance as a whole. Similar possibilities of interpretation appear to be available for all four adverbs illustrated in (68).

In this section, I have investigated the various scope possibilities for parentheticals and adverbials, and reached the following conclusions. First, adverbials and parentheticals seem to behave in identical ways, as would be expected if adverbials are a sub-type of parentheticals. Second, the syntactic position of the adverbial or parenthetical affects its possibilities of interpretation. In some cases, only wide-scope interpretation is possible; in other cases, both wide-scope and narrow-scope interpretations are possible. Third, there is often a preferred interpretation, which is affected by at least the following factors: syntactic structure (main-clause vs subordinate clause), semantic structure (factive vs non-factive) and semantic content (of the parenthetical comment and the clause to which it is attached). Fourth, factive and non-factive structures affect the behaviour of parentheticals and adverbials: when they appear inside factive clauses, narrow-scope interpretation is either preferred or mandatory; when they appear inside non-factive clauses, narrow-scope interpretation becomes much harder. Fifth, I have suggested that the preferred interpretation of factive clauses results from an interaction between 'least effort' parsing principles and the hearer's expectation of relevance. By contrast, the crucial factor in the interpretation of non-factive clauses seems to be the semantic content of the parenthetical and the clause to which it is attached. Finally, I have suggested that even a narrow-scope interpretation is not necessarily truth-conditional, i.e. it need not fall within the scope of truth-conditional connectives to yield a unitary set of truth conditions for the utterance as a whole.

Having shown the essential similarity between adverbials and parentheticals, I shall turn in the next section to their differences in truth-conditional status, and examine how these might be explained.

6.5.3 Parentheticals and truth-conditions

In the last section, I proposed a unified analysis of parentheticals and adverbials, where both wide and narrow-scope interpretations were freely generated, but often filtered out by semantic and pragmatic means. On a 'wide-scope interpretation', the parenthetical fine-tunes the interpretation of the utterance as a whole; on a 'narrow-scope-interpretation', the parenthetical comment fine-tunes the interpretation of some embedded clause. Precisely because of its unified nature, this analysis as yet sheds no light on the differences in truth-conditional status which the various types of sentence adverbial and parenthetical construction seem to exhibit. Why is it that some narrow-scope interpretations seem to fall within the scope of logical connectives and thus contribute to the truth conditions of the utterance as a whole, while others do not? In this section, I shall attempt an explanation of this fact.

The facts about truth-conditional status to be discussed in this section are the following:

1. Evidential and hearsay adverbials (e.g. *clearly, obviously, evidently, apparently, allegedly, admittedly*) seem to be truth-conditional. In particular, they seem to fall within the scope of both factive and non-factive connectives.
2. Illocutionary and attitudinal adverbials (e.g. *frankly, confidentially, seriously, unfortunately, regrettably, happily*) seem to be non-truth-conditional. In particular, they seem to remain outside the scope of both factive and non-factive connectives.
3. Parentheticals (e.g. *I think, Bill says, we all agree*) are hard to test for truth-conditional status, since, although they can take narrow scope in factive environments, in the non-factive environments where I have conducted my tests, they find it difficult or impossible to take narrow scope.

On the double-speech-act analysis, the assumption is that an utterance containing any of these constructions performs two speech acts, one commenting on the other. Thus, the utterances in (70) would make the assertions in (71a–d), with the second of the two speech acts fine-tuning the interpretation of the first:

(70) a. John left, *clearly.*
  b. He's a fool, *frankly.*
  c. He's going to win, *I think.*
  d. He's going to win, *Bill says.*

(71) a. John left. This is clear.
  b. He's a fool. I tell you this frankly.
  c. He's going to win. I think this.
  d. He's going to win. Bill says this.

In speech-act terms, the question is why, for evidential and hearsay adverbials, *both* speech acts seem to fall within the scope of embedding connectives, and why, with illocutionary and attitudinal adverbials, only the ground-floor speech act seems to fall within the scope of embedding connectives. For parentheticals such as *I think, Bill says*, we still need to establish what their truth-conditional status is.

My main claim is going to be as follows. Sometimes, a parenthetical comment alters the truth-conditional status of the ground-floor assertion to which it is attached. It can do this in either of two ways: first, by marking the ground-floor assertion as a case of interpretive rather than descriptive use; and second, by affecting the strength of the assumption communicated (and hence the recommended degree of commitment to the proposition it expresses). A parenthetical comment which functions in either of these two ways will be perceived as making an essential contribution to truth conditions, and, hence, as falling within the scope of embedding connectives. A parenthetical comment which functions in neither of these ways — that is, which does not affect the truth-conditional status of the ground-floor proposition but merely expresses the speaker's attitude to the fact that it is true — will be perceived as non-truth-conditional, and as falling outside the scope of embedding connectives.

The hearsay adverbials *allegedly, reportedly, admittedly,* etc. will be considered first. In relevance-theoretic terms, the key to their behaviour is that they alter the truth-conditional status of the ground-floor proposition by marking it as *interpretively* rather than descriptively used. As shown in chapter 4, an utterance or clause is *descriptively* used when the thought it interprets is one of the speaker's own; it is *interpretively* used when the thought it interprets is attributed to someone other than the speaker (or the speaker herself at another time). Descriptive use implies speaker-commitment; interpretive use does not. Clearly, the function of a hearsay adverbial is to mark the ground-floor assertion as communicating the views of someone other than the speaker. It is, in other words, a marker of interpretive rather than descriptive use. This, however, alters the truth-conditional status of the ground-floor proposition by removing the speaker's commitment to its truth. To illustrate, consider (72):

(72) John is, *allegedly*, a spy.

The question is whether the speaker of (72) is committed to the truth of both the ground-floor proposition in (73a) and the parenthetical comment in (73b):

(73) a. John is a spy.
      b. Someone alleges this.

Clearly, the speaker is *not* necessarily committed to the truth of (73a): this is interpretively, not descriptively, used, to reflect views attributed to someone else.[7]

Thus, we would expect that when (72) is embedded into either factive or non-factive structures, it will be perceived as making an essential contribution to truth conditions: it marks the ground-floor proposition as interpretively rather than descriptively used. And this is, indeed, what we find. Consider (74a) and (74b):

(74) a. Although John is, *allegedly*, a spy, he is a very charming man.
      b. Because John is, *allegedly*, a spy, we must be careful what we say to him.

The speaker of (74) is committed to the truth of (75) and (76):

(75) It is alleged that John is a spy.

(76) a. Although it is alleged that John is a spy, he is a very charming man.
      b. Because it is alleged that John is a spy, we must be careful what we say to him.

But she is not committed to the truth of either (77) or (78):

(77) John is a spy.

(78) a. Although John is a spy, he is a very charming man.
      b. Because John is a spy, we should be careful what we say to him.

The reason for this is that hearsay adverbials 'fine tune' the interpretation of the proposition that falls within their scope by marking it as interpretively rather than descriptively used. Taking into consideration the semantics of *allegedly*, we can conclude that the speaker is not necessarily committed to the truth of this proposition.

Notice, moreover, that the parentheticals we have been considering above, e.g. *I think, we all agree, Bill says,* have the same function as hearsay adverbials: they mark the proposition that falls within their scope as being interpretively rather than descriptively used. In particular, parentheticals such as *Bill says, the newspaper reported yesterday,* which we might call 'hearsay parentheticals', are exactly like hearsay adverbials in that they specifically indicate that the views being interpreted are not the speaker's own. Thus, (79) runs parallel to (72) above:

(79) John is, *you say*, a spy.

Here, the speaker is not committed to the truth of the ground-floor proposition in (80a), as she would be if the parenthetical comment were missing:

(80) a. John is a spy.
      b. You say this.

Similarly, the speaker of (81) is committed to the truth of (82) and (83):

(81) a. Although John is, you say, a spy, he's a very charming one.
      b. Because John is, Bill says, a spy, we should be careful what we say to him.

(82) You say that John is a spy.

(83) a. Although you say that John is a spy, he's a very charming one.
      b. Because Bill says that John is a spy, we should be careful what we say to him.

However, she is not committed to the truth of either (84) or (85):

(84) John is a spy.

(85) a. Although John is a spy, he's a very charming man.
      b. Because John is a spy, we should be careful what we say to him.

Because hearsay parentheticals, like hearsay adverbials, are markers of interpretive use, they are perceived as making an essential contribution to truth conditions.

By contrast, parentheticals such as *I think, I fear,* indicate that the views being interpreted are in fact the speaker's own. In certain cases, e.g. *I think,* the resulting interpretation may be roughly equivalent to a straightforward descriptive use. Consider (86):

(86)   a.   John is, *I think*, a spy.
      b.   John is a spy.

Notice that the presence of the parenthetical comment here is not essential. The speaker of (86a), like the speaker of (86b), commits herself to the truth of *both* the ground-floor proposition in (87a) *and* the parenthetical comment in (87b):

(87)   a.   John is a spy.
      b.   I think this.

And the speaker of (88) is committed to the truth not only of (89) and (90), but of (91) and (92) too:

(88)   a.   Although John is, *I think*, a spy, he is a very charming one.
      b.   Because John is, *I think*, a spy, we should be careful what we say to him.

(89)   I think that John is a spy.

(90)   a.   Although I think that John is a spy, he is a very charming one.
      b.   Because I think that John is a spy, we should be careful what we say to him.

(91)   John is a spy.

(92)   a.   Although John is a spy, he is a very charming one.
      b.   Because John is a spy, we should be careful what we say to him.

In this respect, the truth-conditional status of parenthetical comments will be clearer for some parentheticals than others. When the views being interpreted are not the speaker's own, as in (79), the parenthetical phrase will be perceived as making an essential contribution to truth conditions. When the views being interpreted *are* the speaker's own, as in (86), the parenthetical phrase may be perceived as inessential: the speaker will remain committed to the truth of the proposition that falls within its scope, and a non-truth-conditional reading may be the preferred one. As shown earlier, tests for truth-conditional status are difficult with parentheticals, since they rarely take narrow scope in non-factive environments. Despite the difficulty of conducting tests, the above discussion should shed some light on their behaviour. The case of parentheticals like *I hope*, *I fear* will be discussed in a later section.

Let us turn next to illocutionary adverbials such as *frankly, seriously, confidentially*. These too seem not to affect the truth-conditional status of the propositions that fall within their scope. Consider (93):

(93) a.   *Frankly*, I'm bored.
      b.   *Seriously*, I don't like him.
      c.   *Confidentially*, I intend to resign.

As we have seen, these utterances communicate the information in (94):

(94) a.   I'm bored. I tell you this frankly.
      b.   I don't like him. I tell you this seriously.
      c.   I intend to resign. I tell you this confidentially.

Notice, however, that the same information can be communicated by uttering (95) with the appropriate tone of voice or facial expression:

(95) a.   I'm bored.
      b.   I don't like him.
      c.   I intend to resign.

The illocutionary adverbial may give information about the *manner* in which the speaker intends to make her assertion, but it does not alter the truth-conditional status of the assertion itself, either by marking it as a case of interpretive use, or by altering the strength with which it is put forward. The presence of the adverbial phrase is inessential to the truth conditions of the proposition that falls within its scope. This is, indeed, confirmed by our tests.

In particular, an illocutionary adverbial such as *frankly* appears to be non-truth-conditional even when it takes narrow scope. Consider (96):

(96) a.   I realize that the play is good, although, *frankly*, I'm bored.
      b.   I'm going out this evening, because, *frankly*, I'm bored.

The speaker of (96) is committed to the truth of both (97) and (98):

(97) a.   I'm bored.
      b.   I'm telling you this frankly.

(98) a.   I realize that the play is good, although I'm bored.
      b.   I'm going out this evening, because I'm bored.

(98) suggests that the presence of *frankly* is inessential to the truth conditions of the utterance in which it occurs. The same holds for non-factive environments in which *frankly* takes narrow scope. This is so because *frankly* and other illocutionary adverbials do not alter the truth conditions of the assertion that falls within their scope, but merely indicate the manner in which this assertion is being made.

Consider now the evidential adverbials *apparently* and *seemingly*. Recall that, on conducting the tests, these were classed as truth-conditional. Although I have not investigated whether they mark interpretive or descriptive use, they clearly suspend the speaker's commitment to the proposition that falls within their scope. Consider (99):

(99)   a.   John is, *apparently*, a spy.
      b.   John is, *seemingly*, a spy.

In this case, the occurrence of the adverbial does make a difference to the truth-conditional status of the ground-floor proposition: the speaker of (99a) and (99b) is *not* committed to the truth of (100), but she is certainly committed to the truth of (101):

(100)   John is a spy.

(101)   It seems/appears that John is a spy.

This should mean that these adverbials are truth-conditional, and that they are able to fall within the scope of both factive and non-factive connectives. And this is what we find, indeed. The speaker of (102) is committed to the truth of (103) but not to the truth of (104):

(102)   a.   Although John is, *apparently*, a spy, he is very charming.
      b.   Because John is, *seemingly*, a spy, we should avoid him.

(103)   a.   Although it appears that John is a spy, he is very charming.
      b.   Because it seems that John is a spy, we should avoid him.

(104)   a.   Although John is a spy, he is very charming.
      b.   Because John is a spy, we should avoid him.

As our tests have shown, similar results are obtained when these adverbials appear in non-factive environments.

One way of analysing the situation is as follows. The evidential adverbial makes clear that the speaker is putting forward the proposition that John is a spy with a very reduced degree of strength — a degree determined by the semantic content of the adverbial. As a result, evidence that would have falsified a stronger assertion no longer counts as falsifying evidence. Hence, the truth-conditional status of the utterance is altered, and the speaker's degree of commitment to the proposition expressed — as well as the degree of commitment recommended to the hearer — is affected too. In this way, speech-act accounts of weakened degree of speaker commitment can be reconciled with the fact that the truth conditions of the proposition embedded under the adverbials appear to be altered too.

The evidential adverbials *obviously* and *clearly* alter the truth-conditional status of the ground-floor proposition in a rather different way. In the case of 'Apparently P', the speaker's commitment to P is suspended, but an indication is given that there is some evidence for P. We might call the commitment-suspending evidentials 'weak evidentials'. By contrast, in the case of 'Obviously P', or 'Clearly P', the speaker's commitment to P is strengthened, and it is indicated that there is clear evidence for P. We might call the commitment-strengthening evidentials 'strong evidentials'. The truth-conditional status of the utterance is altered because the range of falsifying evidence is altered. Notice the parallel with non-evidential adverbials such as *necessarily, possibly, probably* and so on, which are invariably perceived as contributing to truth conditions. Just as not every true proposition is necessarily true so not every true proposition is obviously true. In both cases, some modification of the truth-conditional status of the ground floor proposition is achieved. Thus, strong evidentials, like weak evidentials, will be perceived as making an essential contribution to truth conditions, and are expected to fall within the scope of factive and non-factive connectives. As we have seen, they do.

Finally, let us examine how attitudinal adverbials, such as *surprisingly, sadly, unfortunately* etc., are interpreted. Recall that, according to our tests, these are clearly non-truth-conditional. This is so because they indicate the speaker's *attitude* to the proposition that falls within their scope; they do not alter the truth-conditional status of this proposition in any way. Consider (105):

(105)　a.　John is a spy.
　　　　b.　John is, *unfortunately*, a spy.

Regardless of the presence of the adverbial, the speaker is committed to the truth of (106):

(106)　John is a spy.

Also, the fact that the speaker regards it as unfortunate that John is a spy might well be indicated by tone of voice or facial expression, i.e. by non-linguistic means. The adverbial is inessential both to the truth-conditional status of the ground-floor proposition, and of the higher-level explicature in (107):

(107)　The speaker regards it as unfortunate that John is a spy.

We would thus expect attitudinal adverbials to be non-truth-conditional when embedded in factive and non-factive environments. This is, indeed, what we find. Consider (108):

(108) a. Although, *unfortunately*, John is spy, he is very charming.
       b. Because John is, *unfortunately*, a spy, we should avoid him.

The speaker of (108) is committed to the truth of both (109) and (110):

(109) a. John is spy.
       b. This is unfortunate.

(110) a. Although John is spy, he is very charming.
       b. Because John is a spy, we should avoid him.

As (110) shows, the occurrence of *unfortunately* is perceived as inessential to the truth conditions of the utterance, even when it takes narrow scope.

In this section, I have tried to explain the truth-conditional status of parenthetical comments, including sentence adverbials. The argument developed as follows. A parenthetical comment is truth-conditional when and only when it alters the truth-conditional status of the proposition it modifies, i.e. when it makes an essential contribution to the truth conditions of the utterance in which it occurs. It may do this in one of two ways: first, by functioning as a marker of interpretive rather than descriptive use. Such markers necessarily affect the truth-conditional status of propositions that fall within their scope. This is the reason why hearsay adverbials and hearsay parentheticals make an essential contribution to truth conditions. Moreover, I showed why a parenthetical such as *I think*, which indicates that the views being interpreted are the speaker's own, in fact commits her to the truth of the proposition that falls within its scope, and may thus be perceived as roughly equivalent to descriptive use.

Illocutionary adverbials such as *frankly, seriously* do not affect the truth-conditional status of the proposition that falls within their scope, and hence are inessential to truth conditions. Their function is to indicate the manner in which some speech-act is being performed, without altering the truth-conditional status of this speech act in any way.

Parenthetical comments, and sentence adverbials, may be truth-conditional in a second way: by altering the speaker's degree of commitment to the proposition that falls within their scope, and the range of evidence which would count as falsifying evidence. Thus, evidential adverbials such as *obviously, apparently, do* affect the truth-conditional status of the proposition that falls within their scope. In particular, I distinguished between weak evidentials, e.g. *apparently, seemingly*, which reduce the range of falsifying evidence, and strong evidentials, e.g. *obviously, clearly*, which increase the range of falsifying evidence. I drew a parallel with non-evidential items such as the weak *possibly, probably*, versus the strong *necessarily, certainly*, all of which are clearly truth-conditional. The relevance-theoretic notion of strength of assumptions played a crucial role in my account.

Finally, for attitudinal adverbials such as *unfortunately* and *sadly*, I argued that they are non-truth-conditional since they are not interpretive-use markers, and do not affect the speaker's degree of commitment to the proposition that falls within their scope.

Having sketched the way in which the truth-conditional status of parenthetical comments is linked to their semantic content, in the next section, I will return to the pragmatics of parentheticals, and consider their effect on utterance interpretation.

6.5.4 Pragmatic interpretation of genuine parentheticals

In the last section, I suggested that there is a semantic difference between two classes of parentheticals: *Bill says, the newspaper reported yesterday*, on the one hand, and *I think, I fear*, on the other. Parentheticals in the first group specifically indicate that the views being interpreted are *not* the speaker's own. They therefore make an essential contribution to truth conditions. By contrast, parentheticals in the second group indicate that the views being interpreted *are* the speaker's own. For this reason, their presence may be perceived as inessential to truth conditions.

In this section, I intend to investigate how the presence and position in the sentence of parentheticals affects pragmatic interpretation. I shall continue my argument that these parentheticals do not always weaken the speaker's commitment to the proposition that falls within their scope, as speech-act theorists have claimed. Some of them do generally weaken the speaker's commitment (e.g. *I guess*), some others, on the contrary, can strengthen the speaker's commitment (e.g. *Chomsky says*), whereas a few may, depending on the context, have either function (e.g. *I think*). I shall also look at a range of attitudinal parentheticals (e.g. *I hope, I fear*) which seem to fall midway between evidential parentheticals (*I think, I know*) and attitudinal adverbials (*sadly, unfortunately*), and consider their effects on interpretation. Finally, I shall continue my argument that where parentheticals do express an altered strength of, or degree of commitment to, the proposition that falls within their scope, this follows from the semantics of the constructions in question together with considerations of optimal relevance.

Consider, first, an important difference between the examples in (4) above, repeated here as (111):

(111)   a.   John is in Berlin.   *stronger*
        b.   *I think* John is in Berlin.   *weaker*
        c.   John is, *I think*, in Berlin.   *weaker*
        d.   John is in Berlin, *I think*.   *weaker*

There is an obvious difference in the strength of assertions (or speaker commitment) associated with the presence, absence and syntactic position of expressions such as *I think*. Recall that many speech-act theorists regard (111b–d) as equivalent in strength, and weaker than the plain assertion in (111a). In an earlier section, I have pointed out how variations in syntactic position of the parenthetical may affect which proposition it takes within its scope. I have also pointed out a further difference: namely, that the main-clause construction in (111b) involves a single speech act, whereas its genuine parenthetical counterparts in (111c) and (111d) involve a double speech-act structure. I would now like to consider briefly how these various differences in syntactic position and speech-act structure affect the strength of the resulting assertions.

Consider first the differences between (111a), on the one hand, and (111b–d), on the other. (111a) is linguistically the least complex, but contains no indication as to the intended higher-level explicatures or the degree of strength with which the speaker is putting forward the proposition expressed. It follows from relevance theory that the speaker should choose this utterance as long as she can trust the hearer to recover the intended higher-level explicature, and the intended degree of strength, with less effort than would be needed to process an explicit prompt. She would choose one of the other utterances instead if she feels that without explicit guidance the hearer might recover the wrong higher-level explicature, or the wrong degree of strength, or might be in doubt as to which higher-level explicature, and which degree of strength, was intended. If we assume that in normal circumstances the most accessible higher-level explicatures will be drawn from the set *she thinks, she is fairly certain, she is certain* and *she knows*, it will follow that (111b–d) all have a weakening effect.

In fact, as suggested above, it is not always true that parentheticals have a weakening effect. This is indeed the main function of parentheticals such as *I think, I guess, I suppose*, as illustrated in (112a–c):

(112) a. John is in Berlin, *I think*.
     b. John is in Berlin, *I guess*.
     c. John is in Berlin, *I suppose*.

However, parentheticals such as *I know*, *I insist*, and often those such as *Bill thinks*, *Chomsky says*, can have a strengthening function. Compare (113a) and (113b):

(113) a. UG provides a fixed system of principles and a finite set of parameters, each language setting the values for these parameters.
     b. UG provides a fixed system of principles and a finite set of parameters, each language setting the values for these parameters, *Chomsky says*.

Clearly, given an appropriate speaker and hearer, the parenthetical in (113b) would have a strengthening effect. The fact that Chomsky says something provides strong evidence for its truth. The use of such commitment-strengthening parentheticals is particularly common in academic speech, as in all cases where the speaker refers to some authority in order to endorse her own views. As we have seen, parentheticals of this type are always perceived as truth-conditional.

Parentheticals such as *I know*, *I insist*, can also strengthen the speaker's degree of commitment, as in (114a–c):

(114) a. Susan will win the elections.
     b. Susan will win the elections, *I know*.
     c. Susan will win the elections, *I insist*.

As shown above, according to relevance theory, the speaker should add such indications only if the hearer cannot be trusted to supply them for himself without explicit guidance. For example, the speaker should add *I know* to (114) only if she thinks that without such guidance some weaker higher-level explicature (e.g. *I think*) might be supplied. Parentheticals, then, can encourage the hearer to move away from a default interpretation that would otherwise be constructed. As (112) and (114) show, movement may be towards either a weaker or a stronger degree of commitment.[8]

Let us consider now the differences in pragmatic interpretation of (111b–d) that result from differences in syntactic position of the parenthetical *I think*. Intuitively, the earlier the parenthetical occurs in the utterance, the greater the effect on interpretation. Thus, where *I think* has a weakening effect, this will be greater in (111b) than (111c), and in (111c) than in (111d). How can these facts be explained?

One point to notice is that genuine parentheticals, as in (111c) and (111d) have a characteristic, low-key intonation. While *I think* in (111b) can carry main stress, and thus constitute the main point of the utterance, *I think* in (111c–d) are invariably backgrounded. A second point to notice is that the later the position of the parenthetical expression, the more likely it is to have a 'repair', or 'afterthought', interpretation. So, for example, as utterance (111d) proceeds, it may occur to the speaker that the hearer might misinterpret or be in doubt about how to interpret the intended degree of strength, and add a parenthetical to clarify her intentions. By contrast, in planning (111b) the speaker must already have foreseen these possibilities of misinterpretation and have taken steps to eliminate them. Typically, then, the parenthetical in (111b) should make a substantial and integrated contribution to overall relevance, whereas (111c–d) will be perceived as merely 'fine-tuning' an already accessible interpretation.

So far, I have considered evidential parentheticals such as *I think, I know, I guess*, whose primary function is to determine the strength of the assumptions which fall within their scope. I would now like to look at a further range of parentheticals, such as *I hope, I fear*, which seem to perform two simultaneous functions: on the one hand they tend to weaken the strength of assumptions that fall within their scope, and on the other hand, they determine the speaker's *emotional attitude* to these assumptions. Thus, they appear to fall midway between weakening parentheticals such as *I think* and attitudinal adverbials such as *unfortunately, sadly*. Consider (115a–c):

(115) a. Susan will win the elections.
       b. Susan will win the elections, *I hope.*
       c. Susan will win the elections, *I fear.*

By adding *I hope*, and *I fear*, the speaker of (115) reduces her commitment to the truth of the proposition that Susan will win the elections, while simultaneously expressing her emotional attitude towards the state of affairs described: positive in (115b) and negative in (115c). As we have seen, attitudinal adverbials are perceived as truth-conditionally irrelevant, and evidential adverbials such as *I think* are also typically perceived as inessential to truth conditions. We should therefore expect attitudinal parentheticals such as *I fear, I hope* to be irrelevant to truth conditions too, and I will argue that this is the case. Consider (116):

(116) I'm afraid that it will rain tomorrow.

This utterance has two possible interpretations: on one interpretation, the speaker is simply expressing a fear that it will rain, and makes no commitment to the claim that it will actually rain. On the other interpretation, the speaker is asserting that it will rain, and simultaneously expressing her emotional attitude to this fact. The interesting point about the parentheticals in (115b) and (115c) is that they only have this latter interpretation: that is, in both cases the speaker is putting forward the proposition that it will rain, with *some* degree of strength, and simultaneously expressing her emotional attitude. This supports my claim, made earlier, about the difference between utterance-initial and utterance-final parentheticals: that an utterance-initial parenthetical can have a much greater weakening effect than one that occurs utterance-finally. These examples seem to show that, whereas an utterance-initial parenthetical can suspend the speaker's commitment entirely, its utterance-final counterpart can not.

It also sheds light on a curious fact about the behaviour of illocutionary adverbials such as *frankly, confidentially* in the antecedents of conditionals. Consider (117):

(117)   a.   If your book has *frankly* sold very little, you should blame yourself.
         b.   If your book has, *confidentially*, sold very little, I don't think you should blame me.

It has often been noticed that many conditionals have two possible readings: a 'standard' reading, on which the speaker is not committed to the truth of the antecedent, and a 'concessive' reading, where the speaker *is* committed to the truth of the antecedent. The addition of parentheticals such as *frankly* and *confidentially* forces a concessive reading. Thus, the speaker of (117a–b) is conceding that the book has indeed sold very little, whereas in the non-parenthetical counterparts in (118a) and (118b), no such commitment need be made:

(118)   a.   If your book has sold very little, you should blame yourself.
         b.   If I tell you frankly that your book has sold very little, you should blame yourself.

Clearly, much more needs to be said about these examples, but they seem to fit the general pattern noted above.

CHAPTER 7

Evidential particles

7.1 Introduction

In the first chapter of this book, I argued that the notion of an evidential could be more or less narrowly defined. In its broadest sense, an utterance has an evidential function if and only if it overtly *communicates* evidential information, whether this information is linguistically encoded or pragmatically inferred. More narrowly, we can regard a linguistic construction as being evidential if and only if this information is not only communicated but *encoded*. More narrowly still, we can regard a construction as being evidential if and only if it plays a highly restricted syntactic role — e.g. as a clitic, particle, 'discourse marker', bound morpheme or some other minor syntactic category.

In chapter 4, I discussed the role of pragmatic inference in the communication of evidential information. In chapters 5 and 6, I have looked at the evidential role of two types of major syntactic construction: sentence adverbials and parenthetical clauses. I would now like to turn to evidentials in the narrowest sense, and examine various particles[1] and 'discourse markers' with an evidential function. The constructions I have chosen to look at are those generally seen as performing a 'hearsay' function, indicating that the information being offered was obtained from someone else.

Preliminary analyses of hearsay particles were offered within the framework of relevance theory by Blass (1989, 1990). This important work established many points that will be summarized and adopted here. However, Blass's work was completed at a time when the conceptual/procedural distinction, and its interaction with the explicit/implicit and truth-conditional/non-truth-conditional distinctions, was only beginning to be explored. I am interested in showing how hearsay and evidential particles fit into the more fully developed framework outlined in this book. I will use the Modern Greek particle *taha* to argue that not all 'evidentials' encode the same sort of meaning. My main claim will be that hearsay and evidential particles, unlike hearsay and evidential adverbials, encode procedural rather than conceptual meaning; I will also consider their truth-conditional status, which was left unresolved by earlier work.

Finally, I will look briefly at the 'hearsay' function performed by inflectional morphology, and at the use of quotation marks in written language, as still further types of 'hearsay' device.

7.2   'Hearsay' markers as markers of interpretive use

Palmer (1986) treats hearsay markers as a type of 'evidential' (1986: 51, 71) used to indicate reported speech, and hence to mark information for which the speaker has less evidence than if it was experienced first-hand. In fact, it is not always clear whether Palmer considers 'hearsay' markers as *weakly* committing the speaker to the proposition expressed or *not* committing the speaker to the proposition expressed. He describes 'hearsay' markers as 'evidential' or 'modal', i.e. as degree-of-commitment indicators (p. 51, 53–54), but sometimes hints that they actually suspend commitment (p. 7, 51, 53) as in the following remarks: "... many languages grammaticalize "report" or "hearsay" to indicate that what is said has been told to the speaker (who is therefore, not committed to its truth). This can be handled in terms of the modal feature Quotative, ..." (Palmer 1986: 7)

and:

> The Quotative, ... looks *prima facie* to be wholly objective, indicating not what the speaker believes, but what has been said by others. But if this is taken together with other evidentials, e.g. those that indicate the kind of observation (e.g. visual versus non-visual) on which the statement is based, it becomes clear that their whole purpose is to provide an indication of the degree of commitment of the speaker: he offers a piece of information, but qualifies its validity for him in terms of the type of evidence he has. In this sense evidentials are not indications of some objective modality, but are subjective in that they indicate the status of the proposition in terms of the speaker's commitment to it. (ibid.: 53–54)

These remarks connect up with the discussion on parentheticals in chapter 6, where I argued that genuine parenthetical use of *I fear*, *I hope*, etc. favours the stronger of two interpretations available for non-parenthetical uses. Palmer seems to be suggesting that even a hearsay parenthetical such as *Bill says* leaves the speaker to some extent committed to the truth of the host clause: it is put forward on the responsibility of the speaker, on the basis of a hearsay report. Palmer comments:

There are at least four ways in which a speaker may indicate that he is not presenting what he is saying as a fact, but rather:

i.   that he is speculating
ii. that he is presenting it as a deduction
iii. that he has been told about it
iv. that it is a matter only of appearance, based on the evidence of (possibly fallible) senses.

...

All four types are concerned with the indication by the speaker of his (lack) of commitment to the truth of the proposition being expressed. (Palmer 1986:51)

Blass (1989, 1990) argues against this analysis on several grounds. She points out that conveying the speaker's attitude to reported speech is not the only function of hearsay markers. They might indicate attitudes other than diminished commitment; they might indicate attitudes not to what was said, but to what was thought, or to the implicatures of an utterance rather than the proposition directly expressed (Blass 1990:94). With reference to Sissala, a Niger-Congo language, and its potential hearsay marker *ré*, Blass showed that *ré* also occurs in irony and interrogatives. She argued that it was best analysed not as a hearsay marker but as a marker of *interpretive* use. The distinction between descriptive and interpretive use of language and thought was introduced in chapter 4, section 5. I will use it in examining Blass's arguments against Palmer's claim, and in analysing certain morphological evidentials from other languages.

7.2.1   *Ré* and interpretive use

Blass (1989, 1990) drew two main conclusions from her analysis of 'hearsay' markers:

> ... first, that 'hearsay' constructions are best analysed, not as a type of modal or evidential, weakening the speaker's commitment to the truth of the proposition expressed, but as a variety of interpretive-use marker, with all the functions attributed to interpretive use by Sperber and Wilson; second, that other so-called "hearsay" particles might be usefully re-examined to see whether they, like *ré*, occur in other than true "hearsay" constructions, and should thus be reanalysed as markers of interpretive use. (Blass 1990:95)

Blass based her claims on the Sissala particle *ré*, which has, among others, a 'hearsay' function (Blass 1989:304–306, 1990:97–99), i.e. it is a marker of direct and indirect speech. *Ré* can occur either as a complementizer (COMP), or a 'hearsay' particle which occurs at the end of the quoted clause, and which Blass calls an 'interpretive-use marker' (IM). This use is illustrated in (1):

(1) *Náŋá sʊsɛ. Ba kaa konni yo   ta   ré*
     some died they took cut   throw leave IM
     'Some died and were untied and left there RE' (It is said)

However, *ré* occurs in other, *non*-hearsay types of constructions too. For example, in (2) and (3) it co-occurs with verbs of propositional attitude, such as *think* and *know*:

(2) *U pio bʊnɛ   ʊ wí gbee ri.*[2]
     he took thought he NEG play IM
     'He gathered that he (Kofi) was not joking RE'.

(3) *[zɪŋ rí-í   ká ánáwa ré*
     you know COMP-you are parents IM
     'You know that you are parents RE.'

As Blass observes (1989: 306, 1990: 100), the fact that *ré* occurs with *think* and *know* suggests that 'hearsay' markers are not only used for reporting speech. The fact that it co-occurs with *I know* suggests that it is not always used to indicate diminished speaker commitment.

Moreover, *ré* occurs in questions, and their answers. This is also difficult to reconcile with the view that it is a 'hearsay' marker; or with Palmer's claim that it weakens the speaker's commitment to the proposition expressed (Blass 1989: 307, 1990: 100). Consider (4) and (5):

(4) J: *[lísé   namíé ná ré-ɛ́?*
         you taken-out meat   DEF IM-Q
         'Have you taken out the meat RE?'

     C: *Oó, á lísɔ́   ré hāā ká tá*
         yes we taken-out IM AH and left
         'Yes we have taken out (some) RE and left (some).'

(5) S: *'Ba fa-á   pɛ ɛré ré?*
         they PAST-IPF sleep how IM
         'How did they sleep RE?'

     A: *'Ba fa-á   pé dáhá   ré*
         they PAST-IPF slept standing IM
         'They used to sleep standing RE.'

Blass observes that "The occurrence of *ré* in questions is unexpected on Palmer's evidential account. In asking a question, the speaker does not commit himself to the truth of the proposition expressed, so how could the addition of *ré* weaken the speaker's commitment?" (Blass 1990: 100)

Blass claims that *ré* is more adequately analysed as an *echoic interpretive use* marker (IM), because in this way, its different uses can be explained. For example, it might be used in an utterance which expresses an *attitude* towards an opinion echoed (Blass 1989: 312, 1990: 104–105), as in (6) and (7):

(6) M: *'Ba dula   á   wérí.*
       they this-year done well
       'They have done well this year.'

    A: *'Ba há keŋ séminéré ná mʋ Buro.*
       they who took seminar DEF go Boura
       'They, who conducted the seminar at Boura.'

    N: *'Ba bɪéná á   weri é rí.*
       they really done well F IM
       'They have really done well RE.'

(7) D: *| bínɔ́ ná sɪé keŋ susi fé.*
       your thing DEF so catch pity much
       'Your thing (taperecorder) arouses pity.'

    N: *Susi rí. ʋ má nʋsɔ né.*
       pity IM its also make SDM
       'Pity RE. It is just its make.' (Things of that make are always small.)

Blass points out that N's utterances in (6) and (7) do not report speech, but "indicate the speaker's attitude to what has just been said" (Blass 1989: 313, 1990: 105). In (6) N repeats the preceding utterance in order to endorse it, whereas in (7) N repeats the preceding utterance in order to dissociate himself from it. These are, clearly, not cases of the speaker's weakened commitment to the proposition expressed.

Another use of the particle *ré* is in echoing an *implicature* of a preceding utterance, rather than a proposition explicitly expressed. Implicatures can be echoed with various attitudes too (Blass 1989: 315, 1990: 107), as in (8):

(8) D: *'Ba né pɔ́wɔ́   ná kaa lɛ ba-á kaa lí tá*
       they SDM gather-them there take leave they-IPF take leave leave
       ká baa zʋ́ ja   bɪfɛlɛ a baa cɛsɛ, cɛsɛ a baa
       and again enter house new and again break break and again
       cíínɛ lɛ.
       carry leave

'They (ants) gather them (grains) and take them out and leave them there. They enter the house again, break (grains) again and take them out.'

A: *E! cuŋcumó tuŋ ré!*
   Eh! ants   work IM!
   'Eh! Ants work RE!'

Here, A echoes not an utterance, a proposition explicitly expressed by D, but a contextual implication of D's utterance. This contextual implication is derived using the following contextual assumption:

(8′) If ants break grains and carry them out of the house all the time
      then they work hard.

A further contextual implication intended by D is that ants are very effective in destroying his grain. A's utterance conveys this implication too, and thus reinforces the implicature conveyed by D. Such cases, Blass claims, cannot be explained by Palmer's evidential account of hearsay markers (Blass 1989: 315, 1990: 107).

Similarly, the particle *ré* is used to echo *thoughts* and beliefs of people in general, as, for example, in proverbs or sayings. Thus, consider (9):

(9) *[-ı   máŋsé wíwie,   wıı   wuu pɛ-ı   tıı, cie   ı   é di*
     if-you learn thing-small, matter every give-you self tomorrow you F eat
     υ   yυɔrɛ ré.
     your fruit IM
     'Whatever small thing you learn, tomorrow you will eat its fruit RE.'
     (You will gain from it.)

Here, *ré* occurs in an utterance that echoes traditional wisdom, i.e. a thought which is not attributed to anyone in particular. This case too does not easily fit into an evidential account of hearsay particles: we often invoke thoughts or beliefs held by people in general, or in authority, to *strengthen* our commitment to the proposition expressed, rather than weaken it (Blass 1989: 314, 1990: 106).

If *ré* is, indeed, an echoic/attributive marker, it is not surprising that it marks *ironical* utterances in Sissala (Blass 1990: 109). Recall that irony is analysed in the framework of relevance theory as a type of interpretive echoic use (see chapter 4, section 4.5.2). Consider (10):

(10) a. *[zaa   iso   ká tá   ŋ dυŋɔ rí ya-a?*
        you today get-up and leave me alone IM or-Q?
        'Are you leaving me alone today?'

b. *Anɛ Luc ha sɛ́   ŋ́ é dí kıŋkaŋ.*
   as Luc   said I F eat a-lot
c. *U keŋ taŋa   rɛ́.*
   he has wisdom IM
   'As Luc said, I eat a lot. He is right RE.'

In (10c) the speaker did not, in fact, intend to communicate that she eats a lot. In echoing Luc's comment about her, she is being ironical, i.e. she is dissociating herself from the proposition expressed and expects her audience to do the same on the basis of certain assumptions, i.e. that she was the one to prepare the meal, started eating later than the others, and thus did not have as much time to eat as the others (Blass 1990: 87–88, see also 1989: 109–110).

The occurrence of *rɛ́* in propositional-attitude constructions, as illustrated in examples (2)–(3), is also explained naturally on the interpretive-use hypothesis. As Blass points out:

> For Sperber and Wilson, these [propositional-attitude constructions] are typical cases of interpretive use: the proposition embedded in such constructions is entertained not as a description of a state of affairs but as an interpretive representation of an attributed belief or desire. (Blass 1989: 315–316)

Moreover, the use of *rɛ́* in questions and answers, as illustrated in examples (4)–(5), fits naturally with the assumption that it is a marker of attributive use. Questions and answers with *rɛ́* seem to have an echoic element: 'Am I right in thinking ... ?', 'Do you think ... ?', and *rɛ́* might be seen as indicating this extra echoic element.

Note, finally, that 'hearsay' particles used in irony, or in other *non*-evidential functions, have also been reported in other languages. This seems to be the case with *-mis* in Turkish, which is used to convey not only hearsay, but irony, sarcasm, surprise or compliments (Slobin and Aksu 1982), and with *kono*, found in a number of Philippine languages which is used in Bible translation to convey sarcasm and irony (Ballard 1974). According to Blass, all these uses are explained on the assumption that the markers in question are markers of interpretive use, rather than being 'hearsay' in the strictest sense (Blass 1990: 107–109).

This raises the more general issue of whether *all* so-called 'hearsay markers' might be better re-analysed as attributive-use markers, as Blass has proposed for *rɛ́*. Blass has shown that one particular particle, in one particular language, is *not just* a marker of hearsay; this is precisely why it is better analysed as an attributive-use marker. The relevant examples are those which show *rɛ́* occurring in reporting not only what was said, but also what was thought (as in example (9)), what was implied (as in example (8)), and in echoic interrogatives (as in examples (4)–(5)). However, there may be other cases which are genuine 'hearsay' markers. Itani (1996, 1998), for example, has argued convincingly that the particle *tte* in Japanese is a genuine hearsay marker, whose function is to indicate that a report of speech (as opposed to thought) is being attempted. I will look at her analysis in section 7.4.

Another related issue is whether hearsay markers (or attributive-use markers) are best analysed, as Palmer and others have proposed, as indicating weakened speaker-commitment to the proposition expressed. As shown above, Blass has argued convincingly that this is *not* the case (see examples (3)–(5) and (10). It seems, then, that we can reject Palmer's view, presented at the beginning of this chapter, that 'hearsay' parentheticals leave the speaker to some extent committed to the truth of the proposition expressed, so that these propositions would be descriptively rather than interpretively used. To examine this claim further, let us briefly consider a few more 'hearsay' particles.

Some typical morphological evidentials from other languages seem to be analysable along similar lines to Blass's examples. The evidential suffix *-boti/ -beti* in Hill Patwin serves a number of evidential functions, including hearsay, inference and rhetorical use (Whistler 1986:70). Consider the following examples:

(11) *yirma   hayba²a-boti pi.*
     leg(OBJ) hurt-EVID   he
     '[He told me] his leg hurts.'

(12) *la·bakʰe·,   sulʰi-to   pepelet   ²i-boti.*
     elder brother(VOC) kill-INT.FUT us two(OBJ) do-EVID
     'Elder brother, he [seems to be] trying to kill us two.'

(13) *he·ti   win   hene·-boti.*
     from somewhere person arrive-EVID
     'Someone has [apparently] come here from someplace.'

(14) *likku·n hatʰu! ²ilayin   berečoyi-boti.*
     quickly pick   children hungry-EVID
     'Gather up [greens] quickly! [Your] children must be hungry.'

(15) *ma-ne·n   we·ł tiwnana hara· -boti.*
     your-mother salt to buy go-EVID
     'Your mother must have gone to buy salt.'

In (11), -*boti* serves as a hearsay evidential. In (12) and (13), it serves as a marker of logical inference based on suspicion, appearance or circumstance, i.e. an evidential marker of lack of direct sensory evidence. However, in (14) and (15), the evidential is used rhetorically to express what is a patently false claim in the context of the narrative: in (14), the speaker, Bear Old Lady, is imagining a reason why Deer Old Lady should gather greens quickly for her children, who are not present, so there is no evidence of them being, in fact, hungry; in (15), the speaker is imagining a reason for the mother's absence. In both cases, the evidential marker has been used to make patently false claims, a function that can hardly be reconciled with Palmer's evidential account of hearsay markers as expressing the speaker's weakened commitment to the proposition expressed: the point in (14) and (15) is that the speaker does not know, or even believe, that 'the children are hungry' or that 'the hearer's mother has gone to buy salt'.

I would suggest, along lines similar to Blass, that -*boti* in the above examples can be analysed as an explicit indicator of attributive use. On this account, what -*boti* does in (14) and (15) in particular, is mark thoughts attributed to somebody other than the speaker, and which the speaker does not endorse. The effect would be similar to Blass's cases of irony. In (12) and (13), -*boti* functions in a similar way to English *apparently*, which is not a hearsay marker (i.e. a marker of echoic attributive use), but may nonetheless be an indicator of interpretive rather than descriptive use. The relevance-theoretic framework allows for the self-attribution of thoughts or utterances, as in *I think, I infer. Seemingly* and *apparently* may function in this way, and -*boti* might plausibly be analysed as having a similar function.[3] I will discuss these ideas further below.

The evidential marker *soo da* in Japanese is also commonly used to mark hearsay evidence, as in (16) (Aoki 1986: 230–233):

(16) *Ame ga   hutteiru -soo da*
      rain s.m. fall
      'They say it is raining'.

However, *soo da* is also used as an inference marker to indicate a self-attributed thought. Thus, (17) is ungrammatical:

(17) **Ame ga   huri soo da ga   hur-ru to   wa   omowa -na   -i.*
      rain s.m. fall   but fall-NP Q.M. T.M. think -NEG -NP
      'It seems it is going to rain but I don't think it will.'

This function clearly does not fit with the traditional notion of a 'hearsay' marker, whereby speakers pass on responsibility for the truth of an assertion to someone else. As with -boti, the most plausible hypothesis seems to be that *soo-da* may be either self-attributive (like *apparently*) or other-attributive (like regular hearsay-markers). Below, I will look more closely at another particle of this type, and propose a more detailed analysis.

I will now consider the status of hearsay and evidential markers with respect to our three distinctions, i.e. truth-conditional vs. non-truth-conditional, explicit vs. implicit, conceptual vs. procedural. Using the Modern Greek particle *taha* as a case in point, I will argue that hearsay and evidential markers, as well as typical morphological evidentials in other languages, share their truth-conditional status with their English adverbial counterparts, and also contribute to the explicit aspect of communication. However, they are procedural rather than conceptual, and this is where their difference from English sentence adverbials lies. Blass simply hinted at the direction in which answers to these questions are to be sought. She claims that:

> In this case [particle *ré*], the contribution is an explicit, truth-conditional one. Sissala has a means of explicitly indicating whether a certain utterance is intended as an ordinary assertion or a free indirect report of speech. ... at the level of explicit truth-conditional content, or the proposition expressed. (Blass 1990: 123)

She did not, however, consider the status of hearsay markers with respect to the conceptual/procedural distinction. Nor did she seriously investigate whether *all* 'hearsay' markers can be reanalysed as attributive-use markers, or whether there might indeed be a class of genuine hearsay markers, restricted to the indication of reported speech (as with Japanese *tte* above). I will consider these questions in turn.

7.3   *Taha* and procedural encoding[4]

The Modern Greek (MG) particle *taha* is used in informal conversations and written prose in sentence-initial, mid or final position. *Taha* in Ancient Greek carried the manner adverbial meaning 'fast, straightaway' and the evidential meanings 'maybe, perhaps, possibly, undoubtedly, certainly'. In Modern Greek, it carries the evidential meaning 'maybe', 'it seems' and 'apparently', the latter also indicating information obtained through hearsay. In the few existing accounts, it is often referred to as a 'hesitation' adverb or particle, in the sense that it expresses the speaker's hesitation to commit herself to the propositional content of the utterance. As for the sentence types in which it occurs, the examples in the literature show that *taha* can occur in declaratives, interrogatives and imperatives, as indicated below:

(18) **Taha efige**   (declarative)
       left-3D
       'Supposedly, he left.'

(19) **Taha tha figi?**   (interrogative)
       will leave-3D
       'Is he supposedly leaving?'

(20) **Fige taha**   (imperative)
       leave
       'Supposedly, leave.'

The characterization 'hesitation' particle, originally put forward in Triandaphyllides' Grammar (1988 [1941]: 382), has been challenged by Pavlidou (1988). Pavlidou claims that *taha*, rather than expressing hesitation on the speaker's part, expresses "(indirectly) (subjective) certainty" (1988: 541), meaning that (18) is an indirect expression of the speaker's certainty that the referent didn't in fact leave. In interrogatives, Pavlidou claims that *taha* turns a genuine request for information into a rhetorical question, and hence turns (19) into an indirect assertion that he will not come. In this case, *taha* is interpreted as conveying 'I doubt (indirectly) that p'. Alternatively, *taha* turns a genuine request for information into a mere expression of doubt. In this case, *taha* is interpreted as conveying 'I wonder if/I express doubt as to …'. In imperatives, *taha* may be interpreted as conveying 'Pretend to perform A' or 'I doubt (indirectly) that p' or 'I do not really ask you to perform A', so (20) is an indirect request that the hearer should not leave, but merely pretend to do so.

Although I generally agree with Pavlidou's intuitions as illustrated in (18)–(20) above, I do not consider her account fully satisfactory on either descriptive or explanatory levels. Little is said about the semantic nature of *taha*, and I will argue that the pragmatic account fails to offer a straightforward explanation.

My main claim will be as follows. *Taha* is a procedural marker which directly encodes weak evidential information, i.e. something like the meaning 'it seems', and is thus a marker of interpretive (attributive) use. As a weak evidential, it affects the strength of the assumption communicated (and hence the recommended degree of commitment to the proposition expressed). The hearsay and other implicatures communicated, are pragmatically derived from its evidential meaning. On its hearsay interpretation, it marks the ground-floor assertion to which it is attached as a case of other-attributive rather than self-attributive use. In both cases, it alters the truth-conditional status of the ground-floor assertion to which it is attached, and will be perceived as making an essential contribution to truth conditions. Which interpretation (evidential or hearsay) the hearer is intended to recover, or does in fact recover, is determined by considerations of relevance.

7.3.1   A speech-act account of *taha*

The pragmatic functions of *taha* illustrated in examples (18) and (20) above are explained in Pavlidou's speech-act framework as resulting from cancellation of the sincerity condition, required for the satisfactory performance of any speech act in which *taha* occurs. In particular, she claims that for assertive speech acts, the addition of *taha* cancels the sincerity condition that the speaker believes the proposition expressed, and indirectly indicates that she believes the opposite (Pavlidou 1988:539) (see example 18). Similarly, in directive speech acts, the addition of *taha* cancels the sincerity condition that the speaker wants the hearer to perform the act described in the proposition expressed. The result is a request to *pretend* to perform the act described, rather than actually perform it (see example 20). The question is how this is brought about. Moreover, no explanation is offered concerning the functions of *taha* in interrogatives, which leaves the analysis incomplete.

It seems, then, that in Pavlidou's speech-act account, the pragmatic functions of *taha* would have to be explained in terms of a deviation from the norm, because it overrules a condition of truthfulness or sincerity that should otherwise be adhered to. However, contrary to what such an account suggests, *taha* is very common in conversational speech, marks such speech as particularly informal and personal, and is equally used by speakers of different social and educational levels, of standard MG as well as of dialects spoken in rural Greece. The claim that sincerity conditions on speech acts are generally overruled is a rather inelegant way of handling a naturally occurring particle in MG. Within the framework of relevance theory, the fact that in assertions speakers rarely intend to convey exactly the proposition strictly and literally expressed has been seen as evidence against any maxim of truthfulness or sincerity. Sperber and Wilson (1985/6; 1986/95, chapter 4)[5] have argued that this is the case not only with the well-known examples of metaphor and irony, but also with loose talk and indirect speech:

(21) Bill is a tiger! (Metaphor)

(22) That's a clever thing to do! (Irony)

(23) Darwin College is 10 minutes' walk from the station. (Loose talk)

(24) a. John just called.
      b. Mary is held up by traffic. (Free indirect speech)

where Susan may utter (24b) with the aim of communicating (25):

(25) *John said* Mary is held up by traffic.

Similarly, Wilson and Sperber (1988) surveyed a range of directives in which the speaker often does not sincerely desire the hearer to perform the act described in the proposition expressed, as advice, permission, or threats:

(26) John: I need an Introductory Coursebook in Linguistics.
      Mary: Buy *The study of Language* by Yule. (Advice)

(27) a. John: Can I have your pencil-sharpener?
      b. Mary: Here it is, take it. (Permission)

(28) (Mother to child): Come on. Jump. Just you dare. (Threats and dares)

In this framework, such examples are seen not as violating a sincerity condition of the type generally proposed, but as evidence against such a condition. The fact that in assertions *taha* is compatible with the speaker's not believing the proposition explicitly expressed follows naturally from the claim made in relevance theory that literal truth is a limiting case rather than the norm. The fact that *taha* in imperatives is compatible with the speaker's desire that the hearer not perform the act described in the proposition expressed follows naturally from the claim made in relevance theory that imperative mood conveys something weaker than the desire for the hearer to perform the act described in the proposition expressed, which is again a limiting case rather than the norm (Clark 1991; Rouchota 1994).

More importantly, suspending the sincerity condition on its own will not explain why *taha* communicates that the speaker of (18) believes the opposite, or that the speaker of (20) wants the hearer to *pretend* to perform the act described. A sincerity-suspender alone should be found in jokes, fictions, metaphors, ironies, hyperboles, maybe loose talk and free indirect speech. However, if its function is more restricted than merely suspending the sincerity condition — e.g. communicating that the speaker believes the opposite, or wants the hearer to pretend to perform the act described — it is not clear why the suspension of the sincerity condition needs to be mentioned at all.

Note that if it really functions in the way Pavlidou claims, *taha* should be a regular irony marker, or disagreement marker, of the type Grice would have envisaged, enabling the speaker to say one thing and mean the opposite. For example:

(29)   a.   *Iste*   *o   Neil Smith?*
            are you-PL the Neil Smith?
            'Are you Neil Smith?'

       b.   *Taha ime.*
            I am
            *'Taha I am' (meaning 'I am not')

(30)   a.   *Afto to   fagito itan apesio.*
            this the meal was terrible
            'This meal was terrible.'

       b.   *Taha afto to   fagito itan apesio.*
            this the meal was terrible
            *'Taha this meal was terrible.' (meaning 'The meal was not bad')

(29b) sounds very odd as an ironical utterance and it would clearly never qualify as a regular disagreement answer in MG. Similarly, (30b) would make a rather odd ironical utterance and it could not be interpreted as a regular disagreement answer either.

On Pavlidou's account, *taha* does more than merely suspend a sincerity condition: it also indirectly communicates an assertion or a request. But which assertion is the hearer intended to retrieve? And which act is the hearer requested to perform? Pavlidou confirms our intuitions that the intended interpretation for assertions is the opposite of the one explicitly expressed, and that in imperatives the act to-be-performed is a pretence of performing the one explicitly described; but how does the hearer decide that this is so? In other words, we need an explanation of how the hearer interprets a declarative utterance with the logical form in (31a)

(31)   a.   *taha*   P

as communicating (31b)

       b.   *Speaker communicates not – P*

and how the hearer interprets an imperative utterance with the logical form in (32a)

(32) a. *taha*   P

as communicating (32b)

   b. *Speaker asks hearer to 'pretend P'/ 'not – P'*

(31) and (32) involve an inferential step that is too big to accept without further explanation. Two important issues arise here. First, what is the rationale for such a sincerity-suspender? If you believe 'Not – P, why not just say 'Not – P'? Second, 'asking the H to not – P' is very different from 'asking the H to pretend P'. Pavlidou never explains how this more specific proposition is recovered. And surely by parallel to the treatment of assertions, *taha* in imperatives should mean 'Do not do P', instead of 'Pretend to do P'. It seems, then, as if on Pavlidou's account, *taha* has to encode something different in imperatives and in interrogatives. An answer to these problems will be sketched in subsequent sections.

Another problem with Pavlidou's approach to *taha* is that she does not deal with its hearsay interpretation. In fact, *taha* is one of the few particles in MG that can convey a hearsay interpretation, as illustrated below:

(33) O   Yiannis ine **taha** kataskopos.
      the John   is   spy.
      'It is said that John is a spy.'

The hearsay interpretation has been also pointed out by Tzartzanos (1996 [1953]: 248), who remarks in a footnote that *taha* can sometimes, especially in narratives of dreams or imaginary events, be substituted by *lei*, i.e. 's/he says' or 'the story goes'. Here is his example:

(34) *Ki aksafna mou fanike pos ida   mbrosta mou ti   mikri*
      and suddenly to me seemed that saw-1sg in front of me the little
      pethameni. Sa na erhotan,   lei,   ap'tin   antitheti meria.
      dead.   As if was coming-3d s/he says from the opposite direction.
      'And suddenly it seemed to me that I saw in front of me the little girl
      dead. As if she was coming, the story goes, from the opposite direction.'

According to Tzartzanos, the last sentence can be paraphrased as 'She was coming *taha* from the opposite direction' with the same, hearsay meaning.

But if this is so, i.e. if *taha* may occasionally be interpreted as an evidential particle and occasionally as a hearsay particle, the question that naturally arises is, how does the hearer retrieve the intended interpretation? In the following sections I will sketch an account of *taha* on which its evidential and hearsay interpretations will receive a straightforward explanation.

I would now like to consider whether *taha* is (a) truth-conditional or non-truth-conditional, (b) contributes to explicit communication or implicatures, and (c) encodes conceptual or procedural information. Here, I will examine the ways it patterns with the corresponding English evidential adverbials *apparently*, *seemingly* and the hearsay adverbials *allegedly*, *reportedly*, considered in chapter 5. I will argue that, like hearsay and evidential adverbials, *taha* is truth-conditional and explicit, but unlike hearsay and evidential adverbials, which are conceptual, it encodes procedural information.

7.3.2   Truth-conditional or non-truth-conditional?

In the last chapter, I argued that hearsay adverbials in English, e.g. *allegedly*, *reportedly*, are markers of attributive use, which change the truth-conditional status of the proposition that falls within their scope. I want to claim that *all* markers of reported speech or thought have this function: they indicate that the thoughts being interpreted are not the speaker's own, and thus they automatically suspend the speaker's commitment. In Sperber and Wilson's terms, the speaker is no longer committed to the *truth* of a description, but to the *faithfulness* of an interpretation. Consider (35):

(35)   The president has resigned, I hear.

The use of the parenthetical comment *I hear* makes an essential difference to the truth conditions of (35). The speaker is not automatically committed to the truth of the ground-floor proposition 'The president has resigned'. The same is true when (35) is embedded into factive and non-factive environments. Blass's examples which show that *ré* has a similar effect on the truth conditions of Sissala utterances fit naturally into this framework. The examples in (11), (14), (15) and (16) show that — as attributive use markers (whether echoic or not), -*boti* and *soo da* have the same effect on the truth conditions of Patwin and Japanese utterances respectively, and hence they also fit naturally into this framework.

As we have seen, this suspension of speaker-commitment does not always result in what speech-act theorists call *weakened* commitment. Claims of *weakened commitment* suggest that the speaker does remain committed to the truth of the proposition expressed. However, the crucial idea behind other-attributive use is that it automatically suspends the speaker's commitment, by indicating that the views being interpreted are those of someone other than the speaker. Different degrees of speaker commitment may be pragmatically inferred on the basis of assumptions about how trustworthy that other person is. For example, when attributing a certain belief to Chomsky, to the Bible or to popular wisdom, we may indirectly indicate a high degree of commitment to it. By contrast, when attributing a certain belief to someone who is known as entirely untrustworthy, we may indirectly indicate that we have no faith in it at all. Thus, the *function* of an attributive use marker is in no way to indicate a weakened degree of commitment. Where this is so, it is merely a pragmatic effect, achieved in a certain type of context. And in the case of self-attributive uses of *seemingly*, or *apparently* (equivalent to 'it seems *to me*', or 'it appears *to me*'), the degree of commitment will have to be pragmatically inferred on the basis of the type of evidence available to the speaker. I will return now to a specific evidential — hearsay marker, the MG particle *taha*, and examine its truth-conditional status.

In chapter 5, I showed that, according to a standard test for distinguishing truth-conditional from non-truth-conditional meaning, evidential adverbials *apparently*, *seemingly*, and hearsay adverbials *allegedly*, *reportedly*, are truth-conditional. In this section, the same test will be applied to evidential and hearsay interpretations of *taha*. Recall that the test consists in embedding the item to be tested into the antecedent of a conditional and seeing if it falls within the scope of 'if'. If it does, the item is truth-conditional, if it does not, it is non-truth-conditional.

Notice first that *taha* in (36) may have two interpretations, as an evidential particle in (37a) and as a hearsay particle in (37b):

(36) O Yiannis ine **taha** anaksiopistos.
      the John   is   unreliable

(37) a. 'It seems that John is unreliable.'   (evidential)
      b. 'It is said that John is unnreliable.'   (hearsay)

I will first examine how the test applies to the evidential interpretation of *taha*. In considering (37a), the question is whether its truth conditions are (38) or (39):

(38) O Yiannis ine anaksiopistos.
      the John   is   unreliable
      'John is unreliable.'

(39)   *Kata ta fenomena o   Yiannis ine anaksiopistos.*
    it seems that   the John   is   unreliable
    'It seems that John is unreliable.'

To test (36), we embed it into a conditional, as in (40):

(40)   *An o   Yiannis ine **taha** anaksiopistos, min   ksanasinergastis mazi tou.*
    if the John   is   unreliable   do not work again   with him.
    'If John is apparently unreliable, don't work with him again.'

The question is: under what circumstances is the speaker of (40) claiming that the hearer should not collaborate with John again? Is she saying that he should not collaborate with John again if (38) is true, or is she saying that he should not collaborate with John again if (39) is true? Native speakers agree that (39) does contribute to the truth conditions of the utterance. Hence, *taha*, on its evidential interpretation, is truth-conditional.

Let us now consider how the test applies to a hearsay interpretation of *taha*. In considering (41), the question is whether its truth conditions are (42) or (43):

(41)   *I   fitites   **taha** paraponounte gia   to   fagito.*
    the students   complain   about the food
    'The students reportedly complain about the food.'

(42)   *I   fitites   paraponounte gia   to   fagito.*
    the students complain   about the food
    'The students complain about the food.'

(43)   *Legete   oti   i   fitites   paraponounte gia   to   fagito.*
    it is said that the students complain   about the food
    'It is said that the students complain about the food.'

To test (41), we embed it into a conditional, as in (44):

(44)   *An I   fitites   **taha** paraponounte gia   to   fagito, prepi na milisis*
    if the students   complain   about the food   must to talk
    ston   magira.
    to the chef
    'If the students reportedly complain about the food, you should talk to the chef.'

Under what circumstances is the speaker of (44) claiming that I, the students' representative in College, should talk to the chef? Is she saying that I should talk to the chef if (42) is true, or is she saying that I should talk to the chef if (43) is true?

It is clear again that (43) contributes to the truth conditions of the utterance. Hence, the truth-conditional status of *taha* is confirmed.

Notice that in (36), *taha* weakens the speaker's commitment to the truth of the proposition expressed, and in (41), *taha* suspends the speaker's commitment to the proposition that falls within its scope. In both cases, the occurrence of the particle does make a difference to the truth-conditional status of the ground-floor proposition, because as we have seen, the speaker of (36) is not committed to the truth of (38), but she is certainly committed to the truth of (39). And the speaker of (41) is not committed to the truth of (42) but she is committed to the truth of (43).

If *taha* is truth-conditional, it should also be able to fall within the scope of 'factive' connectives, which entail the truth of their embedded propositions. And this is what we find. The speaker of (45) is committed to the truth of (46), but not to the truth of (47):

(45) a. *Par'olo   pou o   Yiannis ine **taha** anaksiopistos, epagelmatika ine*
    although that the John   is   unreliable   professionally is
    epitihimenos.
    successful
    'Although John is apparently unreliable, he is professionally doing well.'

   b. *Epidi   o   Yiannis ine **taha** anaksiopistos, den ine idietera*
    because the John   is   unreliable   not is particularly
    dimofilis.
    popular
    'Because John is apparently unreliable, he is not very popular.'

(46) a. *Par'olo   pou o   Yiannis ine kata ta fenomena anaksiopistos,*
    although that the John   is apparently   unreliable
    epagelmatika ine epitihimenos.
    professionally is   successful
    'Although it appears that Yiannis is unreliable, he is professionally doing well.'

   b. *Epidi   o   Yiannis ine kata ta fenomena anaksiopistos, den ine*
    because the John   is apparently   unreliable   not is
    idietera   dimofilis.
    particularly popular
    'Because it appears that John is unreliable, he is not very popular.'

(47) a. *Par'olo   pou o   Yiannis ine anaksiopistos, epagelmatika   ine*
          although that the John   is   unreliable   professionally is
          epitihimenos.
          successful
          'Although John is unreliable, he is professionally doing well.'
      b. *Epidi   o   Yiannis ine anaksiopistos, den ine idietera   dimofilis.*
          because the John   is   unreliable   not is   particularly popular
          'Because John is unreliable, he is not very popular.'

So, in terms of truth-conditionality, *taha* is similar to hearsay and evidential adverbials. In the next section, I will show that it is similar to the corresponding sentence adverbials in another respect: they all contribute to the explicit, rather than the implicit, side of communication.

7.3.3   Explicit or implicit?

Blass (1990: 123) suggests that attributive-use marker *ré* contributes to the explicit aspect of communication. I shall argue that this is, indeed, true for hearsay particles in general: they fall on the explicit rather than the implicit side, i.e. they contribute to the explicatures of an utterance rather than its implicatures. In the first place (as we have seen), they automatically suspend the speaker's commitment to the proposition that falls within their scope. As a result, this proposition is not (or not necessarily) an explicature. In the second place, they encode information which contributes to higher-level explicatures. In both cases, they affect the explicatures of the utterance, and fall on the explicit rather than the implicit side.

As suggested in chapter 4, the basic explicature of an utterance (when it has one) is the proposition expressed, but most utterances also communicate higher-level explicatures, obtained by embedding the proposition expressed under a higher-order speech-act or propositional-attitude description, e.g. 'The speaker (S) believes that ...', 'The speaker (S) asserts that ...', and so on. In chapters 5 and 6, I suggested that hearsay and evidential indicators contribute to the explicatures of an utterance rather than its implicatures. For example, the hearsay adverbial *allegedly* communicates the explicature 'It is alleged that ...', the evidential adverbial *obviously* communicates the explicature 'It is obvious that ...', and so on. In this section, I will develop an analysis along these lines, using *taha* as a case in point.

The proposition expressed by an utterance of *taha P* will be P, understood as representing different types of object in different types of utterance (Wilson and Sperber 1988; Clark 1991):

(48) a. P represents an actual state of affairs   (declaratives)
     b. P represents desirable information   (interrogatives)
     c. P represents a desirable state of affairs   (imperatives)

Depending on whether *taha* is attached to a declarative, interrogative or imperative utterance, there is a wide range of higher-level explicatures that the utterance may communicate, such as:

Declaratives
(49) a. S supposes that …
     b. It seems to S that …
     c. It is said that …

Interrogatives
(50) a. S is asking whether P is supposed to be true …

Imperatives
(51) a. S is asking H to pretend to perform A

From these explicatures, in appropriate circumstances the following further inferences might be drawn:

(49) d. S does not believe that …
     e. S weakly believes that …

(50) b. S doubts whether …
     c. S thinks it is unlikely that …

(51) b. S does not want H to perform A

I will argue that all this information is recoverable on the assumption that *taha* means something like 'seemingly, apparently, supposedly', which in English too may often convey a dissociative attitude to the proposition expressed.

As noted in previous chapters, explicatures are recovered by a combination of decoding and inference: the greater the element of decoding, the greater the degree of explicitness. With reference to (49c), note that *any* proposition can be interpretively used, whether or not this fact is linguistically encoded. For example, consider (52):

(52) I've just seen the chef. The quality of the food will improve.

The second part of this utterance can be understood in two different ways: first, descriptively, as an assertion by the speaker that the quality of the food will improve, and second, interpretively (or attributively), as a report of what the chef promised the students' representative. In (52) there is no linguistic indication of how the utterance is to be understood. On the analysis I propose, the function of *taha* when used as a hearsay particle would be to indicate that it is intended as a case of attributive rather than descriptive use, i.e. that the second part of (52) represents an attributed representation with a propositional form which it resembles to some degree. In example (52), the type of interpretive use involved involves the reporting of speech, and the *resemblance* may be in form or in content. If the speaker of (52) is directly quoting, she is using a representation which resembles the original (the chef's utterance), in form, i.e. it has a similar linguistic structure, though it may lack paralinguistic information such as voice quality and accent of the original. If she is indirectly reporting, she is using a representation which resembles the original (the chef's utterance) in content, i.e. the two utterances must share some logical properties and contextual implications in some contexts (For a relevance-theoretic analysis of reported speech, and more generally attributive use, see Noh 2000).

It is important to notice here that an utterance with *taha* may also indicate the speaker's attitude to the thought or opinion being reported. For *taha*, attributive use is generally understood as conveying the speaker's dissociation from the proposition expressed, hence the propositional-attitude information in (49d). In the framework of Sperber and Wilson (1986/95: 238), cases where interpretations achieve relevance not only "by informing the hearer of the fact that the speaker has in mind what so-and-so said" but also by communicating that she has a certain attitude to it, are *echoic*. I want to suggest that *taha* may occur in utterances that are not only attributive but *echoic*, and that the relevance of such utterances may depend largely on this expression of attitude.

(49a–b) and (50a–c) may also communicate the speaker's attitude to the proposition expressed. So, for example, the speaker of (53) may intend to communicate not only the proposition expressed but also the propositional-attitude information in (54):

(53)   The quality of the food will improve.

(54)   S weakly believes that the quality of the food will improve.

and the speaker of (55) may intend to communicate not only a genuine request for information, but also the propositional-attitude information in (56):

(55)   Will the quality of the food improve?

(56)   S doubts that the quality of the food will improve.

In these cases, paralinguistic features, e.g. gestures, tone of voice, facial expression, may help to make certain interpretations more accessible. In other cases, the speaker provides explicit linguistic clues to ensure that propositional-attitude information such as the above is communicated. I want to suggest that *taha* provides explicit linguistic clues to relevant inferences, as do the corresponding *seemingly, apparently, supposedly.*

This account clears up some problems that do not receive a clear-cut answer in Pavlidou's account. First, she does not commit herself on the basic, explicit meaning of *taha*. Second, she leaves open whether the information she describes as "indirectly" communicated (see section 7.3) is implicitly communicated as a result of some linguistically encoded, evidential type of meaning. How exactly are the implicatures derived from the explicit meaning? How is the more specific proposition 'Pretend P' recovered in the case of implicatures?

Recall that according to Pavlidou, *taha* in imperatives may be "paraphrased" not only as (51a) but also as (57) (1988: 540):

(57)   S does not really ask H to perform A

I believe that this second analysis is misguided. (57), i.e. 'asking H *not to perform A*' is surely not equivalent to (51a), i.e. 'asking H to *pretend to perform A*'. The difference between the two analyses is shown by the fact that in the following types of example, where the speaker is simply asking the hearer (indirectly) not to perform the act described, *taha* is unacceptable. (58) may be uttered as a desperate emotional appeal whereby the speaker implicitly communicates the propositional-attitude information in (59):

(58)   *Fige, … ki   as ipofero ego.*
        Leave   and let suffer I
        'Leave, and let me suffer.'

(59)   S is pleading with the hearer not to leave.

And (60) may be uttered as a desperate threat whereby the speaker implicitly communicates the propositional-attitude information in (61):

(60)   *Fige   lipon, tolma mono.*
        Leave then   dare just
        'Leave then, … just you dare!'

(61)   S is resenting the thought that H leave.

In both (58) and (60) the speaker is indirectly asking the hearer 'not to perform A'; but because neither explicitly or implicitly asks the hearer to 'pretend to act in such-and-such a way', *taha* cannot be attached to either of them. Thus, (58a) and (60a) make no sense at all:

(58)   a.   *Taha fige ki   as ipofero ego.*
                 leave and let suffer   I
                 '*taha* leave and let me suffer.'

(60)   a.   * *Taha fige lipon, tolma mono.*
                 leave then dare just
                 '*Taha* leave then, just you dare.'

I would therefore like to suggest that the information directly communicated by *taha* in imperatives is (51a), not (57). In other words, the interpretation in (51a) is largely triggered by the semantics of the particle, i.e. its 'as if, as though' meaning in Modern Greek, or as Tzartzanos (1996[1953]:255) puts it, its primary use to denote "something that is pretended or imaginary (as in dream narratives)". Here, *taha* falls within the scope of the imperative: the speaker presents it as desirable that the hearer make *as if* to perform the action described in the proposition expressed. The equivalent in English would be something like 'Seem to do X', or 'Appear to do X'.

With respect to interrogatives, I do not agree with Pavlidou that *taha* turns a genuine request for information into a rhetorical question or a mere expression of doubt. Notice that an interrogative utterance may be rhetorical or express doubt irrespective of whether *taha* is attached to it. This is the case for (62a) and (63a) respectively:

(62)   a.   *Tha erthi?*
                 will come-3D
                 'Will he come?'

        b.   *Taha tha erthi?*
                 will come-3D
                 '*Taha*, will he come?'

(63)   a.   *Ine i   proti fora pou argi?*
                 is it the first time that is late.
                 'Is it the first time she is late?'

        b.   *Taha ine i   proti fora pou argi?*
                 is the first time that is late.
                 '*Taha* is it the first time she is late?'

(62a) may clearly communicate the propositional-attitude information in (64a), and (63a) may clearly communicate the propositional-attitude information in (64b) (perhaps with the aid of paralinguistic clues):

(64) a. S doubts whether X will come.
   b. S implies that X is usually/always late.

I believe that what *taha* is doing in (62b) and (63b) is making this information a little more accessible, as in 'Is he supposed to come?', or 'Do you think it's the first time he is late?'. The speaker will attach *taha* in an interrogative when she cannot trust the hearer to infer the intended propositional-attitude information for himself, or when she simply wants to ensure that such information will be communicated. Again, the particle falls inside, rather than outside, the scope of the interrogative.

An obvious advantage of this account is that *taha* may be treated as encoding the same linguistic meaning in all sentence types, as indicated below:

Declaratives
(65) **Taha** *ine exipnos.*
     is   clever.
   'Supposedly, he is clever.'

Interrogatives
(66) *Ine* **taha** *omorfi?*
   Is   pretty
   'Is she supposed to be pretty?'

Imperatives
(67) **Taha** *malose ton.*
     scold   him
   'Supposedly scold him.'

In all the above examples, *taha* carries its basic meaning of 'it seems', 'it appears', 'it is supposed', irrespective of sentence type: (65) can be paraphrased as 'It seems he is clever', (66) can be paraphrased as 'Does it seem to people that she is pretty?' and (67) as 'Make it seem as if you're scolding him'. In this way, the problem in Pavlidou's account, pointed out in section 2, whereby *taha* looked as if it encoded something different in imperatives, i.e. 'Pretend P', and in declaratives, i.e. 'not — P', does not arise.

According to this relevance-theoretic account, *taha* guides the hearer to access and consider assumptions which contribute to the explicit content of an utterance, but which may or may be not retrieved in the absence of the particle. Suppose I think that John is a spy but I do not want to be held responsible for expressing this belief myself. Still, I may want to make a colleague aware of the possibility that John could be a spy. By using *taha*, I can communicate not only the higher-level explicature in (68a), but a range of further assumptions illustrated in (68b–f):

(68) a. It seems to S that John is a spy.
      b. S heard that John is a spy.
      c. S does not believe that John is a spy.
      d. S is not certain that John is a spy.
      e. But it may be that case that John is a spy.
      f. If John is a spy, I should be more cautious.
          . . . . I should reconsider our partnership.
      . . .

And it is on such propositional-attitude information that the relevance of the utterance may largely depend.

Consider now the interrogatives in (69), produced by someone talking about me:

(69) a. *Ine i   proti fora pou argi?*
          Is   the first time that is late.
          'Is it the first time she is late?'
      b. *Taha ine i   proti fora pou argi?*
                is   the first time that is late.
          '*Taha* is it the first time she is late?'

Suppose that (69a) and (69b) are both intended by the speaker as rhetorical questions implying that I am usually late for my classes. Both may communicate a range of further assumptions such as:

(70) a. S believes that I am always late for my classes.
      b. S believes that I am unreliable.
      c. S thinks that I am unsuitable for the post.
      . . . .

By using *taha*, the speaker overtly stresses that the relevance of her utterance largely depends on the propositional-attitude information in (70a–c). In the absence of *taha* the same information may be communicated, but not as forcefully as with (69b). So, *taha* not only guarantees that the above propositional-attitude information will be communicated but it also guarantees that it will be communicated with an extra degree of emphasis or force.

Finally, compare the imperatives in (71):

(71) a. *Pigene os tin porta.*
go to the door
'Walk to the door.'
b. ***Taha** pigene os tin porta.*
go to the door
'*Taha*, walk to the door.'

Unless some paralinguistic features provide clear clues to the 'Pretend that you walk to the door' interpretation, (71a) could not be interpreted in this way. Thus, in the case of imperatives, *taha* gives rise to assumptions that would not otherwise be communicated; in the absence of *taha* the information in (71b) could not normally be conveyed. In this way, the difference between a declarative, interrogative or imperative utterance with *taha* and one without is explained, an issue which has not been addressed before.

7.3.4 Conceptual or procedural?

In chapters 5.5.1 and 6.4, I argued that hearsay adverbials and parentheticals are conceptual, i.e. they encode concepts rather than procedures. In chapter 6.5.3, I argued that hearsay adverbials such as *allegedly*, *reportedly*, and hearsay parentheticals such as *Bill says*, *the newspaper reported yesterday*, mark the proposition that falls within their scope as being interpretively rather than descriptively used. In particular, they indicate that the views being interpreted are not the speaker's own. Because of this, they make an essential contribution to truth conditions. The hearsay parentheticals ως γνωστόν (as is known), όπως ακούστηκε/μαθεύτηκε (as has been heard/known), κατά την αντίληψη/μαρτυρία του χ (according to x's opinion/testimony) in Modern Greek have a similar effect on the proposition that falls within their scope. Thus, hearsay adverbials and parentheticals are *conceptual* and *truth-conditional*.

I now want to argue that although hearsay/evidential uses of the particle *taha* in Modern Greek, hearsay particles such as *ré* in Sissala and *tte* in Japanese (to be discussed in more detail in 7.4) and classic morphological evidentials such as *-boti* and *soo da* in Patwin and Japanese respectively, are also truth-conditional, they differ from hearsay adverbials and parentheticals in one major respect: hearsay particles and morphological evidentials are *procedural*, whereas, as we have seen, hearsay adverbials and parentheticals, as well as evidential adverbials, are conceptual. In particular, I shall argue that hearsay particles and morphological evidentials encode procedural constraints on explicatures: they facilitate the construction of the intended higher-level explicatures, which mark the proposition expressed as being attributively rather than descriptively used. The notion of *constraints on explicatures* was introduced by Wilson and Sperber (1993) with reference to pronouns and mood indicators. Pronouns were treated as encoding *procedural constraints on truth-conditional content*, whereas mood indicators were treated as encoding *procedural constraints on higher-level explicatures*. I shall argue that hearsay markers and morphological evidentials fall into the same category as mood indicators: they encode procedural constraints on higher-level explicatures. Let us examine the issues in more detail.

Wilson and Sperber (1993) argue that mood indicators encode information constraining the inferential process of constructing higher-level explicatures: declaratives indicate that the state of affairs described is regarded as actual; imperatives indicate that the state of affairs described is regarded as achievable and desirable. Interrogatives are markers of a certain type of interpretive use (see Wilson and Sperber 1988 for further discussion). The differences between declarative sentences and their non-declarative counterparts are explained in terms of the higher-level explicatures they communicate. Thus, we might expect other types of interpretive-use marker — for example hearsay particles — to be analysable along the same lines as mood indicators, i.e. as encoding procedural constraints on higher-level explicatures. This is what I will attempt to show.

The fact that an utterance or clause is interrogative, and hence interpretively rather than descriptively used, can be indicated by a variety of means: for example, by intonation, by use of a question mark in written texts, by use of 'whether' or 'if' in subordinate clauses, and by the presence of wh-words or subject-aux inversion in main clauses. In several languages, for example Japanese (Itani 1993: 129–147), it can also be indicated by use of an interrogative particle, suggesting that particles can be treated along the same lines as other types of mood indicator. As Wilson and Sperber point out, given the existence of a distinction between conceptual and procedural encoding, it would be hard to justify treating a syntactic construction like subject-auxiliary order, or a phonological phenomenon such as intonation, in conceptual rather than procedural terms. At worst, it seems to lead to something like the performative analysis of non-declaratives, which was abandoned many years ago (see Levinson 1983; Lycan 1984).

Wilson (1998–9) suggests two further types of argument in favour of a procedural, rather than a conceptual, treatment of mood indicators. The first involves embedded infinitival clauses. Many semanticists provide plausible analyses of infinitival clauses as representing *possible* states of affairs. But if this information were conceptually encoded, then the sentences in (72) should have something like the semantic representations in (73):

(72) a. To pass the exam would be good for John.
     b. John wants to pass the exam.

(73) a. For it to be possible for John to pass the exam would be good for John.
     b. John wants it to be possible to pass the exam.

As Wilson observes, these semantic representations do not capture the meanings of these utterances. For (72a), the meaning is not that it would be good for John to be *able* to pass the exam, but that it would be good for John to *pass* it. Similarly, for (72b), the meaning is not that John wants to be *able* to pass the exam, but that he wants actually to *pass* it. To preserve the insights of these semantic analyses, infinitival clauses are better analysed as conveying the required information procedurally rather than conceptually. As Wilson observes, procedural information need not be thought of as contributing separate assumptions which the hearer must automatically pay attention to, but merely as providing clues to information which may be confirmed or independently encoded elsewhere in the utterance. In (72b), for example, the verb 'want' already indicates that the embedded clause represents a desirable — hence possible — state of affairs, and the morphological infinitival marking merely confirms this independently encoded information (see Rouchota 1994 for further discussion).

The second type of argument is based on the fact that not all the clues in a given sentence may point in the same direction. If indicators *encode* their associated assumptions, the result should be a contradiction, and yet no contradiction is perceived. An example might be declarative sentences uttered with interrogative intonation. Consider (74b):

(74) a. Which train will you catch tomorrow?
     b. I'll catch the 5 o'clock train?[6]

According to relevance theory, declarative indicators mark the utterance as a case of *saying that*, whereas interrogative indicators mark it as a case of *asking whether*. There is a danger that (74b) would result in something approaching a contradiction if this speech-act information were treated as conceptually encoded.

By contrast, treating mood indicators as encoding procedural information, i.e. as merely providing clues to the direction in which the intended relevance is to be sought, might allow this information to be integrated without contradiction.

As noted above, many languages contain interrogative particles which function as mood indicators, and should, on the above account, be analysed in procedural rather than conceptual terms. These arguments generalize straightforwardly to hearsay particles and other morphological evidentials. Reported speech and attributive use can be indicated by a variety of means — for example, quotation marks in written text, certain types of intonation in spoken language, various inflectional markings such as the French 'reportative conditional' which can, among other things, be a marker of interpretive use. Similarly, degrees of commitment to the proposition expressed, and, more generally, the speaker's attitude to an opinion echoed, can be indicated by intonation and prosodic structure (e.g. pitch, rate, voice quality) as well as by the mood indicators and particles noted above. Again, there is no advantage in treating these phenomena in conceptual terms, given that the alternative of procedural encoding exists.

In fact, there seems to be *no* evidence that either interrogative or hearsay particles encode conceptual information: they cannot be negated, they cannot be the focus of cleft sentences, they cannot be combined with other words to create more complex expressions with a compositional semantic structure. It is no surprise, then, that these arguments generalize straightforwardly to *taha*.

Note first that a speaker who uses the particle *taha* in (75) cannot lay herself open to charges of untruthfulness in its use:

(75) a. John: *Taha itan   arosti.*
                  was-3D ill
                  'Apparently/She says she was ill.'

     b. Mary: **Then les   alithia.*
                  do not tell-2SG truth
                  'You are not telling the truth.'
                  Tin ida   simera k' edihne   mia hara.
                  her saw-1SG today and seemed-3SG fine
                  'I've seen her today and she seemed fine.'

Mary's reply in (75b) sounds odd. This can be explained on the assumption that *taha* in (75a) encodes procedural rather than conceptual meaning, which cannot be brought into the forefront of attention enough to be challenged. Compare the conceptual English versions 'Apparently she was ill', or 'She says she was ill', which are, of course, open to challenge on the ground of untruthfulness, as we have seen in previous chapters. These differences are explained on the assumption that *taha* is procedural rather than conceptual.

Moreover, *taha* cannot be a constituent of more complex particle phrases which undergo the regular compositional rules, in a way parallel to adverbial phrases. Consider (76):

(76) a. *Ine ohi mono ipothetika plousios, alla pragmatika.*
          is   not only supposedly rich,   but truly
          'He is not only supposedly rich, but truly so'.
      b. *Ite   fenomenika plousios, ite pragmatika emena mou aresi.*
          either apparently rich,   or truly   to   me likes
          'Either supposedly rich, or truly so, I like him.'

(77) a. **Ine ohi mono **taha**   plousios, alla pragmatika.*
          is   not only supposedly rich,   but truly
          'He is not only supposedly rich, but trully so'.
      b. **Ite   **taha**   plousios, ite pragmatika emena mou aresi.*
          either supposedly rich,   or truly   to   me likes
          'Either supposedly rich, or truly so, I like him.'

In (76a–b), the MG evidential adverbials *ipothetika* (supposedly) or *fenomenika* (apparently), which carry the same meaning as *taha*, yield perfectly acceptable utterances. In (77a–b), however, where the adverbials are replaced with *taha*, the utterances become clearly unacceptable.

Similarly, *taha* cannot be the focus of cleft sentences, and its meaning is hard to bring to consciousness and analyse in conceptual terms. All this suggests that it is better analysed in procedural rather than conceptual terms, as encoding a constraint on the inferential phase of comprehension. Similar arguments should be able to be produced for the other evidential/hearsay particles considered in this chapter.

A question that has been raised in the course of this chapter is how the hearer recovers the intended interpretation of *taha*, i.e. a hearsay or an evidential one. That is, how does the hearer decide whether the speaker intended him to recover the higher-level explicature in (78) or (79):

(78)   It is said that P   (hearsay)

(79)   It seems to the speaker that P   (evidential)

I have suggested that both these explicatures can be derived via pragmatic enrichment of a basic meaning along the lines of 'supposedly', or 'it is supposed'.

More precisely, in the course of interpretation, the question may arise of *who* supposes, or *why* it is supposed. Just as *apparently* in English often has a hearsay interpretation (the evidence is obtained from what someone said), so *taha* may be enriched to a hearsay interpretation. Alternatively, it may be enriched to 'it seems *to the speaker*', in which case a weak evidential (self-attributive) reading will be derived.

In either case, the communicative principle of relevance should warrant the selection of a single interpretation at most. Let us examine this process in more detail with reference to example (80):

(80)   *O   Yiannis itan **taha** arostos.*
     the John   was   ill
     'John was taha ill.'

The particle *taha* is vague: it may undergo enrichment to mean either 'X says that …' or 'it seems to the speaker that …'. In normal circumstances, the first interpretation of (80) to occur to the hearer will be one or other of these enrichments, along the lines of either (78) or (79). Suppose that the first interpretation the hearer recovers is the hearsay one, i.e. 'John says that he's been ill'. This will then be tested using the relevance-theoretic comprehension procedure (Sperber and Wilson 1998a):

Relevance -theoretic comprehension procedure

a.   Follow a path of least effort in deriving cognitive effects.
b.   Stop when your expectation of relevance is satisfied.

Clause (a) favours the most accessible interpretation, as long as this give rise to enough cognitive effects to satisfy the hearer's expectation of relevance. If the assumption that John says he's ill does satisfy the hearer's expectation of relevance, then according to clause (b), he should look no further: the first satisfactory interpretation is the only satisfactory interpretation, and is the one the hearer should choose.

I would now like to end this chapter by returning to a question raised earlier, about whether there are any strictly hearsay markers, as opposed to more general markers of interpretive or attributive use.

7.4   Some genuine hearsay markers?

Itani (1996, 1998) argues that the Japanese particle *tte* has a genuine hearsay function. Consider her examples (81)–(82):

(81)   Mary wa kashikoi *tte*.
       Mary is smart, *I hear*.

(82)   Mary wa kashikoi *tte*!
       Mary is smart, *did she say that?*

These examples suggest that the function of *tte* corresponds almost exactly to that of *X said* — i.e. it indicates that the proposition that falls within its scope is a direct or indirect report of speech. Unlike the Sissala particle *ré, tte* is restricted to reports of *speech*, rather than thought. It may occur with a report of thought only if that thought has been verbally expressed to the speaker. To illustrate, consider (83):

(83)   A: What does Mary's teacher think of her?
       B: Mary wa kashikoi *tte*.
            Mary is smart, *she thinks*.

According to Itani, (83B) could only be used if the teacher had verbally expressed the thought in question, and this is indicated by the use of *tte*. As Itani puts it, "*tte* carries a strong aspect of the hearsay or quotative, and in fact covers only a subset of types of 'attributive use': it is used, precisely, to attribute *utterances*, not thoughts." (Itani 1993: 145)

   Thus, the Japanese particle *tte* seems to be the best candidate for a genuine hearsay particle, which can be attached to all and only reports of speech. Such a device would have an obvious function: it would inform the hearer about what someone actually said, rather than thought, and this is what we often want to know. The *tte* particle would simply encode this information by procedural rather than conceptual means: it would trigger the construction of a conceptual representation along the lines of 'X said that ...', 'X expressed the view that ...', 'X uttered the words that ...' etc. (see Wilson 2000 for further discussion).

   A second possible type of genuine hearsay device might be quotation marks, discussed briefly above. However, their function is more restrictive: quotation marks are used mainly for *direct* quotation: we do not normally put quotation marks round indirect reports of speech. Moreover, we do use quotation marks for other reasons — for example, to mention (rather than use) a word or phrase. Consider (84):

(84)   How do you spell 'acknowledgement'?

Here, the quotation marks indicate mention rather than use of a word. They are attached to an abstract rather than an attributed representation: they do not indicate that the word was actually uttered by someone. We can imagine a speaker introducing a new word that has never been uttered by anyone, and putting it into quotation marks to show that it was being mentioned rather than used. These quotation marks do not function as 'hearsay' devices. Quotation marks can also indicate that a word is being loosely used. Consider (85):

(85)   Your arguments are, so to speak, 'fuzzy'.

Here, the quotation marks indicate some type of loose use or rough approximation. (85) is not a report of actual speech, but a report of what someone *might* say. Again, the function is not strictly attributive, and goes beyond what we expect from a regular hearsay device.

Notice that this suggests another argument against the idea put forward by linguists such as Palmer, Chafe etc., that hearsay markers invariably indicate weakened commitment. That analysis presupposes that the whole proposition is being reported rather than used. But what very often happens is that most of an utterance is descriptive, with just one word, or phrase, or clause, being reported speech or interpretive use. This again shows the importance of distinguishing between the notion of interpretive use and the notion of diminished commitment.

In this chapter, I have considered a variety of 'hearsay' particles and other devices which have been treated as having evidential function. My main claim has been that these indicate a shift from descriptive use to some form of interpretive representation, or representation by resemblance, of which the most notable subtype is attributive interpretive use. I have also argued that although they share this function with hearsay adverbials and parentheticals, they perform it in a rather different way: by procedural rather than conceptual encoding. If I am right, then 'evidentials' in general, and 'hearsay devices' in particular, do not form a unitary class from the semantic point of view, despite their similarities in pragmatic function.

Chapter 8

Conclusions

A survey of the literature on 'evidentiality' in the *Introduction* of this book showed that the notion of 'evidential' has been mostly applied to a class of linguistic expressions with a particular pragmatic function. This function is twofold: evidentials indicate the source of knowledge, and the speaker's degree of certainty about the proposition expressed. In my initial survey of the literature, I pointed out that these functions could be performed without being linguistically encoded, and that even linguistically encoded evidentials require a substantial amount of pragmatic interpretation. I therefore chose to approach the study of evidentials from the broadest possible perspective, looking at both semantic and pragmatic questions and trying to develop a unified approach. The three main questions I set out to answer were the following: (i) is there a pragmatic framework which adequately accounts for the role of pragmatic inference in the interpretation of evidentials? (ii) are evidentials semantically truth-conditional or non-truth-conditional? (iii) is evidential information explicitly or implicitly communicated? Having considered the two main existing semantic/pragmatic frameworks, speech-act theory and Grice's framework of communication, I tried, using the more recent framework of relevance theory, to develop answers to these questions which would preserve the insights of earlier approaches while avoiding their defects. In this concluding chapter, I will briefly summarise my result.

8.1 Evidentials and pragmatic inference

The framework of relevance theory, outlined in chapter 4, seems to provide an adequate account of the role of pragmatic inference in the interpretation of evidentials. In relevance theory, satisfying the hearer's expectation of relevance is supposed to shed light on every aspect of utterance interpretation, from the identification of explicit content to the identification of intended contextual implications and cognitive effects. At various points in my analysis of evidentials, I have shown how satisfying the hearer's expectation of relevance interacts with linguistically encoded content and a context of available assumptions to yield the expected results.

One important difference between relevance theory and previous frameworks such as Grice's is that it contains no maxims of Quality, i.e. no principle corresponding to Grice's maxims of truthfulness and evidence. Since these are precisely the principles that Griceans would use to account for pragmatically inferred information, this led me to examine the question of how commitment is ever communicated at all in a framework that lacks them. Here I looked at two features of the relevance-theoretic framework: first the notion that assumptions may differ in strength, and second the notion of optimal relevance itself. My main claim was as follows. An assumption with no strength (i.e. a totally unevidenced assumption, for example a groundless speculation) can achieve no relevance. Relevance is achieved by modifying a set of existing assumptions, by strengthening them, contradicting and eliminating them, or combining with them to yield contextual implications. An assumption with no strength can achieve relevance in none of these ways. Yet a speaker aiming at optimal relevance must intend her utterance to be relevant enough to be worth the hearer's attention. It follows that she must expect at least some of the assumptions expressed and implied by her utterance to be strong enough (i.e. evidenced enough) to achieve the intended effects. The results are similar to those achieved by Grice's maxims of Quality, but much weaker: in particular, in the framework of relevance theory, a speaker can achieve optimal relevance by *saying* something false, as long as enough of the intended implications of her utterance are true. Regarding pragmatic inference of degrees of speaker commitment, relevance theorists have repeatedly emphasized that not only the proposition expressed, but the speaker's intended *attitude* towards the proposition expressed is recovered through the process of enrichment, — an inferential process of filling in partially specified representations. Thus, propositional-attitude information is also recovered by satisfying the hearer's expectation of relevance: the hearer is justified in choosing only the first, i.e. most accessible interpretation, which yields adequate effects for no unjustifiable effort, in a way the speaker could manifestly have foreseen. When no specific linguistic guidance is given, the circumstances of an utterance will provide clues to the intended degree of commitment. If the circumstances make highly accessible a particular hypothesis about the speaker's degree of commitment, and if that hypothesis leads us to a manifestly satisfactory interpretation, then this is the only interpretation satisfying the hearer's expectation of relevance, and all other interpretations are disallowed. When there is no single highly accessible hypothesis in the circumstances, or when the most accessible hypothesis is not the intended one, then considerations of relevance dictate that additional linguistic clues, for example some illocutionary force indicator, should be given.

8.2 Evidentials and the explicit/implicit distinction

Coming to the explicit/implicit distinction, Sperber and Wilson introduce a notion of explicature, parallel to Grice's notion of implicature. The propositions recovered from developing a linguistically encoded logical form, either by disambiguating, assigning reference, resolving semantic vagueness, completing ellipsed material, or by optionally embedding the proposition expressed under a speech-act or propositional-attitude description, are the *explicatures* of an utterance. Among these, Sperber and Wilson distinguish between the *proposition expressed* and the *higher-level explicatures*. The proposition expressed determines the truth-conditions of the utterance, whereas its higher-level explicatures, although explicitly communicated, make no contribution to truth conditions. An utterance may offer the hearer more or less linguistic guidance as to what explicatures are intended; the greater the amount of linguistic decoding involved, the greater the explicitness. I suggested that in this framework, both encoded and inferred evidentials may be analysed as communicating information about higher-level explicatures, i.e. about the speaker's attitude to the proposition expressed or the speech act being performed. Thus, linguistically encoded evidentials contribute to the explicit aspect of communication. For example, the speaker of 'Clearly, John is qualified' communicates the higher-level explicature 'The speaker strongly believes that John is qualified'. Pragmatically inferred evidential information contributes to higher-level explicatures too. For example, someone who says *firmly* 'John is qualified', communicates the higher-level propositional-attitude explicature 'The speaker strongly believes that John is qualified', and performs the higher-level speech-act explicature 'The speaker asserts that John is qualified'.

This approach fills an obvious gap in Grice's framework, which I referred to in several points. Speech-act and propositional-attitude information of the type just described satisfies neither Grice's definition of what is said, nor his definition of what is (conventionally and conversationally) implicated. Sperber and Wilson's notion of explicature and higher-level explicature provide a useful means of filling this gap, into which a large amount of evidential information falls.

8.3   Evidentials and truth-conditional/non-truth-conditional semantics

Regarding non-truth-conditional meaning, I pointed out that, for both speech-act theorists and Grice, all non-truth-conditional meaning is of the same type: mood indicators, sentence adverbials, parentheticals, discourse or pragmatic connectives are all treated as non-truth-conditional indicators of the speech act the speaker intends to perform. Sperber and Wilson, following Blakemore 1987, draw a distinction between *conceptual* and *procedural* meaning, and examine on which side of the distinction each non-truth-conditional type of linguistic construction falls. The meaning of a word or other linguistic construction is *procedural* if it constrains the inferential phase of comprehension by indicating the type of inference process that the hearer is expected to go through. In this framework, discourse connectives have been analysed as encoding constraints on the implicatures of an utterance. Mood indicators are also dealt with in procedural terms, but these are analysed as constraints on explicatures: they guide the hearer towards the intended higher-level explicatures of the type described above.

Chapters 5–7 of this book were largely concerned with these distinctions between truth-conditional and non-truth-conditional semantics and conceptual and procedural meaning. In chapter 5, I looked at four types of sentence adverbials, illocutionary, attitudinal, evidential and hearsay, which, though syntactically similar, pattern in very different ways with respect to the truth-conditional/non-truth-conditional distinction. Using a standard test for truth-conditional versus non-truth-conditional meaning, I argued that while illocutionary and attitudinal adverbials are non-truth-conditional, as speech-act theorists would predict, evidential and hearsay adverbials have clearly truth-conditional readings, contrary to the predictions of speech-act theory, which treats all these adverbials as external to the proposition expressed. Despite these differences in truth-conditional status, I showed that all four classes of adverbial encode conceptual rather than procedural information, thus confirming Sperber and Wilson's claims that not all non-truth-conditional meaning is procedural, and that the conceptual/procedural distinction does not coincide exactly with the truth-conditional/non-truth-conditional distinction.

In the course of chapter 5, it became clear that sentence adverbials had much in common with a variety of syntactically parenthetical constructions, including parenthetical evidentials such as *I think, I know*. In chapter 6, I therefore examined parenthetical constructions in general, with two main questions in mind: first, can we provide a descriptive framework in which a unified treatment of evidential adverbials and parentheticals is possible? and second, is there some explanation for the differences in truth-conditional status between the various types of adverbial expression investigated in chapter 5?

The descriptive problems genuine parentheticals present were successfully dealt with in the framework of relevance theory. I showed that they pattern like sentence adverbials in two important respects: (1) They encode elements of *conceptual representations*, which may be true or false in their own right, even if they do not contribute to the truth conditions of the utterances in which they occur. (2) They contribute to explicit, rather than implicit, communication. To the extent that they are non-truth-conditional, they contribute not to the proposition expressed, but to *higher-level explicatures*. In this framework, where the explicatures of an utterance typically include (a) the proposition expressed, which determines the truth conditions of an utterance, and (b) higher-level explicatures, which make no contribution to its truth conditions, though they may be true or false in their own right, both the fact that genuine parentheticals encode concepts, and the fact that they may nonetheless be non-truth-conditional, can be described. For example, if the parenthetical *I think* in 'John is, *I think*, at the airport' is genuinely non-truth-conditional, it can be analysed as providing the hearer with explicit guidance as to the intended higher-level explicature 'Mary thinks John is at the airport'. Main-clause "parentheticals" encode concepts too, and these appear to contribute to the truth conditions of utterances in the regular way — e.g. 'I think that Bill has cheated in the exams' communicates the information 'Mary thinks that Bill has cheated in the exams'. But this information would constitute the proposition expressed by the utterance, and hence contribute to truth conditions.

It still remained to provide an explanation of why some true parenthetical constructions appear not to contribute to the truth conditions of utterances, whereas their main-clause counterparts do. In developing such an explanation, I adopted the view shared by many linguists that utterances containing genuine parentheticals create a double speech-act effect, with the parenthetical constructions being phonologically, syntactically and semantically independent of their host clauses. On this approach, the parenthetical is seen as performing a speech act which qualifies or comments upon the speech act performed by the main clause. Thus, an utterance such as 'That painting is, *I think*, the best in the museum' would make two assertions: (a) 'That painting is the best in the museum' (b) 'The speaker thinks that painting is the best in the museum'. The function of the assertion in (b) is to guide the interpretation of the assertion in (a) by encoding information about the intended higher-level explicature of this 'ground floor' assertion. The parenthetical comment has a 'fine-tuning' function, narrowing down the interpretation of the speech act to which it is appended. Similar remarks apply to the analysis of illocutionary and attitudinal adverbials. Without the parenthetical comment, the content of the higher-level explicature would have to be pragmatically inferred.

In more complex utterances, the speech act whose higher-level explicatures are 'fine-tuned' is determined by the scope possibilities for parentheticals. These may vary according to the position of the parenthetical comment in the utterance: it may occur within an embedded clause, or in complex utterances, between the two conjuncts, or at the end of each. Thus, the question I raised was: what is the phrase or clause whose interpretation the parenthetical comment modifies? Here, the following conclusions were reached. First, adverbials and parentheticals seem to behave in identical ways, as would be expected if adverbials are a sub-type of parentheticals. Second, the syntactic position of the adverbial or parenthetical affects its possibilities of interpretation. In some cases, only wide-scope interpretation is possible; in other cases, both wide-scope and narrow-scope interpretations are possible. Third, there is often a preferred interpretation, which is affected by at least the following factors: syntactic structure (main-clause vs subordinate clause), semantic structure (factive vs non-factive) and semantic content (of the parenthetical comment and the clause to which it is attached). Fourth, factive and non-factive structures affect the behaviour of parentheticals and adverbials: when they appear inside factive clauses, narrow-scope interpretation is either preferred or mandatory; when they appear inside non-factive clauses, narrow-scope interpretation becomes much harder. Fifth, I suggested that the preferred interpretation of the scope of parentheticals results from an interaction between 'least effort' parsing principles, the semantic content of parenthetical and host clauses, and the hearer's expectation of relevance. Finally, I suggested that even a narrow-scope interpretation is not necessarily perceived as truth-conditional, i.e. it need not be perceived as falling within the scope of truth-conditional connectives to yield a unitary set of truth conditions for the utterance as a whole.

Precisely because of its unified nature, this analysis sheds no light on the differences in truth-conditional status which the various types of sentence adverbials and parenthetical construction seem to exhibit. Thus, the question I raised next was: why is it that some narrow-scope interpretations seem to fall within the scope of logical connectives and thus contribute to the truth conditions of the utterance as a whole, while others do not? In speech-act terms, the question is why for evidential and hearsay adverbials, *both* speech acts seem to fall within the scope of embedding connectives, and why, with illocutionary and attitudinal adverbials, only the ground-floor speech act seems to fall within the scope of embedding connectives? My main claim was as follows: A parenthetical comment is truth-conditional when and only when it alters the truth-conditional status of the proposition it modifies. It may do this in one of two ways: first, by functioning as a marker of interpretive rather than descriptive use. Such markers necessarily affect the truth-conditional status of propositions that fall within their scope. This is the reason why hearsay adverbials and hearsay parentheticals are perceived as making an essential contribution to truth conditions. Moreover, I showed why a parenthetical such as *I think*, which indicates that the views being interpreted are the speaker's own, may be perceived as roughly equivalent to descriptive use. Illocutionary adverbials such as *frankly, seriously* do not affect the truth-conditional status of the proposition that falls within their scope, and hence are inessential to truth conditions. Their function is to indicate the manner in which some speech-act is being performed, without altering the truth-conditional status of this speech act in any way. Parenthetical comments, and sentence adverbials, may affect truth conditions in a second way: by altering the strength of the assumption communicated, and hence speaker's degree of commitment to the proposition that falls within their scope. Thus, evidential adverbials such as *obviously, apparently, do* affect the truth-conditional status of the proposition that falls within their scope. In particular, I distinguished between weak evidentials, e.g. *apparently, seemingly*, which reduce the range of potential falsifying evidence, and strong evidentials, e.g. *obviously, clearly*, which increase the range of such evidence. I drew a parallel with non-evidential items such as the weak *possibly, probably*, versus the strong *necessarily, certainly*, all of which are clearly truth-conditional. Finally, for attitudinal adverbials such as *unfortunately* and *sadly*, I argued that they are non-truth-conditional since they are not interpretive use markers, and do not affect the strength of the proposition that falls within their scope.

Towards the end of chapter 6, I investigated how true parentheticals and their non-parenthetical counterparts differ pragmatically, i.e. how their presence and position in the sentence affects utterance interpretation. I argued that genuine parentheticals do not always weaken the speaker's commitment to the proposition that falls within their scope, as speech-act theorists have claimed. Some of them weaken the speaker's commitment, whereas others may strengthen the speaker's commitment. These effects follow from an interaction between context, semantic content and the hearer's expectation of relevance. I ended the chapter by looking at a range of attitudinal parentheticals (e.g. *I hope*, *I fear*), which seem to fall midway between evidential parentheticals and attitudinal adverbials.

Finally, in chapter 7, I turned to evidentials in the narrowest sense — i.e. various particles and discourse markers. By analysing the Modern Greek particle *taha*, I showed that hearsay — evidential particles share their truth-conditional status with their English adverbial counterparts, they also contribute to the explicit aspect of communication but unlike hearsay and evidential adverbials, which are conceptual, they encode procedural information. Other constructions I looked at are those generally seen as performing a 'hearsay' function: in particular the 'hearsay' particles *ré* in Sissala and *tte* in Japanese, which have both been analysed within the relevance-theoretic framework. I argued that these should be analysed in much the same way as mood indicators: as procedural constraints on higher-level explicatures. The main point of this chapter was to show that not all encoded evidential information is semantically homogeneous: whereas hearsay adverbials and parentheticals encode concepts, hearsay particles are best analysed in procedural terms. I also argued that the term 'hearsay particle' has been used to cover a variety of rather different constructions, some of which (e.g. *ré* from Sissala) are quite general markers of interpretive use, or interpretive attributive use, whereas others (e.g. *tte* from Japanese) are indeed used only for reporting speech.

The book leaves several questions unanswered. In particular, I have only begun to investigate the very complex scope possibilities for evidential, and more generally parenthetical, expressions in embedded clauses; and I have not investigated the scope possibilities for procedural expressions, e.g. hearsay particles, at all. Moreover, my explanation of the differences in truth-conditional status between various types of sentence adverbial and parenthetical is fairly rudimentary and vague in many respects. However, I hope to have shown that the investigation of evidential expressions can yield rich and interesting results when pursued within a unified semantic/pragmatic framework such as that provided by relevance theory.

Notes

Chapter 1: Introduction

1. This is a compilation of papers presented at a conference in Berkeley (1981), especially organized to compare evidentiality and the nature of evidential devices in a variety of languages, mainly those where evidentiality is encoded in the inflectional morphology.

2. Some of the arguments in this book were first outlined in my PhD dissertation (Ifantidou 1994).

Chapter 2: Speech-act theory

1. Searle (1979: 13) claims that Austin's verdictives, e.g. *assessing, interpreting as, analysing, calculating,* (Austin 1962: 153) as well as most of his expositives, e.g. *deducing, concluding by, ?doubting, ?knowing, ?believing* (Austin 1962: 162–3) are further types of assertives. However, these are not, strictly speaking, speech acts since they can be performed silently and mentally.

2. In this section, I am drawing on Deirdre Wilson's Semantic Theory Lecture Notes (1998–9) and on Wilson and Sperber (1993).

Chapter 3: Grice and communication

1. My aim in this book is not to justify the truth-conditional/non-truth-conditional distinction, but to see how a variety of evidentials pattern with respect to it, taking *but* — the clearest case of non-truth-conditional meaning — as a base line. For analyses of *but* from truth-conditional and non-truth-conditional perspectives, see Bach 1994; Blakemore 1989; Lycan 1984; Neale 1992; Grice 1961; Wilson and Sperber 1993.

Chapter 4: Relevance theory

1. Gutt (1991) applied Sperber and Wilson's distinction between descriptive/interpretive use in interesting ways to the study of translation.

Chapter 5: Sentence adverbials

1. For a shorter version of this chapter, see also Ifantidou-Trouki (1993).

2.   Sadock, like many generative semanticists, defended the 'abstract (higher) performative hypothesis', which attempted to account for the distribution of sentence adverbials, etc., by syntactic means, i.e. by positing an abstract performative verb in syntactic deep structure. This hypothesis has long since been abandoned, and I am here considering a purely semantic/pragmatic version, on which an utterance like Sadock's (68) would be analysed as communicating the information in (72), without necessarilly encoding all this information by syntactic means. See Levinson (1983) for arguments against the abstract performative analysis.

3.   For arguments that these constructions are synonymous, see Greenbaum (1969:94–95) and Jackendoff (1972:56–57, 72). In later sections, I will look at some cases where movement of the adverb is not required.

4.   The above examples have been tried on several lecture classes and conference audiences, and they all agreed with our intuitions. Some questionnaire results supporting the analysis proposed in this chapter are reported in Koizumi (1997), who also compares this analysis with the proposal of Lycan (1984). Notice how, given a context, 'clearly' and 'obviously' clearly contribute to truth conditions. The following is an exchange I often heard, or had, during the period of the alleged economic scandal with Papandreou's government in Greece, the accusations and the trial.

X: The Government haven't been embezzling public money.
Z: A trial is in process. If the governing party clearly haven't been embezzling public money, they may even get re-elected!

5.   Both ways of eliminating the 'frankly' examples in problem (b) have been suggested to me by Deirdre Wilson.

Chapter 6: Parentheticals

1.   For a shourter version of this chapter, see also Ifantidou (1993).

2.   Note that, as Blakemore points out (1990/1), Urmson, at least, does not treat (3a) as synonymous with (3b) and (3c). The verb is a true performative only in (3a); in (3b) and (3c) it is more like a parenthetical — i.e. a two-utterance construction.

3.   Of course it is only the speaker's opinion that the clauses embedded under 'although' are facts — but that is not the point. The point is that they are *presented* as facts, and that's what the terminology 'factive' means (see Kiparsky 1971). For questionnaire results on similar examples, see Koizumi 1997.

4.   Notice that the term 'contrastive' as referring to 'although' is just a shorthand for the correct analysis, which may involve denial of expectation.

5.   The principle of Full Interpretation is a syntactic principle which requires that sentences are fully interpreted, i.e. all syntactic constituents of a sentence must receive some interpretation, for example, arguments must have theta-roles.

6.   Being a non-native speaker, I have relied quite heavily on Deirdre Wilson's intuitions on the scope possibilities for parenthetical comments.

7.   Such a commitment may be indirectly conveyed: for example, if it is assumed that the speaker of (72) would not report an allegation unless she thought there were some truth in

it. In this case, (72) would be equivalent to a descriptive use. The issue will be discussed further below in connection with the parenthetical *I think*.

8.   Context-dependent expressions of evidentiality in Balkan Slavic languages (see chapter 1: 1.3.1) can be analysed along similar lines to *I think*. In Bulgarian, for example, the definite past specifies that the speaker personally confirms the truth of the statement. This is generally taken as indicating that the speaker has direct experience of the event, hence the form's frequent description as marked for witnessing. However, as Friedman notes, in the following utterances

a.   *Beše tamo.*
'(She) was there.'

the only source of the speaker's information was a report. Similarly, the Bulgarian third person indefinite past without an auxiliary is said to mark report. However, in the following utterances

b.   *Sto na sto **bili**   pokaneni.*   (Conversation)
100%   (they) were invited
'Absolutely, they were invited'

the speaker's conviction was not based on any kind of report, but on assumptions and expectations about the normal course of similar events, i.e. a delegation being invited to a congress. In the above, and other types of data cited by Friedman, it is the speaker's attitude toward the reliability of the information, and not the evidence (report, deduction etc.) on which it is based, that affects the choice of forms. In relevance-theoretic terms, the Bulgarian definite past may, depending on the context, have either the 'direct experience' or the 'reported' interpretation, and the Bulgarian third person indefinite past without an auxiliary may, depending on the context, have either the 'reported' or the 'assumption-driven' interpretation. The speaker of either (a) or (b) should choose this utterance as long as she can trust the hearer to recover the intended higher-level explicature, and the intended type of evidential interpretation, with less effort than would be needed to process an explicit evidential marker. She would choose an utterance with an explicit evidential marker if she feels that without explicit guidance the hearer might recover the wrong higher-level explicature, and the wrong evidential interpretation.

Chapter 7: Evidential particles

1.   By the use of the term 'particle' here, I do not mean to imply the existence of a syntactic category 'particle', but merely to pick out a class of items which perform similar semantic and pragmatic functions to the sentence adverbials discussed in previous chapters, but clearly differ in syntactic status.

2.   The phonological form of the hearsay marker *ré* (or *é*) varies depending on both its syntactic and phonological environment. Thus, it is sometimes realized as *rí (í)* (see Blass 1990: 96–97).

3.   For further discussion of these varieties of interpretive use, see Wilson (2000) and Noh (2000).

4.   See also Ifantidou 2000.

5.   See also Wilson 1995.

6.   The rising intonation in (74b) is a procedural indicator of the speaker's weakened degree of commitment to the proposition expressed.

Bibliography

Anderson, Lloyd B.
  1986 "Evidentials, paths of change and mental maps: typologically regular assyme-tries". In *Evidentiality: The linguistic coding of epistemology*, W. Chafe and J. Nichols (eds), 273–312. Norwood, NJ: Ablex.
Aoki, Haruo
  1986 "Evidentials in Japanese". *In Evidentiality: The linguistic coding of epistemology*, W. Chate and J. Nichols (eds), 223–238. Norwood, NJ: Ablex.
Austin, John. L.
  1962 *How to do things with words*. Oxford: Clarendon Press.
  1979 [1946] "Other minds". In *Philosophical Papers*, J.O. Urmson and G.J. Warnock (eds), 76–116. Oxford: Oxford University Press.
Avramides, Anita
  1989 *Meaning and mind*. Cambridge, Mass: MIT Press.
Bach, Kent
  1975 "Performatives are statements too". *Philosophical Studies* 28: 229–36.
  1994a "Semantic slack: What is said and more". In *Foundations of speech-act theory: Philosophical and linguistic perspectives*, S. Tsohatzidis (ed.), 267–291. London: Routledge.
  1994b "Conversational implicature". *Mind and Language* 9: 124–162.
Bach, Kent and Harnish, Robert N.
  1979 *Linguistic communication and speech acts*. Cambridge, Mass: MIT Press.
Ballard, D. Lee
  1974 "Telling like it was said, Part 1:4 The "hearsay particle" of Philippine languages". *Notes on Translation* 51: 28. [Summer Institute of Linguistics, Dallas, TX].
Barnes, Janet
  1984 "Evidentials in the Tuyuca verb". *International Journal of American Linguistics* 50: 255–271.
Bennett, Jonathan
  1976 *Linguistic behaviour*. Cambridge: Cambridge University Press.
Benveniste, Emile
  1971 [1958] "Subjectivity in language". In *Problems in general linguistics*, E. Benveniste, 223–230. Florida: University of Miami Press.
Blackburn, Simon
  1984 *Spreading the word*. Oxford: Oxford University Press.
Blakemore, Diane
  1987 *Semantic constraints on relevance*. Oxford: Blackwell.

1989   "Denial and contrast: a relevance-theoretic analysis of *but*". *Linguistics and Philosophy* 12: 15–38.

1990/1 "Performatives and parentheticals". *Proceedings of the Aristotelian Society* LXXXXI: 197–213.

1992   *Understanding utterances.* Oxford: Blackwell.

1994   "Evidence and modality". In *The encyclopedia of language and linguistics*, R. Asher and J. Simpson (eds), 1183–1186. Oxford: Pergamon Press.

Blass, Regina

1989   "Grammaticalization of interpretive use: the case of *ré* in Sissala". *Lingua* 79: 299–326.

1990   *Relevance relations in discourse: A study with special reference to Sissala.* Cambridge: Cambridge University Press.

Boas, Franz

1911a   "Introduction". In *Handbook of American Indian languages*, Part I (Smithsonian Institution, Bureau of American Ethnology, Bulletin 40), F. Boas (ed.), 1–83. Washington: Government Printing Office.

1911b   "Kwakiutl". In *Handbook of American Indian languages*, Part I (Smithsonian Institution, Bureau of American Ethnology, Bulletin 40), F. Boas (ed.), 423–557. Washington: Government Printing Office.

1947   "Kwakiutl grammar, with a glossary of the suffixes". *Transactions of the American Philosophical Society* 37(3): 201–377.

Brockway, Diane

1981   "Semantic constraints on relevance". In *Possibilities and limitations of pragmatics*, H. Parret, M. Sbisa and J. Verschueren (eds), 57–78. Amsterdam and Philadelphia: John Benjamins.

1983   "Pragmatic connectives". Paper delivered to the Linguistic Association of Great Britain.

Burton-Roberts, Noel

1999   "Apposition". In *The Concise Encyclopaedia of Grammatical Categories*, K. Brown and J. Miller (eds), 25–29. Amsterdam: Elsevier.

Bybee, Joan

1985   *Morphology: a study of the relation between meaning and form* [*Typological Studies in Language 9*]. Amsterdam and Philadelphia: John Benjamins.

Carston, Robyn

1988   "Implicature, explicature and truth-theoretic semantics". In *Mental representations: The interface between language and reality*, R. Kempson (ed.), 155–182. Cambridge: Cambridge University Press.

1993   "Conjunction, explanation and relevance". *Lingua* 90, 1/2: 27–48.

(forthcoming) *Thoughts and utterances: The pragmatics of explicit communication.* To b published by Blackwell, Oxford

Chafe, Wallace L.

1979   "Caddoan". In *The languages of native America: Historical and comparative assessment*, L. Campbell and M. Mithun (eds), 213–235. Austin and London: University of Texas Press.

1986   "Evidentiality in English conversation and academic writing". In *Evidentiality: The linguistic coding of epistemology*, W. Chafe and J. Nichols (eds), 261–272. New Jersey: Ablex.

Chomsky, Noam

1980   *Rules and representations*. Oxford: Blackwell.

1986   *Knowledge of Language: Its nature, origin, and use*. New York: Praeger.

Clark, Billy

1991   *Relevance theory and the semantics of non-declaratives*. University of London Ph.D. Thesis.

1993   "Let and let's: Procedural encoding and explicature". *Lingua* 90, 1/2: 173–200.

Cresswell, Max

1979   "Review of Lyons 1977". *Linguistics and Philosophy* 3 (2): 289–295.

Crystal, David

1991   *A Dictionary of Linguistics & Phonetics* (3d ed.) Oxford: Blackwell.

DeLancey, Scott

1986   "Evidentiality and volitionality in Tibetan". In *Evidentiality: The linguistic coding of epistemology*, W. Chafe and J. Nichols (eds), 203–213. New Jersey: Ablex.

Derbyshire, Desmond C.

1979   *Hixkaryana*. Amsterdam: Lingua Descriptive Series, 1.

Emonds, Joseph

1979   "Appositive relatives have no properties". *Linguistic Inquiry* 10: 211–243.

Espinal, Teresa

1991   "The representation of disjunct constituents". *Language* 67: 726–762.

Fabb, Nigel

1990   "The difference between English restrictive and nonrestrictive relative clauses". *Journal of Linguistics* 26: 57–78.

Fodor, Jerry A.

1983   *The modularity of mind*. Cambridge, Mass: MIT Press.

Friedman, Victor A.

1986   "Evidentiality in the Balkans: Bulgarian, Macedonian, and Albanian". In *Evidentiality: The linguistic coding of epistemology*, W. Chafe and J. Nichols (eds), 168–187. New Jersey: Ablex.

Ginet, Carl

1979   "Performativity". *Linguistics and Philosophy* 3: 245–265.

Givón, Talmy

1982   "Evidentiality and epistemic space". *Studies in Language* 6: 23–49.

Goral, Don

1974   "How adverbs can be unbelievably strange". *Berkeley Studies in Syntax & Semantics* 1: XIII-1–XIII-12.

Greenbaum, Sidney

1969   *Studies in English adverbial usage*. London: Longmans.

Grice, H. Paul

1961   "The causal theory of perception". *Proceedings of the Aristotelian Society*, Supplementary vol. 35: 121–152, reprinted in *Studies in the way of words*, P. Grice 1989: 224–247. Cambridge, Mass: Harvard University Press.

1967   *Logic and conversation*. William James Lectures, reprinted in *Studies in the way of words*, P. Grice 1989: 1–143. Cambridge, Mass: Harvard University Press.

Gutt, Ernst-August

1991   *Translation and relevance*. Oxford: Blackwell.

Haegeman, Liliane

1984   "Remarks on adverbial clauses and definite NP anaphora". *Linguistic Inquiry* 15: 712–715.

1991   "Parenthetical adverbials: The radical orphanage approach". In *Aspects of Modern English Linguistics: Papers presented to Masamoto Ukaji on His 60th Birthday*, C. Shukim, A. Ogawa, Y. Fuiwara, N. Yamada, O. Koma and T. Yagi (eds), 232–254. Tokyo: Kaitakushi.

Hand, Michael

1993   "Parataxis and parentheticals". *Linguistics and Philosophy* 16: 495–507.

Hare, Richard M.

1971 [1970] "Meaning and speech acts". In *Practical inferences*, R. M. Hare, 74–93. London: Macmillan.

Harman, Gilbert

1968   "Three levels of meaning". *Journal of Philosophy* 65: 590–602.

1974   "Review of Schiffer 1972". *Journal of Philosophy* 71: 224–229.

1975   "Language, Thought and Communication". In *Language, mind and knowledge* [Minnesota Studies in the Philosophy of Science, VII], K. Gunderson (ed.), 270–298. Minneapolis: Univ. of Minnesota Press.

Harnish, Robert M.

1977   "Logical form and implicature". In *An integrated theory of linguistic ability*, T. Bever, J. Katz and T. Langendoen (eds), 313–391. Sussex: The Harvester Press.

Hartvigson, Hans H.

1969   *On the intonation and position of the so-called sentence modifiers in present-day English*. Odense: Odense Univ. Press.

Hedenius, Ingemar

1963   "Performatives". *Theoria* 29: 115–136.

Holdcroft, David

1978   *Words and deeds*. Oxford: Oxford University Press.

Horn, Larry

1984   "Towards a new taxonomy for pragmatic inference: Q-based and R-base implicature". In *Meaning, form and use in context (GURT 1984)*, D. Schiffrin (ed.), 11–42. Washington: Georgetown University Press.

Ifantidou-Trouki, Elly

1993   "Sentential adverbs and relevance". *Lingua* 90, 1/2: 69–90.

Ifantidou, Elly

1993   "Parentheticals and relevance". *UCL Working Papers in Linguistics* 5: 193–210.

1994   *Evidentials and relevance.* University of London PhD thesis.

2000   "Procedural encoding of explicatures by The Modern Greek particle *taha*". In *Pragmatic markers and propositional attitude*, G. Andersen and T. Fretheim (eds), 119–143. Amsterdam and Philadelphia: John Benjamins.

Itani, Reiko

1993   "The Japanese sentence-final particle *ka*: A relevance-theoretic approach". *Lingua* 90: 129–148.

1996   *Semantics and Pragmatics of hedges in English and Japanese.* Tokyo: Hituzi Syobo.

1998   "A relevance-based analysis of hearsay particles: With special reference to Japanese sentence-final particle *tte*". In *Relevance theory: Applications and implications*, R. Carston and S. Uchida (eds), 47–68. Amsterdam and Philadelphia: John Benjamins.

Jackendoff, Ray

1972   *Semantic interpretation in generative grammar.* Mass: MIT Press Cambridge.

Jacobsen, William H.

1986   "The heterogeneity of evidentials in Makah". In *Evidentiality: The linguistic coding of epistemology*, W. Chafe and J. Nichols (eds), 3–28. Norwood, NJ: Ablex.

Jakobson, Roman

1944   "Franz Boas' approach to language". *International Journal of American Linguistics* 10: 188–195. Reprinted in *Selected writings 2: Word and language*, R. Jakobson (ed.), 1971:477–488. The Hague and Paris: Mouton.

1957   "Shifters, verbal categories, and the Russian verb". Department of Slavic Languages and Literatures, Harvard University. Reprinted in *Selected writings 2: Word and language*, R. Jakobson (ed.), 1971:130–147. The Hague and Paris: Mouton.

1959   "Boas' view of grammatical meaning". In *The anthropology of Franz Boas: Essays on the centennial of his birth*, W. Goldschmidt (ed.), 139–145 (American Anthropological Association, Memoir 89). Reprinted in *Selected writings 2: Word and language*, R. Jakobson (ed.), 1971:489–496. The Hague and Paris: Mouton.

Kaplan, David

1989   "Demonstratives". In *Themes from Kaplan*, J. Almog, J. Perry and H. Wettstein (eds), 481–563. Oxford: Oxford University Press.

Katz, Jerrold

1972   *Semantic theory.* New York: Harper and Row.

Keenan, Edward L. and Keenan, Elinor O.

1976   "On the universality of conversational implicatures". *Language and Society* 5: 68–81.

Kiparsky, Carol and Kiparsky, Paul

1971   "Fact". In *Semantics: An interdisciplinary reader*, D. Steinberg and L. Jakobovits (eds), 345–369. Cambridge: Cambridge University Press.

Koizumi, Yuko

1997   *Semantics and pragmatics of sentence adverbials.* University of London MA Thesis.

Lee, Dorothy Demetracopoulou

1938   "Conceptual implications of an Indian language". *Philosophy of Science* 5: 89–102.

1944   "Linguistic reflection of Wintu thought". *International Journal of American Linguistics* 10: 181–187. Reprinted in *Freedom and culture* (Spectrum Books S-6), D. Lee 1959: 121–130. Englewood Cliffs: Prentice-Hall.

Lehrer, Adrienne
1975   "Interpreting certain adverbs: Semantics or pragmatics?" *Journal of Linguistics* 11: 239–248.

Lemmon, Edward J.
1962   "On sentences verifiable by their use". *Analysis* 22: 86–89.

Levinsohn, Steven H.
1975   "Functional perspectives in Inga". *Journal of Linguistics* 11: 1–37.

Levinson, Stephen C.
1983   *Pragmatics*. Cambridge: Cambridge University Press.

Lewis, David
1970   "General semantics". In *The semantics of natural language*. D. Davidson and G. Harman (eds), 169–218. Dordrecht: Reidel.

Lycan, William G.
1984   *Logical form in natural language*. Cambridge, Mass: MIT Press.

Lyons, John
1977   *Semantics*. Cambridge: Cambridge University Press.
1982   "Deixis and subjectivity: Loquor, ergo sum?" In *Speech, place and action*, R. J. Jarvella and W. Klein (eds), 101–124. Chichester: John Wiley & Sons Ltd.

Mayer, Rolf
1990   "Abstraction, context, and perspectivization — Evidentials in discourse semantics". *Theoretical Linguistics* 16: 101–163.

Meyer, Charles
1992   *Apposition in contemporary English*. Cambridge: Cambridge University Press.

McCawley, James D.
1982   "Parentheticals and discontinuous constituents". *Linguistic Inquiry* 13: 91–106.

McConnell-Ginet, Sally
1982   "Adverbs and logical form: A linguistically realistic theory". *Language* 58: 144–184.

Mithun, Marianne
1986   "Evidential diachrony in Northern Iroquoian". In *Evidentiality: The linguistic coding of epistemology*, W. Chafe and J. Nichols (eds), 89–112. New Jersey: Ablex.

Mittwoch, Anita
1977   "How to refer to one's own words: speech-act modifying adverbials and the performative analysis". *Journal of Linguistics* 13: 177–189.
1979   "Final parentheticals with English questions — their illocutionary function and grammar". *Journal of Pragmatics* 3: 401–412.
1985   "Sentences, utterance boundaries, personal deixis and the E-hypothesis". *Theoretical Linguistics* 12: 137–152.

Neale, Stephen
1992   "Paul Grice and the philosophy of language". *Linguistics and Philosophy* 15: 509–559.

Noh, Eun-Ju
    2000   *Metarepresentation: A relevance-theoretic approach.* Amsterdam and Philadelphia: John Benjamins.

Nuccetelli, Susana
    1992   "Review of Vanderveken 1990; Vol. 1". *Journal of Pragmatics* 18: 59–69.

Palmer, Frank
    1986   *Mood and modality.* Cambridge: Cambridge University Press.

Pavlidou, Theodosia
    1988   "Ta distahtika epirimata". *Studies in Greek Linguistics* (Proceedings of the 9th Annual Meeting of the Department of Linguistics, Faculty of Philosophy, Aristotle University of Thessaloniki), 527–546.

Pylyshyn, Zinon
    1984   *Computation and cognition.* Cambridge, Mass: MIT Press.

Recanati, Francois
    1987   *Meaning and force.* Cambridge: Cambridge University Press.

Rochette, Anne
    1990   "The selectional properties of adverbs". In *CLS 26(1): Papers from the 26th Regional Meeting of the Chicago Linguistic Society,* M. Ziolkowski, M. Noske and K. Deaton (eds), 379–391. Chicago: Chicago Linguistic Society.

Rouchota, Villy
    1994   *The semantics and pragmatics of the subjunctive in Modern Greek — a relevance-theoretic approach.* University of London PhD thesis.

Rouchota, Villy and Jucker, Andreas (eds)
    1998   *Current Issues in Relevance Theory.* Amsterdam and Philadelphia: John Benjamins.

Sadock, Jerrold M.
    1974   *Toward a linguistic theory of speech acts.* New York: Academic Press.

Safir, Ken
    1986   "Relative clauses in a theory of binding and levels". *Linguistic Inquiry* 17: 663–689.

Sapir, Edward
    1921   *Language: An introduction to the study of speech.* New York: Harcourt, Brace.

Schiffer, Stephen
    1972   *Meaning.* Oxford: Clarendon Press.

Schreiber, Peter A.
    1971   "Some constraints on the formation of English sentence adverbs". *Linguistic Inquiry* 2: 83–101.
    1972   "Style disjuncts and the performative analysis". *Linguistic Inquiry* 3: 321–347.

Searle, John
    1968   "Austin on locutionary and illocutionary acts". Reprinted in *Essays on J. L. Austin,* Sir I. Berlin et al. (eds), 1973: 141–159. Oxford: Clarendon Press.
    1969   *Speech acts.* Cambridge: Cambridge University Press.
    1974   "Chomsky's revolution in linguistics". In *On Noam Chomsky: Critical essays,* G. Harman (ed.), 2–33. New York: Anchor Press.

1975 "Indirect speech acts". In *Syntax and semantics 3: Speech acts*, P. Cole and J. Morgan (eds), 59–82. New York: Academic Press. Reprinted in *Pragmatics*, S. Davis 1991 (ed.), 265–277 Oxford: Oxford University Press.

1979 *Expression and meaning*. Cambridge: Cambridge University Press.

Searle, John R. and Vanderveken, Daniel

1985 *Foundations of illocutionary logic*. Cambridge: Cambridge University Press.

Slobin, Dan I. and Aksu, Ayhan A.

1982 "Tense, aspect and modality in the use of the Turkish evidential". In *Tense-aspect: Between semantics and pragmatics*, P. J. Hopper (ed.), 185–200. Amsterdam and Philadelphia: John Benjamins.

Smith, Neil and Wilson, Deirdre

1992 "Introduction". *Lingua* 87: 1–10.

Sperber, Dan

1982 "Comments on Clark and Carslon's paper". In *Mutual knowledge*, N. Smith (ed.), 46–51. London: Academic Press.

1994 "Understanding verbal understanding". In *What is intelligence?*, J. Khalfa (ed.), 179–198. Cambridge: Cambridge University Press

Sperber, Dan and Wilson, Deirdre

1983 Draft of Relevance, Chapter VIII, Dept. File, UCL.

1985/6 "Loose talk". *Proceedings of the Aristotelian Society* NS LXXXVI: 153–171. Reprinted in *Pragmatics*, S. Davis 1991 (ed.), 540–549. Oxford: Oxford University Press.

1986/95*Relevance: Communication and cognition*. Oxford: Blackwell.

1987 "Précis of relevance, and presumptions of relevance". *Behavioural and Brain Sciences* 10(4): 697–710; 736–754.

1990 "Rhetoric and relevance". In *The ends of rhetoric: History, theory, practice*, J. Bender & W. David (eds), 140–155. Stanford, CA: Stanford UP.

1998a "The mapping between the mental and the public lexicon". In *Language and thought: Interdisciplinary themes*, P. Carruthers and J. Boucher (eds), 184–200. Cambridge: Cambridge University Press.

1998b "Irony and relevance: A reply to Seto, Hamamoto and Yamanashi". In *Relevance theory: Applications and implications*. R. Carston and S. Uchida (eds), 283–293. Amsterdam and Philadelphia: John Benjamins.

Strawson, Peter

1971 "Intention and convention in speech acts". Reprinted in *Logico-linguistic papers*, P. Strawson, 149–169. London: Methuen.

1973 "Austin and 'locutionary meaning'". In *Essays on J. L. Austin*, Sir I. Berlin et al. (eds), 46–68. Oxford: Clarendon Press.

Swadesh, Morris

1939 "Nootka internal syntax". *International Journal of American Linguistics* 9: 77–102.

Thompson, Laurence C.

1979 "Salishan and the Northwest". In *The languages of native America: Historical and comparative assessment*, L. Campbell and M. Mithun (eds), 692–765. Austin and London: University of Texas Press.

Thomason, Richmond H. and Stalnaker, Robert C.
    1973   "A semantic theory of adverbs". *Linguistic Inquiry* 4: 195–220.
Travis, Lisa
    1988   "The syntax of adverbs". *McGill Working Papers in Linguistics: Special issue on comparative Germanic syntax*: 280–310.
Triandaphyllides, Manolis
    1988   [1941]   *Neoelliniki grammatiki.* Thessaloniki: Aristotelio Panepistimio Thessalonikis, Institouto Neoellinikon Spoudon.
Tsohatzidis, Savas
    1994   *Foundations of speech-act theory.* London: Routledge.
Tzartzanos, Achilleas
    1996   [1953]   *Neoelliniki syntaxis.* Thessaloniki: Kyriakides.
Urmson, James O.
    1963   "Parenthetical verbs". In *Philosophy and ordinary language*, C. Caton (ed.), 220–240. Urbana: University of Illinois Press.
    1977   "Performative utterances". In *Contemporary perspectives in the philosophy of language*, P. French, T. Uehling and H. Wettstein (eds), 260–267. Minneapolis: Univ. of Minnesota Press.
Vanderveken, Daniel
    1990   *Meaning and speech acts*, Vol. 1. Cambridge: Cambridge University Press.
Walker, Ralph
    1975   "Conversational implicatures". In *Meaning, reference and necessity*. S. Blackburn (ed.), 133–181. Cambridge: Cambridge University Press.
Warnock, Geoffrey J.
    1971   "Hare on meaning and speech acts". *The Philosophical Review* 80: 80–84.
Whistler, Kenneth W.
    1986   "Evidentials in Patwin". In *Evidentiality: The linguistic coding of epistemology*, W. Chafe and J. Nichols (eds), 60–74. Norwood, NJ: Ablex.
Wiggins, David
    1971   "On sentence-sense, word-sense and difference of word-sense. Towards a philosophical theory of dictionaries". In *Semantics: An interdisciplinary reader*, D. Steinberg and L. Jakobovits (eds), 14–34. Cambridge: Cambridge University Press.
Willett, Thomas
    1988   "A cross-linguistic survey of the grammaticalization of evidentiality". *Studies in Language* 12: 51–97.
Williams, Edwin S.
    1977   "Discourse and logical form". *Linguistic Inquiry* 8: 101–139.
Wilson, Deirdre
    1991   "Varieties of non-truth-conditional meaning". Paper delivered to the Linguistics Association of Great Britain, Spring meeting, Oxford.
    1994   "Relevance and understanding". In *Language and understanding*, G. Brown, K. Malkmjaer, A. Pollitt and J. Williams (eds), 35–58. Oxford: Oxford University Press.
    1995   "Is there a maxim of truthfulness?" *UCL Working Papers in Linguistics* 7: 197–212.

1998   "Linguistic structure and inferential communication". In *Proceedings of the 16th International Congress of Linguists* (Paris, 20–25 July 1997), B. Caron (ed.). Oxford: Pergamon, Elsevier Sciences.

2000–1 Pragmatic Theory Lectures, University College London.

1998–9 Semantic Theory Lectures, University College London.

2000   "Metarepresentation in linguistic communication". In *Metarepresentations*, D. Sperber (ed.), 411–448. Oxford: Oxford University Press.

Wilson, Deirdre and Sperber, Dan

1981   'On Grice's theory of conversation'. In *Conversation and discourse*, P. Werth (ed.), 155–178. London: Croom Helm.

1987   "An outline of relevance theory". *Notes on Linguistics* 39: 5–24. Dallas: SIL.

1988   "Mood and the analysis of non-declarative sentences". In *Human agency: Language, duty and value*, J. Dancy, J. Moravcsik and C. Taylor (eds), 71–101. Stanford: Stanford UP.

1992   "On verbal irony". *Lingua* 87: 53–76.

1993   "Linguistic form and relevance". *Lingua* 90: 1–25.

2000   "Truthfulness and relevance". *UCL Working Papers in Linguistics* 12:215–254.

Wilson, Deirdre and Matsui, Tomoko

1998   "Recent approaches to bridging: truth, coherence, relevance". *UCL Working Papers in Linguistics* 10: 173–200.

Wilson, Norbert L.

1970   'Grice on meaning: The ultimate counter-example'. *Nous* 4: 295–302.

Woodbury, Anthony C.

1986   "Interactions of tense and evidentiality: A study of Sherpa and English". In *Evidentiality: The linguistic coding of epistemology*, W. Chafe and J. Nichols (eds), 188–202. Norwood, NJ: Ablex.

Yu, Paul

1979   "On the Gricean program about meaning". *Linguistics and Philosophy* 3 (2): 273–288.

Ziff, Paul

1967   "On H. P. Grice's account of meaning". *Analysis* 28: 1–8. Reprinted in *Semantics: An interdisciplinary reader*, D. Steinberg and L. Jakobovits (eds), 1971:60–65. Cambridge: Cambridge University Press.

Name Index

Subject Index

In the PRAGMATICS AND BEYOND NEW SERIES the following titles have been published thus far or are scheduled for publication:

1. WALTER, Bettyruth: *The Jury Summation as Speech Genre: An Ethnographic Study of What it Means to Those who Use it.* Amsterdam/Philadelphia, 1988.
2. BARTON, Ellen: *Nonsentential Constituents: A Theory of Grammatical Structure and Pragmatic Interpretation.* Amsterdam/Philadelphia, 1990.
3. OLEKSY, Wieslaw (ed.): *Contrastive Pragmatics.* Amsterdam/Philadelphia, 1989.
4. RAFFLER-ENGEL, Walburga von (ed.): *Doctor-Patient Interaction.* Amsterdam/Philadelphia, 1989.
5. THELIN, Nils B. (ed.): *Verbal Aspect in Discourse.* Amsterdam/Philadelphia, 1990.
6. VERSCHUEREN, Jef (ed.): *Selected Papers from the 1987 International Pragmatics Conference. Vol. I: Pragmatics at Issue. Vol. II: Levels of Linguistic Adaptation. Vol. III: The Pragmatics of Intercultural and International Communication* (ed. with Jan Blommaert). Amsterdam/Philadelphia, 1991.
7. LINDENFELD, Jacqueline: *Speech and Sociability at French Urban Market Places.* Amsterdam/Philadelphia, 1990.
8. YOUNG, Lynne: *Language as Behaviour, Language as Code: A Study of Academic English.* Amsterdam/Philadelphia, 1990.
9. LUKE, Kang-Kwong: *Utterance Particles in Cantonese Conversation.* Amsterdam/Philadelphia, 1990.
10. MURRAY, Denise E.: *Conversation for Action. The computer terminal as medium of communication.* Amsterdam/Philadelphia, 1991.
11. LUONG, Hy V.: *Discursive Practices and Linguistic Meanings. The Vietnamese system of person reference.* Amsterdam/Philadelphia, 1990.
12. ABRAHAM, Werner (ed.): *Discourse Particles. Descriptive and theoretical investigations on the logical, syntactic and pragmatic properties of discourse particles in German.* Amsterdam/Philadelphia, 1991.
13. NUYTS, Jan, A. Machtelt BOLKESTEIN and Co VET (eds): *Layers and Levels of Representation in Language Theory: a functional view.* Amsterdam/Philadelphia, 1990.
14. SCHWARTZ, Ursula: *Young Children's Dyadic Pretend Play.* Amsterdam/Philadelphia, 1991.
15. KOMTER, Martha: *Conflict and Cooperation in Job Interviews.* Amsterdam/Philadelphia, 1991.
16. MANN, William C. and Sandra A. THOMPSON (eds): *Discourse Description: Diverse Linguistic Analyses of a Fund-Raising Text.* Amsterdam/Philadelphia, 1992.
17. PIÉRAUT-LE BONNIEC, Gilberte and Marlene DOLITSKY (eds): *Language Bases ... Discourse Bases.* Amsterdam/Philadelphia, 1991.
18. JOHNSTONE, Barbara: *Repetition in Arabic Discourse. Paradigms, syntagms and the ecology of language.* Amsterdam/Philadelphia, 1991.
19. BAKER, Carolyn D. and Allan LUKE (eds): *Towards a Critical Sociology of Reading Pedagogy. Papers of the XII World Congress on Reading.* Amsterdam/Philadelphia, 1991.
20. NUYTS, Jan: *Aspects of a Cognitive-Pragmatic Theory of Language. On cognition, functionalism, and grammar.* Amsterdam/Philadelphia, 1992.
21. SEARLE, John R. et al.: *(On) Searle on Conversation.* Compiled and introduced by Herman Parret and Jef Verschueren. Amsterdam/Philadelphia, 1992.

22. AUER, Peter and Aldo Di LUZIO (eds): *The Contextualization of Language*. Amsterdam/Philadelphia, 1992.
23. FORTESCUE, Michael, Peter HARDER and Lars KRISTOFFERSEN (eds): *Layered Structure and Reference in a Functional Perspective. Papers from the Functional Grammar Conference, Copenhagen, 1990*. Amsterdam/Philadelphia, 1992.
24. MAYNARD, Senko K.: *Discourse Modality: Subjectivity, Emotion and Voice in the Japanese Language*. Amsterdam/Philadelphia, 1993.
25. COUPER-KUHLEN, Elizabeth: *English Speech Rhythm. Form and function in everyday verbal interaction*. Amsterdam/Philadelphia, 1993.
26. STYGALL, Gail: Trial Language. *A study in differential discourse processing*. Amsterdam/Philadelphia, 1994.
27. SUTER, Hans Jürg: *The Wedding Report: A Prototypical Approach to the Study of Traditional Text Types*. Amsterdam/Philadelphia, 1993.
28. VAN DE WALLE, Lieve: *Pragmatics and Classical Sanskrit*. Amsterdam/Philadelphia, 1993.
29. BARSKY, Robert F.: *Constructing a Productive Other: Discourse theory and the convention refugee hearing*. Amsterdam/Philadelphia, 1994.
30. WORTHAM, Stanton E.F.: *Acting Out Participant Examples in the Classroom*. Amsterdam/Philadelphia, 1994.
31. WILDGEN, Wolfgang: *Process, Image and Meaning. A realistic model of the meanings of sentences and narrative texts*. Amsterdam/Philadelphia, 1994.
32. SHIBATANI, Masayoshi and Sandra A. THOMPSON (eds): *Essays in Semantics and Pragmatics*. Amsterdam/Philadelphia, 1995.
33. GOOSSENS, Louis, Paul PAUWELS, Brygida RUDZKA-OSTYN, Anne-Marie SIMON-VANDENBERGEN and Johan VANPARYS: *By Word of Mouth. Metaphor, metonymy and linguistic action in a cognitive perspective*. Amsterdam/Philadelphia, 1995.
34. BARBE, Katharina: Irony in Context. Amsterdam/Philadelphia, 1995.
35. JUCKER, Andreas H. (ed.): *Historical Pragmatics. Pragmatic developments in the history of English*. Amsterdam/Philadelphia, 1995.
36. CHILTON, Paul, Mikhail V. ILYIN and Jacob MEY: *Political Discourse in Transition in Eastern and Western Europe (1989-1991)*. Amsterdam/Philadelphia, 1998.
37. CARSTON, Robyn and Seiji UCHIDA (eds): *Relevance Theory. Applications and implications*. Amsterdam/Philadelphia, 1998.
38. FRETHEIM, Thorstein and Jeanette K. GUNDEL (eds): *Reference and Referent Accessibility*. Amsterdam/Philadelphia, 1996.
39. HERRING, Susan (ed.): *Computer-Mediated Communication. Linguistic, social, and cross-cultural perspectives*. Amsterdam/Philadelphia, 1996.
40. DIAMOND, Julie: *Status and Power in Verbal Interaction. A study of discourse in a close-knit social network*. Amsterdam/Philadelphia, 1996.
41. VENTOLA, Eija and Anna MAURANEN, (eds): *Academic Writing. Intercultural and textual issues*. Amsterdam/Philadelphia, 1996.
42. WODAK, Ruth and Helga KOTTHOFF (eds): *Communicating Gender in Context*. Amsterdam/Philadelphia, 1997.
43. JANSSEN, Theo A.J.M. and Wim van der WURFF (eds): *Reported Speech. Forms and functions of the verb*. Amsterdam/Philadelphia, 1996.
44. BARGIELA-CHIAPPINI, Francesca and Sandra J. HARRIS: *Managing Language. The*

discourse of corporate meetings. Amsterdam/Philadelphia, 1997.
45. PALTRIDGE, Brian: *Genre, Frames and Writing in Research Settings.* Amsterdam/Philadelphia, 1997.
46. GEORGAKOPOULOU, Alexandra: *Narrative Performances. A study of Modern Greek storytelling.* Amsterdam/Philadelphia, 1997.
47. CHESTERMAN, Andrew: *Contrastive Functional Analysis.* Amsterdam/Philadelphia, 1998.
48. KAMIO, Akio: *Territory of Information.* Amsterdam/Philadelphia, 1997.
49. KURZON, Dennis: *Discourse of Silence.* Amsterdam/Philadelphia, 1998.
50. GRENOBLE, Lenore: *Deixis and Information Packaging in Russian Discourse.* Amsterdam/Philadelphia, 1998.
51. BOULIMA, Jamila: *Negotiated Interaction in Target Language Classroom Discourse.* Amsterdam/Philadelphia, 1999.
52. GILLIS, Steven and Annick DE HOUWER (eds): *The Acquisition of Dutch.* Amsterdam/Philadelphia, 1998.
53. MOSEGAARD HANSEN, Maj-Britt: *The Function of Discourse Particles. A study with special reference to spoken standard French.* Amsterdam/Philadelphia, 1998.
54. HYLAND, Ken: *Hedging in Scientific Research Articles.* Amsterdam/Philadelphia, 1998.
55. ALLWOOD, Jens and Peter Gärdenfors (eds): *Cognitive Semantics. Meaning and cognition.* Amsterdam/Philadelphia, 1999.
56. TANAKA, Hiroko: *Language, Culture and Social Interaction. Turn-taking in Japanese and Anglo-American English.* Amsterdam/Philadelphia, 1999.
57 JUCKER, Andreas H. and Yael ZIV (eds): *Discourse Markers. Descriptions and theory.* Amsterdam/Philadelphia, 1998.
58. ROUCHOTA, Villy and Andreas H. JUCKER (eds): *Current Issues in Relevance Theory.* Amsterdam/Philadelphia, 1998.
59. KAMIO, Akio and Ken-ichi TAKAMI (eds): *Function and Structure. In honor of Susumu Kuno.* 1999.
60. JACOBS, Geert: *Preformulating the News. An analysis of the metapragmatics of press releases.* 1999.
61. MILLS, Margaret H. (ed.): *Slavic Gender Linguistics.* 1999.
62. TZANNE, Angeliki: *Talking at Cross-Purposes. The dynamics of miscommunication.* 2000.
63. BUBLITZ, Wolfram, Uta LENK and Eija VENTOLA (eds.): *Coherence in Spoken and Written Discourse. How to create it and how to describe it.Selected papers from the International Workshop on Coherence, Augsburg, 24-27 April 1997.* 1999.
64. SVENNEVIG, Jan: *Getting Acquainted in Conversation. A study of initial interactions.* 1999.
65. COOREN, François: *The Organizing Dimension of Communication.* 2000.
66. JUCKER, Andreas H., Gerd FRITZ and Franz LEBSANFT (eds.): *Historical Dialogue Analysis.* 1999.
67. TAAVITSAINEN, Irma, Gunnel MELCHERS and Päivi PAHTA (eds.): *Dimensions of Writing in Nonstandard English.* 1999.
68. ARNOVICK, Leslie: *Diachronic Pragmatics. Seven case studies in English illocutionary development.* 1999.

69. NOH, Eun-Ju: *The Semantics and Pragmatics of Metarepresentation in English. A relevance-theoretic account.* 2000.
70. SORJONEN, Marja-Leena: *Responding in Conversation. A study of response particles in Finnish.* 2001.
71. GÓMEZ-GONZÁLEZ, María Ángeles: *The Theme-Topic Interface. Evidence from English.* 2001.
72. MARMARIDOU, Sophia S.A.: *Pragmatic Meaning and Cognition.* 2000.
73. HESTER, Stephen and David FRANCIS (eds.): *Local Educational Order. Ethnomethodological studies of knowledge in action.* 2000.
74. TROSBORG, Anna (ed.): *Analysing Professional Genres.* 2000.
75. PILKINGTON, Adrian: *Poetic Effects. A relevance theory perspective.* 2000.
76. MATSUI, Tomoko: *Bridging and Relevance.* 2000.
77. VANDERVEKEN, Daniel and Susumu KUBO (eds.): *Essays in Speech Act Theory.* 2001.
78. SELL, Roger D. : *Literature as Communication. The foundations of mediating criticism.* 2000.
79. ANDERSEN, Gisle and Thorstein FRETHEIM (eds.): *Pragmatic Markers and Propositional Attitude.* 2000.
80. UNGERER, Friedrich (ed.): *English Media Texts – Past and Present. Language and textual structure.* 2000.
81. DI LUZIO, Aldo, Susanne GÜNTHNER and Franca ORLETTI (eds.): *Culture in Communication. Analyses of intercultural situations.* 2001.
82. KHALIL, Esam N.: *Grounding in English and Arabic News Discourse.* 2000.
83. MÁRQUEZ REITER, Rosina: *Linguistic Politeness in Britain and Uruguay. A contrastive study of requests and apologies.* 2000.
84. ANDERSEN, Gisle: *Pragmatic Markers and Sociolinguistic Variation. A relevance-theoretic approach to the language of adolescents.* 2001.
85. COLLINS, Daniel E.: *Reanimated Voices. Speech reporting in a historical-pragmatic perspective.* 2001.
86. IFANTIDOU, Elly: *Evidentials and Relevance.* 2001.
87. MUSHIN, Ilana: *Evidentiality and Epistemological Stance. Narrative retelling.* 2001.
88. BAYRAKTAROĞLU, Arın and Maria SIFIANOU (eds.): *Linguistic Politeness Across Boundaries. The case of Greek and Turkish.* 2001.
89. ITAKURA, Hiroko: *Conversational Dominance and Gender. A study of Japanese speakers in first and second language contexts.* 2001.
90. KENESEI, István and Robert M. HARNISH (eds.): *Perspectives on Semantics, Pragmatics, and Discourse. A Festschrift for Ferenc Kiefer.* 2001.
91. GROSS, Joan: *Speaking in Other Voices. An ethnography of Walloon puppet theaters.* 2001.
92. GARDNER, Rod: *When Listeners Talk. Response tokens and listener stance.* 2001.
93. BARON, Bettina and Helga KOTTHOFF (eds.): *Gender in Interaction. Perspectives on femininity and masculinity in ethnography and discourse.* n.y.p.
94. McILVENNY, Paul (ed.): *Talking Gender and Sexuality.* n.y.p.
95. FITZMAURICE, Susan M.: *The Familiar Letter in Early Modern English. A pragmatic approach.* n.y.p.
96. HAVERKATE, Henk: *The Syntax, Semantics and Pragmatics of Spanish Mood.* n.y.p.